PRAISE FOR *THE LAST AMERICAN EDITOR*

"Ken Tingley not only writes from the heart, but he writes about the hearts of others. He tells great stories for those who live in his unique part of the world. Buy his book. Put it on the table next to your bed. When you've had a hard day, open it up: You can turn almost to any page and feel your heart restored."

— Terry Pluto,
author and columnist for the *Cleveland Plain Dealer.*

"You'll find the spirit of America in Ken Tingley's columns. He has the compassionate voice of a man determined to tell stories that might otherwise have gone untold about people who might otherwise have gone uncelebrated."

— Ken Paulson, J.D.,
Director, Free Speech Center, Middle Tennessee State University and former editor-in-chief of *USA Today.*

"In reading Ken's columns, even many years after they were written, the reader gets a snapshot of a community and its people and their place in time. That's because Ken Tingley was one of them. He *belonged* to them. And through each of his columns, it's very clear that *they* belonged to *him. Ken Tingley was more than a columnist for their newspaper. He was their conscience. Their advocate. Their friend.*"

— Mark Mahoney,
Pulitzer Prize-winning editorial page editor of
The Gazette in Schenectady, N.Y.

D1242622

"Ken Tingley's biggest gift as a writer is that he doesn't tell the reader his version of a person's story. He tells that person's *ACTUAL* story. He finds that certain something that makes his story subjects unique, and paints the picture of what *they're* feeling, what *they're* thinking, who *they* are. He writes about their joys and their pains, finding the strength in each. He makes us feel like we truly know his story subjects. And if we look hard enough, we usually find a lesson that we can apply to our own lives."

— **Tim Reynolds,** *Associated Press.*

"Each of Ken's columns pulls his reader into the story of someone living a life unnoticed, compassionately relating the outline of a life marked by terrible tragedy, a heroic act that only a few neighbors will ever know about, a journey of self-destruction that ends in redemption, or a political career ended by a single courageous vote. During Ken's years as the editor of *The Post Star*, he earned the trust of its readers, many of whom chose him to tell the stories of their lives honestly and with heart."

— **Diane Kennedy,** president,
New York News Publishers Association.

"These columns take readers inside the lives of their friends and neighbors with uncommon insight and provide a fascinating window into life in small-town America. Every town needs a Ken Tingley, who as a sports writer and editor clearly learned that the best stories are not about who won and lost, but about real life. Glens Falls is lucky to have him."

— **Bill Eichenberger,**
executive director of *Associated Press* Sports Editors.

«I've known and admired Ken's writing for years — his way with words, his ability to draw a reader in and take them on a narrative journey. He goes beyond human interest to highlight the deep humanity of the people he profiles. That's powerful stuff, and a true gift."

— **Tamara Dietrich,**
journalist and author of *The Hummingbird's Cage.*

The Last American Editor

Ken Tingley

ISBN – 978-1-954102-02-6

Library of Congress Control Number: 2021943750
Printed in the United States of America
First Printing: 2021

Edited by Mark Heinz
Interior design by Amit Dey
Cover design by Rhonda Triller

Published By: Something or Other Publishing

SOMETHING
OR **OTHER**
PUBLISHING

Madison, Wisconsin 53719
www.soopllc.com
retailers@soopllc.com

DEDICATION

Gillian and Joseph proved the best stories are always sitting right in front of you. Thanks for being part of this great adventure.

TABLE OF CONTENTS

Hometown, USA

Life & Death

Sports

The World

My Life

All the columns in this book were originally published in *The Post-Star* of Glens Falls, N.Y. and are reprinted here with gratitude from Lee Enterprises.

FOREWORD

By Margaret Sullivan
- *The Washington Post*

America's small newspapers are having a tough time these days. Thousands of them have gone out of business over the past fifteen years. Even those which have endured have been forced to shrink their reporting staffs by half or even more. The old, reliable business model for newspapers — based largely on print advertising — has withered, and so has their presence in many communities. To me, these losses are a tragedy.

If I were making an argument in court for the value of small newspapers, I would point, as Exhibit A, to Ken Tingley's work at the Post-Star in Glens Falls, N.Y. For many years, Tingley fostered what small newspapers — at their best — stand for: their tight-knit connection to the community, their focus on people, their indelible sense of place.

Tingley is remarkable, too, in his versatility: He edited the paper expertly, leading it to win a slew of journalism awards during his tenure, including a Pulitzer Prize for editorial writing. And his writing, which is both spare and evocative, is of a national caliber.

So it is a wonderful gift that a generous selection of his columns is collected here, where they can be read, returned to and treasured. Newspaper work is, by its nature, ephemeral. It's of the instant, of the day. Readers absorb it, appreciate it or object to it, and then stack the paper for recycling. And we ink-stained journalists recognize we aren't writing for the ages but for the moment. People will remind us, especially when they aren't happy with our work, that they use the newspaper to line their birdcages or wrap their fish. We're okay with that, too.

But here, once again, Ken Tingley manages something extraordinary. These columns are of their moment, but they also have lasting value. When he writes, for example, about a young soldier, about to ship off to the Persian Gulf after 9/11, the column is not only about specific people — Ed Feulner and his wife Cindy of Hudson Falls — but also about something universal and timeless. At the end of each column collected here, Tingley provides an update or a reflection in the form of a postscript. It says so much about the value of small newspapers that, in the postscript about the Feulners, Tingley recalls that, after he interviewed the couple in December, 2002, he asked The Post-Star's publisher, Jim Marshall, if one of the newsroom's laptop computers could be donated so that Ed could keep in touch with his family more readily from overseas. The publisher agreed and Tingley promptly dropped the computer off at their home as a Christmas and going-away gift.

Once again, that close connection was forged between the columnist and his subject, between the newspaper and the community it serves.

As we read *The Last American Editor*, let's remember that deep and valuable connection. Let's do everything in our power to keep it alive.

Margaret Sullivan is the media columnist for *The Washington Post*, the former public editor of *The New York Times*, and the former chief editor of *The Buffalo News*, her hometown newspaper where she started as a summer intern.

PEOPLE

Being the editor of a small local newspaper can be an all-consuming job. By 2008, I had been editor of the The Post-Star in Glens Falls, N.Y. - a smalltown of about 15,000 fifty miles north of the state capital in Albany, N.Y. - for nine years. I was 51 years old, and perhaps feeling my mortality, I decided to recommit myself to what I loved to do the most - writing columns. When readers called with interesting story ideas, instead of handing them off to a reporter, I took them. Almost immediately, a series of stories about the people who lived in my community landed in my lap. All I had to do was pick up the phone and listen. Ultimately, what small newspapers are all about isn't the news, but the people and their lives.

When Paul Mead told the author he had seen Jesus Christ walk into his heart, he meant it literally and the author did not know what to think. But Mead's story of resurrection from a life of drugs set the tone for the type of stories the author wanted to tell. Over the years, Rev. Mead became the source of several columns. When he celebrated his tenth anniversary as pastor of his church, the author was there to celebrate with him. (Photo courtesy of The Post-Star in Glens Falls, N.Y.)

TEACHER, PASTOR, COUNSELOR

March 23, 2008 - Easter Sunday

The first time he cries is because of what he did to his mother.

It is still painful, hard to talk about and tears flow freely as he tries to gather himself in the small room where he is giving a public confession.

The second time is when he tells you about seeing Jesus. He trembles at the memory. He talks slowly and gradually, his voice gathers strength and he sees the disbelief in your eyes.

"It was just like I was looking at you right here," he says. "It was just like the pictures you see of Jesus with the long hair and flowing robe. It was a door in my chest and I looked down and saw Jesus walk right into my heart."

It was then, he says, that his life changed forever.

It is a perfect metaphor, one usually delivered from a pulpit by a professional preacher who can spin the tale in a revival tent for a big turn on the collection plate. But this is Easter Sunday so perhaps we need to cut him some slack because the absolute reality is that something made him change, something lifted him out of the gutter, so maybe we should all listen closely.

He cried for a third time later, but we don't want to talk about that yet. We don't want to give away the ending.

We all have a story, a path filled with turns and twists that is our life. This is Paul Mead's story.

We all have made wrong turns, tripped, fallen, but Mead didn't just take a wrong turn, he fell off a cliff - almost literally.

It was 30 feet off a roof while working construction as a young man. He broke both his ankles and spent the better part of a year in a wheelchair. It was clear he would never work construction again or play sports.

What followed was a windfall of more than $500,000 in a settlement from his employer's insurance company. He invested half and kept the rest in the bank.

With the injury came the demons. He found himself depressed, lonely, lamenting his injuries, and the fact he would never play sports again.

Sadly, the story is almost a cliche after that.

Mead tried crack cocaine and became "instantly addicted" he said. He blew through $250,000 in a year. He moved from his small hometown in the Catskills to Albany where he lived in hotel rooms and spent his days smoking crack. He was spending $600 to $1,000 a day on drugs. He was soon broke.

"I was helpless, hopeless and could not stop," said Mead. "As long as I had $20, I was going to buy crack."

He described going to Price Chopper and filling up a carriage with meat and walking right out the door. He would trade every $100 worth of beef for $50 worth of drugs. He did the same with cartons of cigarettes. He got caught a lot and spent a lot of time in jail.

"My father told me I would be better off dead because I was killing him," said Mead.

His mother moved out of her home and lived with a friend so he couldn't find her.

He remembers living on the street in Albany with only a pair of pants, a T-shirt and shoes. That was it. No underwear, no socks.

It was Dec. 4, 2002. Mead had been living on the streets for 10 years. He was at rock bottom.

"I was sitting on Clinton Avenue in Albany," said Mead. "Cold, wet and freezing, homeless, hopeless and looking across the street and saw a phone booth."

Over the years, Mead had tried it all, Alcoholics Anonymous, Narcotics Anonymous, rehab, halfway houses and he had always gone back to drugs, to the street. This time he called Teen Challenge in Syracuse.

Teen Challenge is a worldwide Christian drug and alcohol rehabilitation program that provides a faith-based cure.

He told his drug dealer that he was leaving, that he was getting off drugs for good.

"He held out a big bag of crack, 3-1/2 grams, what they call an 8 ball and he rubbed the bag between his fingers and said, 'Are you sure?'"

You can tell that vision is still with Mead, even today.

"It was hard," said Mead. "Several times on the drive to Syracuse I wanted to turn around. My mind could not escape the picture of that cocaine."

You'd like to say that was the fork in the road that changed his life, but it wasn't. Mead married his wife Sharon, relapsed and the marriage was annulled. He came back to Teen Challenge and kept at it.

He was in a church in Syracuse while working and living at Teen Challenge and heard three words over and over again: "Teacher. Pastor. Counselor." It was then that he saw Jesus.

"I had no idea what it meant," said Mead.

He came to Hudson Falls five years ago through his connections at Teen Challenge. He was allowed to live with a local family and work at the church as a volunteer janitor. He wasn't qualified to do much else. He started taking seminary courses from an online organization called Global University.

You see, it would have been unfair to put the Rev. before his name when we started this story. It would have been a shame to spoil the ending.

It would have been unfair to give away the final destination of the journey from the mean streets to Teen Challenge to volunteer janitor to the senior pastor of Gospel Lighthouse Church in Hudson Falls.

That is where I found him when he told me he wanted to tell his story. That is where we started when he shook my hand and started to talk about his life.

He looked ordinary, average, a vanilla milkshake of a man with a Mountain Dew cap and black Dale Earnhardt Jr. T-shirt.

The casual attire, he admits, was by design, a point he wanted to make to his interviewer that Paul Mead is a regular guy, nothing special, one of the flock as they say in the religion game, a NASCAR preacher who gets out the word in just over an hour and is home in time to watch the good old boys trade paint.

But nothing seems further from the truth.

Not with his story.

"I have experienced the favor of God over the last five years and you know, I don't know why," Mead says. His eyes water up again. He is humbled. "Gosh, I've been given so much. I'm really nothing special. There was a time in my life I got to a place where I knew I had to turn right and I turned left anyway. Today, I turn right.

"Even now, it doesn't make sense," said Mead. "God has taken the least likely candidate to share a mission of hope."

Whatever you want to believe about the reasons, the motivations for Mead to turn his life around, this thing is for certain - the journey is anything but ordinary.

It was earlier this month that he was installed as pastor. He tells you 187 people were there including his mother and father. He tells you of the applause and the cheering and how he had never heard anything so loud.

And he tells you of the card from his mother.

And here is where the tears start again for the final time.

"I love you with all my heart," he says choking out the words from his mother. "I'm proud of what you have accomplished."

It is an amazing story and what better day than Easter to share the story of a man who was raised from the dead.

P.S.

Paul Mead is the minister of the Gospel Lighthouse Church, a Pentecostal church, in Hudson Falls, N.Y. He had been there five years when he called me in 2008.

When he described to me that he saw Jesus walk into his heart, I stopped him. "Figuratively," I said. "No," he insisted. "I actually saw him walk into my heart." I am an agnostic, I do not go to church regularly and I struggled with how to write that without making Paul sound ridiculous. I am a cynical journalist with a healthy dose of skepticism, but there was something that made Paul stop taking drugs and reclaim his life and family and ultimately help other people. But maybe most of all, there seemed to be a reason we were brought together. And that stayed with me.

A LOOK AGAIN, ONE YEAR LATER

April 12, 2009

On the message board outside the main entrance to the Gospel Lighthouse Church in Hudson Falls is this message:

> *Go tell the people what I did for you*
> *and tell them I'll do it for them too*
> *…God*

I'll be honest, it's not often that I get to quote God. Might be the first time ever.

The message has been up there for a few weeks. Paul Mead, who is the first pastor of the church, is letting it sink in, letting it settle deep with hope that it will change lives. It's a tough gig changing lives.

I wrote about Paul last Easter, about his drug and alcohol problems, about a ruined life that often left him in an Albany gutter.

He's been the lead pastor for more than a year. His marriage to his wife, Sharon, has been restored. He tells me that so many things have happened. He tells me that the church has grown and that there were more than 200 in attendance for Palm Sunday. There are more families coming, more children and young adults. In other words, business is good.

We are sitting in the same small room where we first talked a year ago, where Paul shed tears over a life gone wrong.

He tells me about the people he meets and all the problems he hears.

"A high percentage of the time I'm dealing with a situation that reminds me of me," said Paul. "It's Groundhog Day. Same pain, same guilt, same alcohol abuse, same drug addiction, same relationship issues. It's the same."

It's just not his life this time. If you talk to Paul, you can be 100 percent sure you are getting an expert when it comes to screwing up your life.

Sometimes, he believes he makes a difference.

"People's lives are being changed because they are staring face to face with a changed life," said Paul.

But he means this in the most humble of ways. He says he is nothing special. He is a man of the cloth with only online training and his one special gift is the ability to relate to people who are at their worst.

At that, he seems quite successful.

But I still sense something is missing. He wants more. He wants more people to embrace Jesus Christ the way he has, to feel the love the way he does.

So I tell him my own confession about his confession.

His story stayed with me. It lingered and every few months I would read the column again. Maybe I needed that fix of inspiration the way he once craved crack.

Meade's story was the first of a renewed commitment on my part to write more, to tell the stories of regular people in the real world. And over the course of the past year those stories piled up one after another:

A young mother fighting MS; a solder in Iraq who could not attend his daughter's college graduation; a young woman who was laid off from her job; a millionaire who funded a building at the local college; a college student with grand dreams.

I want him to know his story had an effect on at least one person – me. And maybe his story led me to write those other stories and along the way I'm hoping they did some good, too. Maybe others, because of those stories, acted out of kindness and charity, and that really all goes back to Paul.

We haven't talked in a year and yet it feels like we have not missed a beat.

We pick up where we left off as if we both know that the story didn't really have an ending and we have to finish it.

We have to go back to Oct. 1 - seven months after the first story - when Paul received an evening phone call. His mother was being rushed to Albany Medical Center. The situation was grave.

When he arrived, they told him she had suffered a brain aneurism and they were stabilizing her. But she was already gone.

Paul was her only child. She had never remarried after the divorce from Paul's father. Paul held his hand over her beating heart and felt its strength.

He stayed for some time and finally told the doctors they could turn off the machines that were keeping her alive.

It was his mother who gave him the letter the day he was installed as first pastor, the letter that told him how proud she was, the letter that made him cry tears of great joy.

"My mother got to live the last six years of her life happy," said Paul.

He said goodbye and watched her slip away.

"She was only 68," said Paul.

In that hospital room, pain welled up inside him and took over. It continued through the funeral and the eulogy, which he gave himself, and into the ensuing weeks.

Paul never could handle pain. With the pain would come the drinking and the drugs and the gutter.

"Without Jesus, there is no way I don't smoke crack," said Paul. "I never could have handled that pain."

Three months after his mother's death, Paul's father came to see him.

He looked at him hard, searching for something and for the first time told him, "You know, I think you are going to make it."

P.S.

A year after the first column, I was drawn to Paul again. Our paths crossed from time to time. He presided over the funeral of six children killed in a fire, there was a community forum addressing the opioid epidemic in our community and he was at the center of a controversy in his town when he hosted a meeting of drug addicts at his church.

After my wife was diagnosed with ovarian cancer in 2011, we talked again and Paul insisted we pray for her there in his office. It made me uncomfortable, but I went along because it made Paul feel good. In September, it will be 10 years since my wife was first diagnosed with cancer. The prayers probably didn't hurt.

MAYBE PASTOR PAUL'S STORY IS JUST BEGINNING

December 17, 2017

Ten years ago, I thought I was coming in at the end of the story, but that was not true.

When I first met Paul Mead in 2007, he was already five years into his sobriety. He had just been named lead pastor of the Gospel Lighthouse Church in Hudson Falls and the story of his redemption from a homeless crack addict in Albany to the leader of a local parish was a perfect story for Easter Sunday.

He was a man who had been raised from the dead.

That's how I ended Act I 10 years ago.

But it wasn't the end at all.

The story was just beginning.

Mead was just months into his tenure as the lead pastor when I talked to him, and he told me this past week that at the time, he was wracked with self-doubt. He related a moment when he lay down all alone on the floor of the vestibule and sobbed.

He was a high school graduate with only a year of Bible study, taking over a church that was in debt, a building that needed repairs and a congregation that was aging and without momentum after seven pastors in 10 years.

It turned out, this was just the beginning of Paul Mead's journey.

What you have to understand is that leading the Sunday prayer doesn't magically transform you into a man of respect and dignity. It doesn'tprovide wisdom, insights and answers for those who so desperately need them. That's a daily commitment. That takes dedication and devotion.

So he kept at it.

He started out as the pastor who used to be the crack addict. That gave him street credibility with the sinners and those struggling with their own demons. Perhaps it made him approachable because he would not judge.

So what he lacked in theology training, he more than made up for in life experiences and insights from his own horror.

He'd seen the gates of hell, so there was little you could say to shock him.

I'm not sure what it is about Paul Mead, but you can talk to him without reservation.

He appears unassuming, with a round face, receding hairline and sad eyes. I believe they speak to his past. He has an aura of ordinariness that allows him to blend in easily among the crowd. His message is soft, gentle and sincere.

After becoming pastor, he hit the ground running with a new purpose in life.

I was not surprised when our paths crossed as the community came together to address the opioid epidemic.

Paul Mead was learning more every day.

He worked with the sheriff and the local assemblywoman and others in the community.

He made himself available to counsel those who wanted it.

He listened.

Oh, how he must have listened.

And when they were done telling him about the tragedy they had made of their lives, he would turn and say brightly, "You know, I think you are doing a lot better than you think you are."

He refused to tell them what was wrong with them. He argues people already know that.

Instead, he tells them what is right with their lives.

It is a starting place, a beginning.

Fewer than 50 were regulars when he started 10 years ago. Most were older people who dragged their grandkids to the service. He got the building fixed. He told the regulars that changes had to be made. Traditional hymns were replaced with modern Christian folk music, and instead of an organ, there were guitars and drums.

Some left, but more came.

Membership and attendance grew each year.

You see them today and there is an energy, a fellowship that bleeds over into the start of the service with smiles, hugs and camaraderie.

I suspect this all has something to do with the mild-mannered preacher who stuck around to make a difference.

What happened is that Paul Mead grew beyond being the pastor who used to be on drugs, to the pastor who will do just about anything to make a difference.

So last Sunday, the Gospel Lighthouse Church scheduled a celebration to honor Mead's 10 years of service and some 235 people showed up.

The county sheriff was there, the village attorney, the local assemblywoman and the Teen Challenge folks who got him straight 15 years ago.

And the local newspaper editor was there, too, because as it turned out, there was still a story to tell.

Perhaps it was to bear witness to what this man has become, the journey he has made and what he means to these people.

Paul Mead saw the guests. He also saw the former parishioners who had moved on to other churches and the people he had counseled at one time or another, and he said he was surprised.

Caught off guard.

Taken aback.

He looks back at you with those sad eyes again, choking with emotions.

"You know, you just don't know sometimes how you are doing," he said. "You don't do these things to get a pat on the back, but when it happens, it feels good."

They sang Pastor Paul's praises last Sunday, and when they tried to sum up all his fine qualities in one word, they needed nearly a dozen.

I'm sure they could have gone on and on. Let me add one of my own — authentic.

He is the real deal.

As the emotions welled up in him again, he was able to choke out a thought to those in front of him: "I need you far more than you need me."

That's Paul Mead.

That's Pastor Paul underestimating what he has meant to so many.

Let me just speak for myself in this regard.

Paul, you done good.

P.S.

Institutional memory is a great thing in a small town. On the 10th anniversary of being pastor at the Gospel Lighthouse Baptist Church in Hudson Falls, Pastor Paul invited me to the ceremony along with other community leaders. Afterward, we hugged and we both had tears in our eyes. It turned out the first column I wrote about Paul was just the beginning for both of us with my column continuing to evolve.

When I decided to retire in the summer of 2020, I published a series of my favorite columns. The first column I chose was this one about Paul Mead and his redemption. It was where the best of my work started and Paul and I will always be linked because of that. That morning, he called me. I could hear his voice breaking over the phone. He said he had been going through some difficult things with his family and he was questioning himself all over again. Then, his wife showed him the column in the newspaper and why it was so important to me. He said it lifted him up. I thought that was his job.

REMEMBERING JEFFRY

October 31, 1993

By the time Jeff Morrison answered the door, his apartment was already a cloud of cigarette smoke.

He was nervous.

It wasn't yet noon and the cigarettes were coming one after another. When he wasn't smoking, he gulped from a tall glass of cola. There was so much to say, so much ground to cover, so much he had to do, so much he wanted other people to know.

"We're doing this because of my son," Morrison said.

They were the first words out of his mouth. They were difficult words to say even now, two years later.

Behind him was a large poster-size photograph of a young boy standing in the kitchen with the baseball uniform of a Queensbury Little League All-Star. There is a look of pride, a look of innocent happiness in the photograph. Below the photograph is a poster of Jeffry's favorite movie "Field of Dreams." On the poster, the words read "Heaven is where dreams come true."

The juxtaposition is not a coincidence.

On Friday, Oct. 11, 1991, Jeffry Dan Morrison II was riding his bicycle on Dixon Ave. in Queensbury where he lived with his mother.

"It was 3:15 in the afternoon," Morrison said, taking a long drag on another cigarette.

It was every parent's nightmare.

There was a collision with a car. Jeffry was thrown from his bicycle.

There was massive head trauma, yet young Jeffry clung to life.

Jeffry was an athlete. His favorite sport — like his dad's — was baseball. And he was good. Very good.

Morrison puts down his cola and shows the photo of young Jeffry swinging a baseball bat at age 2.

"Look how big he is," Morrison says. "Look how perfect the mechanics are."

Jeffry went though the Little League program at Queensbury and was successful. His dad coached him each season.

As a 9-year-old, Jeffry began a strengthening program — designed by his dad — to develop as an athlete. Morrison consulted doctors and nutritionists so that young Jeffry had every advantage to succeed at what he loved — playing baseball.

"Throughout the whole process of his development as a ballplayer, I did not push him," Morrison says. "That's important. It's important that parents don't push."

In Morrison's Queensbury apartment, there is no living room couch, no easy chair or coffee table. He has weight machines. He has barbells. He has even rigged up a makeshift batting cage right there in the living room. The artwork is of life-sized posters of great ballplayers, the entertainment baseball instructional videos and almost every baseball movie ever made.

All for Jeffry.

It is still there, too.

By age 10, Jeffry was already 5 feet tall and close to 100 pounds. Doctors projected he might grow as big as 6-3 or 6-4 and weigh a robust 210 pounds.

"He could have been a great power pitcher," Morrison says as he refills his glass again.

But that was only part of the education. Morrison taught his son sportsmanship. He taught him that what he saw on television in the major leagues wasn't always something to be imitated. He taught him to respect authority, to respect umpires, to work hard and he would reach his goals. He taught him that winning wasn't everything.

After the collision, the strength that Morrison helped Jeffry develop helped keep the young boy alive despite the terrible head trauma. Jeffry lived three more days.

"That was my own personal torment," Morrison said.

On Oct. 15, Jeffry died.

He was buried in Pine View Cemetery in Queensbury.

"After the funeral, someone asked me if I would continue to coach," Morrison said. "I said I didn't know."

Two days later, Morrison got a note from Jeffry's English teacher. It was a short 108-word composition that Jeffry had written the night before the accident.

"My favorite place is the Queensbury Little League Park," it began. "Some of the reasons this is my favorite place is that I get to play against my friends. I also get to play ball.

"Every year I play ball, my dad has been my coach. I hope that continues."

"I read this," Morrison said, "that's when I promised that I would coach until I went on the extended road trip that he was on. That's how I looked at it, as an extended road trip."

The next spring Morrison returned to the Queensbury Little League Park to coach again.

"I spend anywhere from three to four days a week up there at the field," Morrison said. "When I was there, I truly felt my son right there in my heart. He was right there with me. And sometimes, I don't want to say I have visions, but I sense he is there. And before I deal with another child, I stop and think how would I treat Jeffry. It has made me a lot better person.

"It has made me stronger. It has made me a lot better coach," Morrison continued. "He is my only son. He is the only son I will ever have, and it has been very hard to deal with because I loved him more than anything else in the world.

"Little League is what has kept Jeff alive," said Carol Keeton, Morrison's fiancée" and a vice president in Queensbury Little League. "If it wasn't for the kids, Jeff wouldn't be alive."

Returning to Little League was only the start for Morrison.

It filled some of the void but not all of it.

His vision was larger than that. He saw a baseball program that could provide year-round instruction for youngsters interested in baseball.

He researched almost every baseball school in the country, finally settling on the Doyle Baseball Organization, headed by former major league player Denny Doyle.

Last month Morrison became the local representative for Doyle Baseball — a voluntary position — and has set in motion the beginnings of the baseball school.

A clinic for coaches is already scheduled for February. A clinic for players 7 to 18 is scheduled in July. Morrison pictures a foundation in Jeffry's memory that will help area youngsters attend the school.

"I envision a program for every (area) school," Morrison said. "I envision — with some of the (baseball) talent we have here — the whole level of baseball increasing, especially with the coaching clinic."

But maybe most of all, Jeff Morrison would like to keep the spirit of his son, the spirit of what he called his "perfect child" alive forever.

It may already be happening.

"Jeffry had this little habit when he pitched, when he got in a tough situations, he would stop and kind of look up at the sky before he pitched," Keeton remembered.

"It was a little secret I taught him," Morrison said. "You feel pressure, and you know you have to do your best, back off and look to the sky and be thankful where you are and what you are and then focus on what you have to do."

"Well, one of the kids this year on the team did the same thing, stepped back and looked at the sky," Keeton said. "It was just like Jeffry was there. It was phenomenal. And he had never seen Jeffry pitch."

These days Morrison has opened up his apartment to other youngsters.

They go through the same strengthening program Jeffry went through. They lift the weights, they watch the videos, they listen to Morrison's dreams.

"Kids that don't know Jeffry and will never know Jeffry, will know him in one way or another," Keeton says. "Because what happened to Jeff and Jeffry is alive in every child we come in contact with."

A lone tear rolls down the cheek of Jeff Morrison while behind him the boy in the little League uniform smiles innocently forever.

"My son lives in Queensbury Little League Park," Morrison said.

P.S.

I was still sports editor when Jeff Morrison called to tell me about the youth baseball league he was starting in memory of his late son. I can still see the large poster-sized photograph of the little boy in his Queensbury Little League uniform in Jeff Morrison's apartment. It was haunting.

The little boy was hit by a car while riding his bicycle two years earlier and died. It was clear his dad was still not over it. He chain-smoked cigarettes and gulped a soft drink as he struggled to get through the interview. He said he wanted to talk about baseball, but he really wanted to talk about his little boy. And I let him do that.

I probably didn't fully relate until I had my own little boy three years later.

ONE FAMILY'S VERY MERRY CHRISTMAS

December 24, 1996

GREENWICH – It was another stack of Christmas cards on the dining room table.

You know the drill.

Rip open the envelope, read the first couple of verses of "Tis the season…" and "Wishing you and yours…," skip to the bottom to see who signed it and do a quick mental inventory on whether you remembered to send them a card, too.

But this card was different.

> *This has been a wonderful year for me. I've had many opportunities to spend with my wife and children working on our farm, riding our horses and playing with our dogs. I've had the opportunity to teach my 16-year-old son, Leslie, to drive and share his job in having his license. But my greatest satisfaction has been to watch him run and laugh and work and eat. To watch him live."*

This was no ordinary Christmas card.

It was from Steve Wright, a Glens Falls stockbroker who had sold some stock for me last year. He eventually helped me out with a column I did last Christmas on buying sports stocks as Christmas gifts.

He had spoken then of his son and trying to get him interested inhis business with the stock market.

I remembered that now.

I remembered that very deeply.

> *Last year he was diagnosed with bone cancer and began a year-long course of chemotherapy which was completed this June. Several*

weeks ago, he underwent a series of tests which showed no cancer present. There is no greater gift than that to me.

So here I was Monday night winding my way through some back-road somewhere outside Greenwich as I tried to follow the taillights of Steve Wright's car. It was the first day of my vacation. I should have been home with my wife and 10-month-old son having dinner. That Christmas card changed that.

Steve and Michelle Wright live on a modest 35-acre farm with their 16-year-old son Les and 15-year-old daughter Alex. They have some horse, some cows, some other livestock, too.

This time of year, at night, you can see the house from a good half-mile off in the little ravine below the road with Christmas lights hung from the eaves in celebration of the holidays.

Inside, their three dogs greet you at the back door and you can hear laughter from the next room.

The old farmhouse is a work in progress and Michelle is the first to admit that house work isn't one of her major priorities. There are other things more important in life, she tells you.

She is an expert on that.

It was at the end of February in 1995 when the Wrights first took their son to the doctor with pain in his left hip.

The doctors couldn't find anything wrong.

The pain got worse, but the doctors still couldn't find anything wrong.

By Memorial Day weekend, the Wrights had decided to take their son to Boston to get answers they weren't getting locally. But Les' pain was so bad, they took him to the hospital in Bennington, Vt., out of desperation.

The X-rays of Les' hip showed the left side of his pelvis had almost entirely disappeared. The right side was full of holes.

"It was like Swiss cheese," Michelle said.

The Wrights were told their son had cancer.

"You could see the desperation of the faces of the nurses and doctors at the Bennington hospital," Michele said. "There's no worse fear for a parent."

Steve spent that long night in the Bennington hospital with his son. "I thought he was dying right there before my eyes," Steve said.

Les was transferred to Massachusetts General in Boston the next day where he was diagnosed with lymphoma of the bone, a very rare form of cancer. It was only the third case the Boston hospital had ever seen in a child.

After the bone biopsy, the Wrights were given the news.

The doctors came in and said, 'Leslie, you're a winner. You have a cancer we can treat'," Michelle said.

It was the beginning of a year-long chemotherapy treatment. Every three weeks, Michele and Les would travel the four hours to Boston for treatments.

The treatments made him sick.

He lost his hair.

He had to spend time in a wheelchair.

"Once we found out there was a treatment, we figured we could get through anything," Steve said.

Les continued to get better.

The pelvis that had been eaten away by the cancer began to grow back.

In June, he was declared cancer free.

"You feel like you've been given a gift more precious than when you got him the first time," Michele said. "Life is great."

"A lot of people don't get the second chance," Steve said. "There were a lot of people on the ward where we were who didn't get that chance."

This past fall Les ran cross country for Greenwich varsity.

He was up on his horse again too, practicing team roping with his Da - his first love - and he plans on entering his first rodeo in the coming months.

"I really think we got a miracle," Michele said. "It came out of nowhere. We certainly weren't expecting it."

Each Christmas, Steven sends all his clients a Christmas card like hundreds of other people in business. But Steve always tried to personalize his. This year he went further than that, he had a message.

"I just wanted to let everyone know the good news," Steve said.

Ken,

Where ever you be or whatever you may be doing, I hope that this letter finds you and yours well and enjoying a pleasant holiday season. It is my wish for you that your year be filled with the simple but profound joys of life. I wish you all the best.

Steve Wright

I stopped what I was doing.

I thought about my own little boy sleeping in the next room.

What greater gift indeed.

P.S.

By 2021, Steve Wright was still giving me financial advice, although he was now semi-retired.

To take his mind off the cancer, Steve and Michelle had him do research on colleges. Les stumbled on Texas A & M, drawn as much by its rodeo team as its engineering program. He graduated from Texas A & M with an engineering degree and eventually made his way back to upstate New York. By January 2021, he was closing in on his 40th birthday, working as a civil engineer in Rutland, Vermont, married with a three-year-old daughter while being cancer free.

The entire Wright family continues to compete in rodeos across the region and Steve and Les have competed many times in team roping.

'GET ME BACK IN'

December 26, 2002

HUDSON FALLS
    There was such a sadness in Cindy Feulner's eyes, you never, ever would have guessed it was Christmas Eve.

She had curled herself into the corner of the living room couch of her modest two-story Hudson Falls home with the beautiful antique woodwork. She slouched up against a pillow with her legs tucked comfortably underneath her. Her husband Ed sat on the floor a few feet away, her 10-year-old son - Ed's stepson - Keith sat next to him, but Cindy never took her eyes off Ed. It was as if she was trying to draw in every bit of the warmth and safety of his presence, inhale it, embrace it and never let it go.

Ed had just been asked why.

Why was he leaving for the Persian Gulf the day after Christmas? Why after almost five years out of Naval Reserve duty had he had re-enlisted after 9/11? Why had he transferred out of his Glens Falls unit to another unit in Connecticut that almost certainly would be called to active duty to do patrol boat duty as security for the Naval fleet if things got hot in the Middle East? Cindy seemed to need to hear the reasons again - for comfort.

This wasn't a political debate anymore, this was her husband going off voluntarily to a potential war.

"It's going to be hard tonight and then on Christmas," said Ed. "The last night sleeping together will be the worst. Cindy never cries, but I can see her eyes getting watery right now."

Cindy nestled deeper into the safety of the couch never once taking her eyes off of Ed.

Ed Feulner is a 33-year-old Galway native. He works the third shift at a packaging plant in Scotia as a machine operator. He says he loves his job. He served three years in the Navy after high school graduation. He was part of Operation Desert Storm. He then did another six years in the Reserves. He married Cindy five years ago, right about the time he was getting out.

"Ed's the type of person who likes to help people," said Cindy. "He probably has stopped 50 times on the Northway to help someone on the side of the road."

Oddly, that's where this all started.

Ed had finished work and was heading home on the morning of Sept. 11, 2001, when he saw a truck broken down on the side of the road. Ed lent the driver his half-ton jack and got him on his way again. When he got back in his truck, the news was just breaking about the terrorist attacks on the World Trade Center.

"I was angry after 9/11," said Ed.

Nothing new there. There weren't many Americans that weren't. Only Ed did something about it.

"Ed is a doer," said Cindy.

"The next day I called up the recruiter in Glens Falls and said, 'Get me back in,'" said Ed. On Oct. 24, 2001, he was sworn back into the Reserves. "I wanted to get over there then and there."

About six months ago, Ed decided he wanted to switch to a Reserve unit in Connecticut that would almost certainly be called to active duty if there was a war. He talked it over with Cindy first. She refused to stand in his way.

"My main concern was if they were taken care of financially and if they were ready mentally," said Ed. "I know what it will be like to be away a long time. I've experienced that before. This is her first experience. I know it will be tough for Cindy."

Although they work opposite shifts, both live for their weekends together. "I don't think there's been a weekend we've been apart since we got married," said Ed. On this day, both are even dressed alike wearing jeans and gray sweatshirts.

In November, Ed got orders that his unit was being called to active duty and that they would be going somewhere in the Persian Gulf. Ed was told they would leave before Christmas. He was also told he might be away as long as a year.

Keith, Ed's 10-year-old stepson, took it hard. "He put on his Christmas list this year for Ed to stay," said Cindy.

Later, the orders were changed. Ed was to leave the day after Christmas - today.

"I can say that I don't want him to go," said Cindy. "But I know he has to go. I wasn't going to stop him from following his dreams because of my own selfishness."

"Why?" came the voice next to Ed.

It was 10-year-old Keith.

And there was quiet again. A day earlier he had asked Ed again why he had to go. Ed tried hard to explain again, but obviously without much impact.

"It hurts me inside," said Ed.

Then Ed gives Keith the speech about stepping up and being the man of the house while he's away and not giving his mom any trouble. Maybe the pep talk is for Cindy too. Neither one looks any happier.

"He does things for everyone," said Cindy about Ed. "This is a way he can do something for his country."

This afternoon, Ed's parents, Alan and Liz, will drive Cindy, Keith and Ed to the airport in Albany.

Ed says he's feeling excitement, worry, fear and certainly a sense of dread at the impending goodbyes.

"I'm a wimp at goodbyes," said Ed.

"There's pride, but there's fear at the same time," said Cindy.

There is quiet again in cozy living room. They all know the time is growing short and there is little left to say. Finally, Ed speaks up, "Something like this makes you realize what you have."

And maybe that's the best reason of all why Ed Feulner has to go. Over on the couch, Cindy's gaze never wavers.

P.S.

The roots of this story started at a Christmas party that year where I met Ed and Cindy and learned he was about to deploy to the Middle East. Newspaper editors are never off duty. On Christmas Eve, I interviewed them in their living room. Ed talked about how tough it was going to be because he was away from his family. He said he wished he had a laptop so he could better communicate with Cindy and Keith.

After the interview, I went into work and asked Publisher Jim Marshall if we could give Ed and Cindy one of the newsroom laptops. He agreed and I dropped it off at their house with a hearty "Merry Christmas."

Ed went on to do three deployments with the Navy in the Middle East and retired in 2018. Ed and Cindy still live in Hudson Falls, N.Y. In 2014, they became grandparents when 22-year-old Keith had a baby girl. They now have two grandchildren.

CAPTURING HISTORY THROUGH A LENS

May 9, 2003

HUDSON FALLS - Amid the clutter on the living room floor in Bruce Manell's home lies a digital camera. It sits at the foot of his easy chair, at the ready for a quick snapshot of his latest visitor.

It could be an American goldfinch, a black-capped chickadee or some smart-alek squirrel trying to steal the seed from one of the four bird feeders just inches beyond the living room window. It's hard to tell if the easy chair is facing the bird feeders or the television in the corner.

It's a quiet hobby that has evolved over 60 years. Across the room is a new computer sitting on a desk. On the screen, mixed between the brightly colored digital images of his feathered friends are some other photos that Manell took long ago: a group of Marines on Guadalcanal, a leggy showgirl from a Bob Hope Show on the Marshall Islands and one of himself sitting placidly on the wreckage of a burned-out Zero on Okinawa.

That gets your attention.

Okinawa, like Iwo Jima, is one of those places that speaks automatically to the blood spilled in defending the United States during World War II. It was a nightmare of a blood bath.

Bruce Manell was there.

For most of the past 15 years I've known the 81-year-old Manell as a gregarious senior citizen who came in to The Post-Star offices once a week to collect scores for his weekly bowling column. He always had a smile and an easy-going nature, even when he and his computer weren't getting along. He was one of those guys with an easy laugh of whom you might say, "He wouldn't hurt a fly."

He waged his war on the front lines in the Pacific from 1942 to 1945 armed with a camera in his hands and a .45 on his hip.

Now I was staring at this old black and white photograph of Bruce in a white T-shirt with a camera hung around his neck.

Manell speaks of the front-line experience in matter-of-fact tones. There is an odd lack of emotion and even an easy laugh from time to time.

"I was in a rest area," Manell says, as he describes one of his first contacts with the enemy. "We had a hell of a raid the night before. It started at 11 p.m. and ended at 3:30 in the morning. They were coming at us from all angles. The next day I waded out into the rice patties, looking around and then I saw a wounded Jap soldier and he had a grenade in his hand. He was from here to the bedroom (20 feet away). Their grenades were different than ours and they had to tap them on the butt of the rifle or their helmet to arm them. I saw him tap it on his helmet. So I got out my .45."

The story ends there. The conclusion is not in doubt because Manell is telling the story.

"I have the grenade as a souvenir," he says.

Manell, born and raised in Whitehall, was a combat photographer for the Marines during World War II. His job was to take photographs on the front lines. Sometimes for reconnaissance, other times for publication in magazines and periodicals.

He shows you the news clippings. One photo ran full page in LIFE magazine's outstanding news shots of 1944.

If you've lived in these parts long enough, you've probably heard of Manell. He was on the Hudson Falls police force for 34 years, retiring as the deputy police chief in 1984. He was also The Post-Star's bowling columnist for the better part of the past two decades. He even took some photographs for the newspaper on a free-lance basis after he got out of the military service in 1945.

That's why I was visiting.

His war memories were recently showcased on The Veterans Project on the History Channel, where veterans chronicle their war experiences in words and images. It's a half-hour television show where Manell talks about his experiences in the war.

He hands me the photo of the burned-out Zero and begins to talk about the battle for Okinawa. He remembered vividly the day they heard Ernie Pyle, the renowned war correspondent, had been killed on a nearby island. He remembers taking photos of a river outside the capital of Naha so the Army could build a bridge. He remembers getting wounded.

"They were shooting these 150s at us," said Manell. "The first round was way short. The second one was a little closer. The third one went over our heads, so I said to the guy next to me to watch out for the next one. Sure enough, it landed about 30 to 35 feet away."

Manell leaves the room for a second and brings back his camouflaged helmet from that day in 1945. There, prominently displayed is a half-inch wide hole where the shrapnel penetrated. Manell had been wounded in the forehead and ear. He was back with his outfit within a week, after an operation removed the metal from his head.

"I was a little gun-shy after that," he said.

After Okinawa, Manell was sent to Guam, where he was told his next destination was Tokyo Bay. But since he had been overseas for 2-1/2 years, he was granted leave to return to the States. During his 22-day voyage to San Francisco, he heard about the bombing of Hiroshima and Nagasaki.

"I didn't think it could be true," said Manell. "I didn't think there was any way one bomb could wipe out an entire city."

The war was over for Manell, sort of. In some ways it has never left.

"There was always something going on so you couldn't think about things for too long," Manell explained. "A guy you knew pretty well would get killed and you'd think, that's a shame, but then something else would happen. A lieutenant friend of mine got all blown to hell. He got hit with two shells. He was in agony. His legs were just like jelly with the meat rolling off the bones."

Did he take those photos, too?

"Oh yeah," said Manell.

He talked about the sights that no person should ever see, all in an even voice without a hint of tremor or emotion. He talked of the huge 6 by 6 trucks that would roll through the jungle collecting the bodies of fallen servicemen. He described the sights and the sounds and the smells that still seemed to be with him.

"People who haven't actually been in combat, they have no idea what war is like," said Manell. "I still have the nightmares. My wife used to tell me how I would wake up screaming and thrashing around in bed."

That's when he handed me another black and white photo of a pretty showgirl with Betty Grable legs named Patty Thomas, which he says was his most popular photo.

"I must have made 100 copies of that photo," says Manell with a big smile. "Who knows, maybe 1,000."

P.S.

Not long after I wrote this column, my son told me he had an assignment in school to talk to a veteran. I told him I knew a guy. The three of us met for lunch and Bruce answered all of Joseph's questions and then a few of mine. After the lunch, Bruce popped open the trunk of his car in the parking lot and showed Joseph his M-1 rifle and the helmet with the shrapnel hole that had saved his life.

On July 9, 2009, Bruce Manell passed away at the age of 87. The nightmares would finally cease. Joseph and I paid our respects at his wake and there to the side of the casket was his helmet.

In my July 12 column about Bruce's death I wrote, "We as a community are the poorer this week because of the passing of Bruce Manell. His kind, that gave so much and expected so little, are a rare find these days."

READY FOR A SECOND CHANCE

August 14, 2005

Just a couple weeks shy of his 35th birthday, Ken Powers shifts his seat to the front of the green couch, leans forward and declares, "I can still salvage something out of this."

He's talking about his life.

The second chance he has been hoping for arrived in the mail last month in a letter from Mount Sinai Hospital in New York City.

"We are now formally placing you on the UNOS Waiting List, as we have discussed. Although it is impossible to predict when an organ will become available, you now need to be prepared for the fact that it could happen at any time," announced the letter.

Ken Powers is on the list to receive a new liver to begin a new life.

Sober for just more than two years, Powers was first introduced to readers of The Post-Star as part of a series on teen drinking in the spring of 2004. Powers volunteered to come forward and tell his story of growing up in South Glens Falls and how he started drinking at age 15 and didn't stop until he was in his 30s after years of alcoholism.

"I was lost for so long," Powers said. "I was trying to find everything by drinking."

Instead, he almost lost everything.

He never finished college. He was in and out of meaningless jobs and missed out on any meaningful relationship that could have led to marriage and family. He still lives with his mother in the house in which he grew up.

He got sick and came down with a form of jaundice by alcohol-induced hepatitis. His liver was damaged. He got weaker and weaker.

For the past several years, he has been unable to work with a liver that was only partially functioning, but not sick enough to be on the transplant list.

That's when he came forward to tell his story about the dark side of teen drinking. He volunteered to work with the newspaper to tell his stories to kids.

"My story is scary," Powers said.

He has told it a dozen or so times to students in the South Glens Falls school district, where his family is well-known.

"They know my family and would come up to me in the store and tell me about their own family situations," Powers said. "They didn't want to end up like me."

Three months ago, Powers starting working part-time for the Youth Advocacy Program of Warren/Washington Counties working with troubled youth, many who have had their own problems with alcohol and drugs.

"He seems to have a knack of working with kids," said John Kassebaum, the assistant director. "In some ways, he may see this as a way to give the help to kids that he never got when he was young.

For maybe the first time, Powers sees a future for himself.

"I want to catch up on my life," he said.

He laments how his life went nowhere while he was in his 20s. He talks about all that he missed and the opportunity that a new liver would provide.

The tone of his voice quickens and the future pours out of him. He talks about working full time with the kids who have so many problems. He talks about going back to school. "I want to have a degree on the wall," he said. He talks about establishing relationships, getting married and taking future kids to Little League.

"What's important to me is the community. I want to be a strong man in the community and do what so many other people are already doing," said Powers.

But first there is the transplant.

"I'm anxious, but not afraid," Powers said. "I haven't been afraid since I stopped drinking."

Mount Sinai has told him to be on a moment's notice. The liver could come at any time of the day or night. He has a bag packed and is ready to make the drive to New York City.

"I can't wait to recover," Powers said.

P.S.

I first heard Ken Powers' story when he agreed to be part of the newspaper's underage drinking series that looked at the culture of acceptance around teen drinking. He wanted to turn his experience into a learning experience for others.

Later, we were both asked to speak to a group of high school students about the dangers of drinking. We stayed in touch over the years and he remained committed to telling his story.

CHANCE MEETING LEADS TO GIFT OF LIFE

June 29, 2008

It starts with a simple conversation.

That's the odd thing about this story. Two acquaintances, literally bumping into each other between two aisles of canned goods, catching up with each other on the vagaries of everyday life, shooting the breeze, passing the time … and soon they are talking life and death.

Ken Powers needs a new liver.

He wrecked his with a youth filled with too much booze and no control. He is 38 now, and has since righted the ship, established a life-style worthy of a new liver to fight the toxins that today sap him of energy and strength.

Out of the blue, the other man, Tom Casey, asks what it takes to get a new liver. Right there in the market. He's still not sure why he asked.

Powers tells him the donor has to have a healthy liver. He tells him that the blood types have to match. And he tells him the two people have to be about the same size.

That's the lightning bolt, according to Casey.

This is the part where Casey still pauses, unsure of how to explain what happened next.

"I don't ever put a lot into stuff like this, but when I heard him say, 'You have to be about my size,' there was instant goose bumps," said Casey. "I didn't say a word to him, but all I could think about was 'Jeez Ken, I'm about your size.' "

For days afterward, those words echoed in his head, tormented him, overwhelmed him until he finally went to his doctor for a blood test.

O negative, the same as Ken Powers.

That was two years ago and Casey says it was that moment that preordained that in nine days he will give 65 percent of his healthy liver to Ken Powers because "he is about the same size."

Simple as that.

Livers are amazing organs. You whack out a big slice of your own and give it to someone else and yours will grow back. Of course it is not that easy. It is serious surgery that will take place at Mount Sinai Medical Center in New York and will take Casey away from work for two to three months as he grows his liver and gains strength.

It also gives Powers back a life that he had previously tried to destroy.

I've written about Powers before. He came forward four years ago when our newspaper was doing a series on underage drinking.

Powers told his story of being a star athlete at South Glens Falls who left high school with unlimited potential and a drinking problem. He pulled no punches. He spoke to classes and groups about his experience, imploring youths to be responsible and not end up like him. I watched him do it. You could hear a pin drop when he was done.

Powers went back to school and tried to earn himself a new liver with a new lifestyle. He got a two-year degree at ACC and is earning credits there for Plattsburgh State so that he will have a career in counseling to go with a new life.

Here is another mind-bender: Tom Casey was not a close friend.

That will probably surprise you. It surprised me. He knew the Powers family. He knew Ken, but they were hardly best buddies.

It may also surprise you that Tom Casey has a stepson and two boys of his own and is in the middle of a divorce. You think you've got a lot on your plate?

The surgery will force him to miss two to three months from his job at the Target distribution center in Wilton where he loads trucks.

Still, the only thought that resonates is this: "But Ken, I'm the same size as you!"

So put yourself in Tom Casey's shoes. Mull it over awhile and I bet you'll come to the same conclusion that I did. Most of us wouldn't do it.

And there have been those who have wondered about his sanity, those that have come right out and said, "Are you freaking nuts?"

His 18-year-old stepson Lance tells Casey he is proud of him.

His 12-year-old Brandon is worried for him.

His 8-year-old Liam knows what is happening, but still asks, "Dad, why are you doing this?"

Still, Casey remains steadfast.

"All I can say to you is that I have had two years to think about this," said Casey. "I don't want to word it wrong … but I haven't given this decision a second thought. I'm as sure as I can be."

If that doesn't floor you, then you don't have a pulse.

So here is where I do my part and you can do yours.

Ken Powers' brother Jerry is arranging a fundraiser on July 20 at the South Glens Falls American Legion for Ken and Tom to help with the thousands of dollars of expenses. There is an account set up at the bank where people can donate directly to help the two get through the next few months.

This is where you think about your own luck and wonder which one of your friends would have their liver carved out to save your life.

This is also where you have the chance to help two amazing people, one who turned his life around and another who turned his life upside down to make the other whole.

It sort of makes you proud to be a member of the human race again and that's got to be worth something.

P.S.

The surgery took place in New York City in July 2008 and was successful.

Every year after the surgery, Ken Powers returned to the South Glens Falls Middle School to tell his story again to educate young people about the dangers of alcohol before they start drinking.

After the liver procedure, Ken's health returned to normal and he completed a master's in education in 2012. Tom Casey, who donated part of his liver, also recovered in full after his gift of life.

Ken Powers now works for Northern Rivers helping troubled and disadvantaged teens in three counties and says he loves his work. His advice to young people is to find a job you would do for free like he has. He continues to be active in his community as well.

A PAINFUL DIAGNOSIS

September 24, 2008

You think you've got problems, pull up a chair.

Erica Thomas has a story that will park your complaints in an orbit with Jupiter.

The 26-year-old single mom comes to the door of her subsidized two-bedroom Queensbury apartment, looking fit, vibrant and ready for a fight.

There is a cane by the door, a walker by the bed and a wheelchair for the really bad days, but you see the fire in her.

You wonder if the limp is from beating back all that life has thrown at her lately.

She was diagnosed with multiple sclerosis three years ago. Every six to seven months, the disease unleashes another wave of attacks on her nervous system, further weakening her stamina and increasing her pain.

She was working as a private housekeeper for a local doctor with a house up on Lake George when the MS struck again last December.

"It happened so fast," she said. Her left side suffers from regular numbness. She can have double vision in her left eye. There is constant fatigue and the treatment is often worse, leaving her violently ill, unable to sleep and with migraines that make her wish she was never born.

She can no longer work.

Since the original diagnosis, osteoporosis has weakened her bones and made her susceptible to other injuries. She has developed nerve disorders that cause immense pain with just a light touch to her skin.

Simply put, she's a mess.

She grew up in Glens Falls and has an 8-year-old daughter, Desiree. They share their apartment with Bob and Bianca, two pet bunnies, and their next-door neighbor Jen Hickey regularly comes by to help out.

Most of her family still lives in Glens Falls and Queensbury. But until this past year, Erica took pride in her 50-hour work weeks, taking care of other people's homes before coming home to take care of Desiree and her own home.

So here is the worst part about all this.

"I'm a strong-minded, independent woman," said Erica. "I'm not used to waiting for people to help me. I'm not used to people having to do things for me."

This is what makes her mad. This is her real cross to bear. And this is where you need to consider what it would be like to be dependent on someone else.

She doesn't like being interrogated by the government workers or asking for a ride to the doctor's office. But she's out of options. She wants to shout it out that she didn't ask for this, that she would rather be working and have her health back.

"If it wasn't for my daughter, I would lay down and just give up," said Erica. "But I can't."

And this is other part of the story. Got a spoiled kid? Have a teen that's been taking their cushy life a little too much for granted? Go get them right now and have them pull up a chair because they've gotto read this.

This is what Erica has to say about Desiree, and keep in mind the little girl is only in third grade.

"She is amazing," says Erica, the first tears of the day beginning to form. "All she wants to do is help. It always makes me feel bad. I feel like I've taken away her childhood."

Not once did Erica shed a tear over her own predicament, but get her talking about that little girl and she gets to blubbering.

Erica couldn't get anyone to watch Desiree recently so she had to take her with her to therapy at the hospital complex on Bay Road.

"This summer I brought her with me to physical therapy and it just about tore me apart," said Erica. "I'm struggling to spin on the bike or lift 15 pounds with my legs and she is there, 'You can do it Mom. You can do it.'

"It sucks to have her see me like that," said Erica. "It's awful. I'm supposed to be the strong one and she is instead."

But Erica is plenty strong. Most of us would have folded long ago. She takes 23 pills a day.

During the 90 or so minutes I was with her, she was battling with another agency to get transportation to a doctor's appointment in Clifton Park, then treatment at Albany Medical Center. That was going to be her whole Friday.

Her car needs work and new tires and even if it was fixed, she says it's not really safe for her to drive anymore.

Part of her treatment for the MS is a drug called Tysabri. Get a load of the very first line of the disclaimer on this medication: "Tysabri increases your chances of getting a rare brain infection that usually causes death or severe disability."

How about starting your day with that message staring you down?

Erica is drying her tears after talking about Desiree.

You look up at the wall clock that keeps vigil over the life in Erica Thomas' living room and you are confused by the message.

Across the face of the clock are two Chinese symbols and below them is spelled out their meaning: "Good Luck."

You want to tell Erica to get a new clock.

"I hope to God that someday I'm going to wake up and feel good and I can go back to work," said Erica. "The reality, the way it comes back every six or seven months is that in two months, six months, maybe a year, I could be in a wheelchair. I could wake up blind or not be able to use my entire upper body."

So her new motto is to not sweat the small stuff.

To take each day as it comes.

"My life has changed so drastically," she says. "To sit here every day at 26 and not be able to do anything, not be able to afford to do anything."

She stops and stares off into space. Above her, the clock counts the seconds and minutes and Erica waits quietly for the luck.

P.S.

In the days after publishing this column on Erica my spirit was rejuvenated, my soul reinvigorated and my outlook revitalized despite the financial calamity unfolding all around us.

If you want to know what makes communities like Glens Falls special, consider what happened when I arrived at the office the morning the column was published.

The first email wanted Erica to know there was a support group locally for those suffering from MS and wanting her to attend.

Then there was a voice mail message from a woman in Queensbury, saying she had free time to run some of Erica's errands or give her a ride to the doctor. She also said she would be happy to babysit, too.

A man at one of the local car dealerships sent off a note that he had never done anything like this before, but he would be happy to fix Erica's car for free, refurbish her tires, whatever she needed.

The financial world preceding the Great Recession was crumbling all around us and my community was reaching out to a young woman in need.

Two more email messages just wanted to know: How can I help this young woman with MS?

A man who had written a book about his wife's battle with MS wanted to send her a copy. Another woman wanted to send her a gift certificate to a wellness spa, hoping it might help.

The local Caritas chapter said they had a volunteer who would be happy to do shopping and other errands for her if she didn't feel up to it.

Two other young women, who also suffer from MS and have young children, said they knew exactly what Erica was going through and wanted to reach out to her as well.

By the end of the day I had memorized Erica's email address and corresponded a half-dozen times.

When I finally talked to her again in January 2021, Erica said things got better afterward and she went nearly 10 years without taking any medication at all. She met a man 10 years ago and they married, and although she had not planned on having any more children, she had two boys - one nine and the other six in 2021.

In 2017, lesions began appearing on her brain and spine and her doctor insisted she try a new medication or she will end up in a wheelchair. The new medication stabilized her condition.

She was busy working with the boys with their schoolwork when we talked by phone. She lamented she was in the process of getting a divorce, but that her health was stable.

Desiree graduated from Queensbury High School in 2018. She was supposed to be married in 2020, but postponed it because of the pandemic. Desiree was seven months pregnant when we talked in 2021 and Erica was looking forward to being a grandmother at 38.

AN AMERICAN JOURNEY

April 5, 2009

WHITEHALL

She is 73, her hair pure white and as she leans back into the hard-backed chair in her living room, Gunta Krasts Voutyras wants you to know about her love of America.

And we need to hear it.

Especially now.

Especially after another ugly congressional election made both candidates look bad and discouraged the rest of us.

Oust Oprah and give Gunta a television show to broadcast the story of her life.

She arrived by ship on March 12, 1949, at 7:30 in the evening.

"I can't possibly express the feeling of seeing all those lights," said Gunta about the view of Boston Harbor that night. "We all stayed up all night wondering what our new lives were going to be like, if our parents would get jobs and how we would learn the language."

Sixty years later, it is a date she still cherishes.

That is the message that Gunta wants you to know, now more than ever.

"I don't ever want to hear anything negative about this country," Gunta says. "All of us who came here, it was a privilege.

"I think if you were born in the United States that you don't see it," said Gunta. "I don't want to say you take it for granted, but I don't think you see it."

I think Gunta is right.

Liberals are fighting conservatives, few have faith in our leaders and many wonder why the rest of the world seems to despise us. We're a culture that is collectively shaking its head and wondering what happened.

Maybe it's not what we didn't see but what Gunta did see that frees her love of country in ways we can never imagine. Maybe it's because Gunta and her family had to work for this life a little harder.

She takes us back to her childhood as a slight, curly-haired blond girl living in the port city of Liep ja in Latvia.

Her 60 years here have left her with only the hint of an accent. Her story is rich in detail with dates, places and sometimes even times. Her words paint a home movie, a childhood portrait that is simply a nightmare.

One of her first memories is as a 5-year-old who wondered why her father was digging the underground trench in the backyard.

"He knew it was coming," she says.

Latvia was in a literal crossfire during World War II between the Soviets to the north and the Germans to the south. Gunta's port city, hard by the Baltic Sea, was one of the first captured by the Nazis after Germany began its war with the Soviet Union.

Gunta tells you of a childhood spent running to the underground trench her father had dug to keep them safe from the Soviet bombers.

Children quickly learned survival skills.

"When the moon was out we knew the bombers were coming," said Gunta. "When it was overcast, we knew we were safe."

The Nazis quickly exterminated 7,000 Jews. They rounded up men in the city and took them away by train.

Gunta quietly tells about the night the Nazi officer appeared at the door in 1942. She can still see his youthful face, blond hair, shiny boots and terrifying blue eyes.

"They had picked up my father in town and were taking him away and they brought him home to say goodbye," Gunta said. "Can you imagine?"

The answer is obvious. We cannot imagine that in this country.

Gunta lives in a simple apartment in Whitehall now. She gave up the family home on Lake Champlain several years ago after her mother died at age 94. She gets by on a small online business. She has written a novel and had an essay published in a recent book by Hugh Downs on what it means to be an American. Her essay is one of the few not written by a celebrity.

After three months, Gunta's father had not returned.

She remembers her grandmother imploring her mother to move on, saying her husband probably was not coming back.

Can you imagine?

The family was rounded up with other families and loaded into cattle cars. They rode for days and were finally relocated in Germany where they were put to work in a small factory that made parts for airplanes.

Enemy aircraft sometimes strafed their town and Gunta's sister was shot in the leg.

When the war ended, Gunta would go out on the Autobahn and show people a photo of her father and ask if anyone had seen him.

By some miracle, Gunta's father found his way back from Italy where he had been doing forced labor.

"It was a one in a million shot," said Gunta.

Four years later, her entire family immigrated to the United States just days before a mass deportation of Latvians to Siberia in the Soviet Union.

Her family settled in the Bronx, then Long Island and eventually her father and mother moved into an old home on Lake Champlain.

After her father died, Gunta moved here to take care of her mother.

"I feel that those of us that have been allowed to come here have to pay respect to the bread and butter we have been allowed to eat," said Gunta. "Without this country, I would have ended up some miserable creature in Europe."

We should all pay attention to what Gunta has to say.

Gunta gets up out of her chair and brings you her citizenship papers that are more than just legal documents. They are framed like a college diploma and hang on the wall.

You can see the pride.

Sixty years here and she tells you she never, ever wants to return to Latvia.

This is the country she is proud to call her home.

It is a good thing for us to remember, too.

P.S.

Not long after this initial interview, Gunta befriended a young neighborhood girl in Whitehall who was fascinated by Gunta's vast collection of books. The girl's father was in jail and her mother was absent much of the time. Gunta took the teenager in and eventually adopted her. Imagine adopting a teenager in your 70s.

Gunta moved to Glens Falls and began doing citizenship classes for other immigrants like herself and her adopted daughter blossomed into an outstanding student. She graduated from Glens Falls High School and received a scholarship to Holy Cross. She eventually studied overseas. And while the two often found it difficult to live together, her adopted daughter eventually made her way to Gunta's native Latvia.

The column about Gunta was the start of a relationship that continues to this day. There was a time where it was not unusual for Gunta to call me three or four times a week to comment on the news. She was the first to call me when the Capitol was being stormed in January 2021.

Gunta has no-nonsense opinions and is stubborn as a mule. And when I would tell her that, she would get angry. Strong women like Gunta are another part of the American experience that we all need to celebrate. Each April, Gunta marks the anniversary of when she arrived in the United States. It is her Fourth of July, her Declaration of Independence. And she never takes that for granted.

PEOPLE LIKE TERRY MARTIN DON'T RETIRE

June 3, 2009

People like Terry Martin don't retire, ever.

They switch gears, change professions, look for bigger challenges, set higher goals. They are always asking, "What's next?"

She has been a school teacher in the same place for 33 years. Think about that for a second. You can dig a pretty deep rut in 33 years, but she never did.

She taught physical education to junior high kids who would rather decipher algebraic equations than work up a sweat. After school, she was the varsity field hockey coach for 32 years and became one of the most respected coaches in the region. She won close to 400 games and was a respected referee, too.

How good was she?

Her son Jarred loved her sport so much, he donned a kilt and played on the all-girls high school team in Schuylerville. He is now an assistant coach at Duke.

Her daughter Abby got a full ride to North Carolina.

And yet when you ask her about her success, she won't measure it in wins and losses, but in the number of former players who have also become teachers and coaches and have carried on a legacy of quality education.

This is the coach you've always wanted for your son or daughter.

So there she was 11 years ago with all this going for her and they tell her she has breast cancer.

And she vows to beat that, too, because that's "what's next."

The Relay for Life at Queensbury High School - an American Cancer Society all-night walkathon - had only been in existence for a couple of years. Terry never participated. Like most of us, she had other, more important things to do.

"Honest and true, it always fell during the regional field hockey tourney," Terry said. And that came first.

She was finishing up her treatment that spring in 1998 when several of her former students who worked at the pharmacy in the hospital convinced her to participate for the first time.

"I was in awe," Terry said. "I was shocked. It is like a bee biting you. It gets into your system."

And it stays there.

So, of course, the Relay for Life became "what's next" too.

But she wasn't going to just participate, she wasn't just going to raise some money. Before long, Terry was the liaison between the school and the organizers and then the chairperson of the whole darn event and each year the relay got a little bigger.

She got on the board of directors, she helped out on the regional level and then the national level. People like Terry don't hang in the background, they take charge, solve problems and, in this case, try to find a cure for a killer disease.

She has now been cancer-free for more than 10 years.

And at the Relay for Life Saturday, it was announced that this whirling dervish was going to retire.

You could see the smirks on the faces of those who knew her.

Maybe what she meant is that to do more, to make a bigger difference, that 9-to-5 job had to go.

So there we were last Saturday, with the latest Relay for Life coming to a close and only 100 of the original 1,100 still out there on the track, and here comes Terry, bathed in the sunlight of a new day on a motorized mini-flatbed cart, the co-chair of the event pulling garbage detail at 6 in the morning and looking like she could go another 12 hours.

And she's retiring?

I hope the rest of us can just keep up.

P.S.

After retiring in 2009 from coaching, Terry Martin started officiating field hockey around the region and racing up and down the 100-yard pitch. She lamented that she now spends more time in the gym staying in shape than when she was coaching.

Her daughter Abby was an All-American field hockey player at the University of North Carolina and played on the U.S. national team. She is currently an assistant field hockey coach at Skidmore College in Saratoga Springs, N.Y.

Her son Jarred, who loved field hockey so much he played on the girls' team and wore a kilt like the girls, graduated from the University at Albany with a degree in biochemistry. He spent 12 years on the U.S. National Field Hockey Team before retiring in 2012. After being an assistant coach at Skidmore College, he became the associate head coach at Duke University for 12 years before landing the head coaching job at Ohio State in 2016. He still coaches there today.

AN UNUSUAL JOURNEY TO TIARA

August 15, 2009

GANSEVOORT - Mrs. New York answers the door of her Gansevoort home and, of course, she is attractive, but she may be a little overdressed for a casual interview in her kitchen.

She is wearing a long, flowing sun dress, heeled sandals and makeup. She has also made me brownies. Never in my 30 years of conducting interviews has anyone ever made me brownies. They look good, too.

Nicole Palmer, 33, introduces me to her daughters, 11-year-old Alyssa and 8-year-old Jordan, both of whom are dressed a little too fashionably to be just hanging out during summer vacation. And just when I'm about to buy into the notion that I have walked into the perfect house, in the perfect suburban neighborhood, with the perfect children and perfect wife, she admits that the pool is turning green because of algae.

We have established that Nicole Palmer's life is not perfect, even if you have a sash and crown.

For the next hour and a half, we watch Nicole the wife, teacher and the mother of two young girls wrestle with Nicole the beauty pageant contestant and the reigning Mrs. New York.

Each identity seems to be at odds with the other. My first question, and the one she is asked the most, is why she does it.

Her answer - "to better serve her community and work for her charities" - really does sound like the bottled and polished answer we've come to expect from Miss America contestants who claim their top priority is world peace.

Nicole seems to realize that, too.

If you were not aware, beauty pageants are surviving as a cottage industry.

Being a beauty queen can be expensive. Just entering a pageant can cost $500 or more. And that's before you buy the clothes.

If you never realized your dream as Miss America, you've got the rest of your life to chase Mrs. America.

Nicole's journey has followed that thread.

She started entering pageants when she was a freshman in high school. She was named Miss Poughkeepsie in 1992 and Miss Hudson Valley Teenager in 1993. There were many other pageants along the way but she lived her life, too, graduated from college, became a teacher, married her husband, Joe, and had the girls. She has been teaching in the Queensbury Elementary School for the past three years and will teach third grade this year.

But once the girls were back in school, she started thinking about competing again. She entered the Mrs. New York pageant in 2003, but didn't even crack the top 10 out of 28 contestants. It bothered her.

"It gets in your blood," said Nicole. "I enjoy it and am passionate about it. You get to wear these beautiful gowns and get up on stage in your bathing suit and 4-inch heels."

On one hand, you have the dedicated, professional elementary school teacher and on the other you have the beauty pageant contestant who loves to be looked at on stage.

Nicole seems to embrace the one thing - wearing a bathing suit in public - that most women fear.

So you ask the question again: Why does she do it?

She talks about the pageants as a performance that never gets old, about being in the spotlight.

She tells you that winning the Mrs. New York pageant evolved into her dream.

But here's the thing about these pageants - the conundrum if you will. You need to be attractive and you need to carry yourself well, but there is something else the judges are looking for that is an intangible, some bit of character that separates the winner from everyone else, beyond wanting world peace.

Something that makes the contestant real and not just a pretty face.

Nicole may have found that in the emergency room at Saratoga Hospital two years ago.

It was there that she confronted her vanity and what was really important in her life.

She was visiting a friend's house with her two young daughters when she bent over to pet their little dog. She had done it before. She had always been around dogs. It whirled around and sank its teeth into her upper lip.

They rushed Nicole to the hospital where her husband Joe met her. Her upper lip had nearly been torn off her face and the plastic surgeon was looking at a jigsaw puzzle of nerves and tissue.

As the doctor tried to do his work, Nicole was a whimpering mess, fretting over what she would look like. Would her smile be crooked? Would there be a scar? Would she ever be able to compete in a beauty pageant again?

"Four inches lower and you might not be alive," the doctor told her.

Nicole thought about her two daughters and husband and was quiet.

"Any other questions?" the doctor asked.

"No, we're good," Joe said.

So at the very moment when her dream was escaping, her beauty compromised, perhaps this was the piece of her that was missing as a person, and yes, as a contestant.

It took 100 stitches to close the wound, but maybe it made her whole in ways that can't be measured by a doctor's sutures.

During the Mrs. New York pageant in July, the judge asked about life lessons. She told him about the dog attack and the scar and the moment with Joe in the emergency room. She pointed to the scar to see if the judge could see it through the makeup.

She was sure of herself in that regard, of who she was and what was important.

And she won.

She brings one photo to the kitchen table. It is not of her being crowned, but of her stitched lip. She points to her lip so you can see the scar, but it is invisible to you as well.

Nicole will be going to Tucson in September to compete with 50 other women for the Mrs. America title. The finals will be televised on the Women's Entertainment network.

She tells you about the night she won and riding home in the car with Joe and wearing the crown in the car as a goof. She talks about how she and Joe joke about it and how she threatens to wear the crown and sash mowing the lawn or doing the dishes while asking Joe if he can get Mrs. America a drink.

"That's who I am," says Nicole, laughing as you try to figure out which Nicole you are talking to - the serious teacher or the vain beauty queen - and you realize they have merged seamlessly into this complete person and that was what the judges were looking for all along.

P.S.

In October 2009, Nicole was chosen to be the grand Marshall of the South Glens Falls Holiday Parade.

Nicole continued to compete in pageants and was crowned "America's Outstanding Mom 2012" in a pageant in Connecticut and then Mrs. New York International in 2014.

HUSBAND'S IMPOSSIBLE CHOICE

May 25, 2013

Willard F. Skellie of Glens Falls pleaded guilty to manslaughter last week for helping his wife to commit suicide.

What would you have done?

Willard is 69. His wife, Kathy, was 59. She had been suffering from mental illness for years and had attempted suicide in the past. She rarely left her room because of panic attacks, so she finally asked her husband to help her.

Can you imagine the conversation?

Can you imagine the back and forth, the angst, the agony, the tears?

I don't think it was a short conversation. How could it be? I suspect it went on for weeks, maybe months, until Willard finally relented and bought her a 12-gauge shotgun.

Marriage is difficult, but it was never supposed to be this difficult.

Willard said his wife had been despondent, and she was in mental anguish. I imagine Willard changed the subject, stalled and did everything he could in hopes she would change her mind, that she might see a reason to live.

But eventually, Willard showed Kathy how to use the shotgun. He reviewed the details step by step while she took notes on a scrap of paper.

He later tampered with the first two rounds, hoping she would never get to the third.

He gave her the gun on a Friday afternoon this past December before going hunting. When he returned that night, he didn't check on her.

Maybe he couldn't bring himself to check.

He got up the next morning and went hunting again. When he returned mid-morning, he forced his way into her locked bedroom and found her dead of a gunshot wound to the head.

The police found inconsistencies with Willard's story and asked him to take a lie detector test.

He failed.

Willard was not a criminal.

He admitted he bought the gun for Kathy and showed her how to use it. He admitted he picked up the notes she took when he showed her how to use the gun. He also picked up a suicide note before police arrived.

Section 125.15 of the New York State Penal Code states you can be charged with manslaughter in the second degree if you intentionally cause or aid another person to commit suicide. It is a felony.

Willard was charged. He couldn't make the $100,000 bail and spent 25 days in Warren County Jail. He was facing up to 15 years in state prison.

This past week, Willard faced Judge John Hall and quietly answered questions in court.

His children pleaded for leniency. They told the judge Willard loved Kathy.

There had also been an outpouring of community support for Willard.

What would you have done?

We suspect the judge asked himself that question, too.

Judge Hall put Willard on interim probation for a year with a requirement he perform 1,000 hours of community service, about six months' worth of work. If he completes the community service, Hall will impose a five-year term of probation.

Willard did break the law, but I doubt anyone believes Willard Skellie is a criminal, or a threat to society.

I think we all can agree it's up to a power much higher than the New York courts to decide if what Willard did was right or wrong.

One thing is for sure: The man has been through enough.

P.S.

There are times when we all need to put ourselves in the other person's shoes. To walk a few steps and consider what we would have done, how we would handle an impossible situation. Sometimes throwing the book at someone is not the right course. The column also brought up the controversial issue of assisted suicide.

Willard, who was 69 at the time, was charged with manslaughter and spent 25 days in the Warren County Jail. His children pleaded for mercy. They told Judge Hall he loved his late wife. There was an outpouring of sympathy from the community.

Cancer got Willard in 2017. I hope he found peace in those remaining years. He deserved it.

'LOVE YOU TO THE MOON AND BACK'

March 4, 2018

We had been talking for nearly two hours.

Tough, gut-wrenching talk. The kind of conversation that brings tears, sobs, defiance, but in the end a sad emptiness.

There had been no resolution, no redemption, just pain from a world turned upside down.

Karen Caputo-Canale is 68, bright-eyed and well spoken, but this day she was still recovering from a fall that had her left arm in a cast while she used a walker for support.

It was the least of her pain.

As I stood to leave, she struggled to articulate a final time why she needed to tell the story, but her desperation failed her.

She pointed to a white linen shawl draped over a stool.

"You see that shawl," she said. "My sister took her to Spain and she gave me that as a present when she came back. I decided I was going to wrap her in it when she died."

She says it matter-of-factly.

Almost as if it is foretold.

Cara Mia Canale is Karen's daughter.

She was one of those in the boat with Alexander West when his boat crashed into another, killing 8-year-old Charlotte McCue in July 2016.

She was the only one in that boat to testify against West.

"This is a love story of a mother and a daughter," Karen said with steely eyes, as if it's all she has left.

It's the last thing you would expect out of this boating tragedy, especially after hearing a story of an artistic young woman who dropped out of college, got hooked on heroin and overdosed twice while being at the center of a horrific boating accident that left the community disgusted by the young people who ran away.

"I'm tired of going to funerals and wakes," Karen said, again trying to explain, trying to find some meaning in her story and her daughter's life.

You try to nail down the specifics of when and how this started, but Karen jumps from one thought to the next, sometimes overwhelmed by the tears, distracted by something written in a letter, the past and future mashed together in a confusing sob.

Then she stops and stares a hole through you with those piercing eyes.

"She was clean and sober for two years," Karen says slowly, deliberately. It isn't so much a statement as a haunting question that can never be answered, the "why" lingering in the air.

Karen said she is grateful to the McCue family and the compassion they showed her during the trial, but she is also bitter about those who anonymously attacked her on social media, called her daughter a "baby killer" and encouraged her to "shoot herself."

"I want people to know she is a good person," Karen said. "She's a genuine human being. She put others before herself."

Karen said she forgave her daughter when she testified against West, but she does not speak of redemption.

Cara Mia is in rehab now. Her jail sentence will depend on how well she does in putting her life back together.

Karen says she was an enabler.

She tells the story of taking her to Albany because she wanted to look at an apartment.

Karen stares back at me again.

"I was taking her to buy drugs," she said. "I can't be a tough-love mom."

It took its toll on Karen, too.

Twice Cara Mia overdosed. The second time was in Karen's home.

"She did it right in my house," Karen says. "I used his little knife to unlock the bathroom door. She was lying on the floor. She was unconscious and I screamed out the door for my neighbor to call 911. They gave her Narcan at Glens Falls Hospital. She was put on a suicide watch."

"I just turned 68 and I didn't want to," Karen said. The inference is obvious. She had lost her will to live, too.

But that changed recently. A friend talked her through it, convinced her that there was more life to live.

She and Cara Mia write each other every day, with Cara Mia ending each letter, "I love you to the moon and back."

It's their mother and daughter thing. The phrase is stitched on a pillow on the living room couch, a gift from Cara Mia.

Karen shares this letter that Cara Mia wrote last July:

"As angry as I was, I understand how lost and desperate you have been to fix my addiction. Actually, I don't understand how that must feel. But I can relate to some of the emotions you may have been feeling. I know I've felt helpless, hopeless, lost, alone and scared."

Karen goes into her bedroom. I hear her rummaging behind the door and then removing the paper that is covering a large charcoal drawing.

She props it up on the living room sofa.

It draws you in.

It's a self-portrait that Cara Mia drew in high school.

It was a part of a high school art show that was eventually displayed at The Hyde.

It is a self-portrait of a young girl, a swath of hair covering one eye while she peers out from behind her glasses with the other, like she might be keeping a big secret.

But maybe that is just my interpretation from 10 years in the future.

There are no secrets for Cara Mia or her mother now. There can't be.

"I want people to know she is a good person," Karen says.

Maybe that's what she has been getting at for the last two hours. Maybe that is what she has been trying to convince herself of.

She stares at the painting, the promise of a future now stained.

"I think she has a great future," she says to me directly. "She has a heart and soul. I don't see with my eyes. I see through my heart."

As any mother would.

As Karen must now.

It's the only way she can get out of bed in the morning.

P.S.

The boat accident on Lake George, after a day of partying by the young people on board, was one of the most shocking stories that our newspaper covered in years, especially since the young people ran, then refused to be cooperative with police - except Cara Mia.

Three months after this column ran, Cara Mia pleaded guilty to a misdemeanor count of offering a false instrument for lying the day after the fatal boat crash. She was the only passenger in the boat to cooperate with prosecutors. She was sentenced to probation as relatives of the victims advocated for her.

The story of redemption continued. When I checked in with Karen in January 2021, she said Cara Mia was "doing great." She was employed as a nurse at a Capital District hospital and she had delivered Karen a granddaughter five months earlier.

HEART, SOULS AND BRAVERY OF WILL AND BELLA

November 18, 2018

The best of our reporters, our editors, our writers, all of those journalists who serve our communities bring a brutal honesty to their craft.

That doesn't sound good, but it is imperative to accurately tell the stories of our community.

But I fear there are few among us who don't hesitate in some small way.

We are often afraid to go too far, to upset our readers and face some backlash.

That is true today more than ever.

The great ones are not afraid to do that, and they do it without reservation.

It was just over a year ago that *The Post-Star's* Projects Editor Will Doolittle came into my office and said he needed to talk to me.

Will told me that Bella, his 59-year-old wife, had been diagnosed with early onset Alzheimer's and the two of them wanted to do a weekly podcast on *The Post-Star's* website to talk about Alzheimer's and what they were going through.

This did not surprise me.

Will and I are about the same age, and about the time my son was born 22 years ago, Will and Bella — after raising two children of their own — adopted an African-American baby. Not long after that, Bella's young great-niece came to live with them as well. They eventually adopted her as well. Both recently graduated from college.

At work, Will is our de facto writing coach, showing patience and skill while successfully guiding young reporters to career opportunities at larger, more prestigious media outlets.

When we took on newsroom-wide projects, it was Will who sorted out the egos and brought them together as a team that produced national-award-winning projects on underage drinking, the working poor, domestic violence, the heroin epidemic and suicide.

It made our community better, stronger, as it faced stern challenges.

But this past year, it has been Will and Bella facing the stern challenges.

Over the past nine months, they have settled into a routine with regular podcasts to go along with columns from Will called, "The Alzheimer's Chronicles."

In that first column, Will showed the brutal honesty I believe is needed: "The doctor who delivered the diagnosis told Bella she had eight years left, based on the average. Other doctors have said the progression is unpredictable and can take much longer. But they all agree Alzheimer's is fatal and there is no cure."

Consider the bravery it took to write those words for all to see.

To let the world know their most personal challenges and heartache.

Bella never wanted to be identified in any of his Will's past columns, including the ones about the kids, but she agreed to do it for this project.

In another column, he described their agreement going forward. Will would let Bella know when she had done something "Alzheimerish," but Will admitted he often did not have the heart to tell her.

He walked readers through Bella's early retirement and the crunch that would put on their finances.

He recounted the reaction of readers across the region when their story was recounted in a segment on North Country Public Radio that went national, and then wrote this heartbreaking line, "We know the hours we have left are fewer than we expected."

I believe Will and Bella's goal has always been to express that brutal honesty in the hopes it would help the next couple down the road.

"I notice what she doesn't as the disease progresses," Will wrote a year after Bella was diagnosed. "I notice the way the interval of forgetfulness gets shorter, so we will exchange the exact same sentences twice or three times within the same number of minutes."

He explains how her concerns are narrowing to familiar things — family, pets and home.

"But those are the important things, after all, and if she can't observe what is happening to her, then that is a blessing that dwells inside the curse of this disease. Because I do notice, I carry a feeling of loss around, although sometimes it is light as a shadow and hard to spot as it trails behind me. Sometimes, it is all around me like a coat."

You never know that from seeing him at work as he makes good stories great for all of you to read.

This past week, Lee Enterprises announced that Will was the recipient of its "Spirit Award" for sharing the story none of you would want to share.

Kevin Mowbray, Lee's chief executive officer, told me that Will was chosen from about 30 entries across Lee's 50 newspapers, but it wasn't even close.

Kevin said that when he announced the honor in a company-wide conference call earlier this week, he hesitated about whether there should be applause.

"It didn't really seem like the kind of thing to applaud," Mowbray said.

It really isn't "Spirit" that Will and Bella have shown; it's heart and soul and a large dose of bravery.

Will said this in a recent column:

"But the dread of the worst of the decline hangs over you, and it's hard to put out of your mind, because the symptoms, even when they're mild, are constant reminders. Not everyone who has Alzheimer's is able to admit what is happening or is as sensitive as Bella is to what their spouse is going through. Looking at myself, I see someone obsessed with this ordeal, and I'm not even the one who has a fatal disease. Maybe success as an Alzheimer's caregiver comes in accepting failure. Your loved one will not recover. Your life will be changed. You will not handle this well."

I think they have handled it perfectly by addressing it head on with the brutal honesty and bravery that few of us would be able to manage.

Will Doolittle is just one example of the type of people that work at our newspaper. You need to know that, appreciate that and be grateful for that. I know I do.

"We like our routine," Will wrote in a column this summer, "because it gives us each time to do things we enjoy and also spend hours together, not necessarily speaking but sitting with the heightened awareness of each other's presence that people have when they are saying goodbye."

If you are wiping away a tear, I understand.

P.S.

Over the years, Will had been night editor, Sunday editor, features editor and projects editor at the newspaper. He has regularly won state and national journalism honors for his reporting and writing. In 2011, Suburban Newspapers of America named him their Journalist of the Year.

By the beginning of 2021, Will and Bella were still doing their podcasts and Will was still updating readers with his column with the stark reality that Bella continued to get worse.

In June 2020, the podcast was honored with another first place award. The judges said: "This is an absolutely beautiful podcast. Anyone who has a loved one with Alzheimer's should listen to this."

HOMETOWN, USA

A Look Magazine article in 1946 proclaimed Glens Falls, N.Y. to be "Hometown, USA" for its small-town values and charm. The community has proudly worn that moniker ever since. And while Glens Falls still sports that small-time charm and is unique in so many ways, the city and the surrounding communities have many of the problems that other communities do. It also has plenty of those small-town values.

REDEMPTION AND HOPE IN A SMALL TOWN

June 30, 2005

When Michael Jahne stood up to give his speech at Cambridge High School's graduation this year, you can be sure there were a few people holding their breath.

This was what Cambridge school officials had feared last year.

Michael and his twin brother, Daniel, were two of the smartest students in their class.

Past newspaper articles showed that the two competed in a regional competition of the school's Odyssey of the Mind competition in 2000 and 2002. They were also named "Commended Students" in the 2005 National Merit Scholarship Program.

But they both had disciplinary problems on their school records.

So Cambridge school officials took action.

They enacted a policy last June - in the twins' junior year - that allowed the superintendent to withhold the top two academic awards if a student had a history of behavioral problems in or out of school.

It was a pretty transparent attempt, some felt, to ward off a possible embarrassing situation should the Jahne brothers earn valedictorian or salutatorian honors for their 2005 graduation.

What followed was one of those small-town furors that divides communities and causes ill will for years. The argument spilled over into other schools and communities throughout the Capital District, as Cambridge's policy was debated for being arbitrary and subjective and especially aimed at the Jahnes.

After much turmoil and debate, school officials returned to the traditional policy.

That was not the end of the story, though.

Michael and Daniel Jahne were arrested Oct. 1, 2004, by Washington County sheriff's officers, who found several marijuana plants in the trunk of Michael's Mazda after a routine traffic stop. There were 2 pounds of marijuana in the car.

The brothers eventually pleaded guilty to felony marijuana charges and admitted in court they were addicted to marijuana. They agreed to take part in the county's drug treatment program to stay out of jail.

That set the stage for Cambridge's graduation.

Michael earned salutatorian honors as the student with the second-best grades in the senior class. Daniel was third.

Yes, it was what some school officials had feared almost a year earlier. But what they never anticipated was that Michael Jahne would stand up before everyone in his small town and tell them he was sorry.

He told the hundreds assembled outside on a warm Friday evening that he had made mistakes, but that he wanted to carry a message to his classmates that "nothing is a mistake as long as you learn from it."

It was almost the same message that acting Washington County Judge John Hall had recited to the twins at their sentencing six months earlier.

"Proud," said LoisAnn Jahne when asked how she felt about her son's speech. "Proud. A lot of adults couldn't have done what they did."

She was right.

It takes a special person to admit his mistakes in front of hundreds of his closest friends and relatives in a small town.

According to LoisAnn, Cambridge Principal Dan Severson led a standing ovation after Michael's speech, as almost everyone in attendance stood and applauded. Dozens congratulated the young man after the ceremony.

Instead of an embarrassment, instead of a black eye for the school and the community, what Cambridge experienced was a shining moment, a redemption that should go a long way toward healing old wounds.

Redemption for two young men who still have their entire lives ahead of them and obviously lots to offer the world and their community.

And redemption for school officials, for listening to the voices of their community and doing the right thing.

Superintendent Frank Greenhall, who initially recommended the valedictorian and salutatorian changes, said in an earlier Post-Star story that he learned a lot from watching the class of 2005 mature.

That was good to hear.

We all need to remember that people can change. They can redeem themselves. They can surprise us in ways we could never imagine.

The Jahne brothers still have to complete their yearlong drug rehabilitation program. They plan on attending Adirondack Community College in the fall.

They are not out of the woods yet, but the way they handled their graduation means they have learned a lot already from the stumbles they have made in their young lives.

I asked LoisAnn what it meant to her.

"We're back to where we were," she said. "We had our boys back."

P.S.

Things turned out pretty well for the Michael and Daniel. The twins spent a year at Adirondack Community College where they both made the Dean's List. From there, Daniel transferred to Rensselaer Polytechnic Institute in Troy, N.Y. where he graduated with a computer science degree and now works in the Capital District as a software engineer.

Michael, who made the graduation speech, transferred to Clarkson University in Potsdam, N.Y. where he received a bachelor's degree in 2009, a master's in 2012 and a doctor of philosophy degree in environmental science and engineering in 2015. He is currently working for the Environmental Protection Agency on a water revitalization project. He married in May 2019.

Lois Ann and her husband continue to be in the news with their political activism. They were regularly involved in protests at Rep. Elise Stefanik's office in Glens Falls, N.Y. in recent years.

SHUFFLING THROUGH AN UNIMAGINABLE LIFE

March 30, 2008

It is a bleak, drafty storefront with dirty blinds and a couple of plants that don't look like they will make it through the week.

The people that walk through the door often look that way, too.

They walk through the door often.

Glen Street merchants would kill for this type of foot traffic. It is a constant, unrelenting march of folks trying to get through the next day by getting through this door. There is no cash register.

No place in downtown Glens Falls does better business than Community Action's food pantry on Maple Street.

Pat Reynolds sits at the desk facing the door. She answers the phone, keeps track of the paperwork, sends out thank-you notes to those who donate and takes the information from people who need food immediately.

A young woman with short brown hair sits down at the desk.

There is more than just a sadness about her. Her eyes betray something older than her 20-something years. She is uncomfortable in this chair, meekly chirping out the grim statistics of her finances.

"Do you have any income," Reynolds asks.

"No," she says quietly. "I get child support sometimes."

Reynolds asks how much she pays for rent, heating and other expenses while also keeping a wary eye on the next person to come through the door.

Within a few minutes, Mark Carroll, one of the volunteers here, brings out an emergency food basket, a nice way of describing a cardboard box filled with peanut butter, pasta, juice, hot dogs and maybe a steak, although they are just about out of meat this day. The basket is supposed to get the family through the next three days.

Fred Stone, who runs the program that procures leftover food from area markets and stores, says the baskets can last longer if people scrimp.

It isn't quite noon yet and this is the eighth food basket to go out this morning.

Another 75 people have signed the clipboard that allows them to fill a plastic shopping bag filled with day-old bread and bagels, a dessert and some non-fat yogurt with an expiration date from two weeks ago.

But not everyone has bothered to sign in and with so many people coming through the door, it is hard to keep track.

Later, bruised fruit and wilted lettuce will be added to the menu.

But here's what strikes you about the souls who walk through that door.

They shuffle quietly around the room choosing the food they need. Their eyes hug the floor and they rarely talk above a whisper. It's as if they did something wrong just coming through that door.

Here's what else strikes you.

People like me, and maybe you, don't really care.

"The part of the community that is capable of helping us, people like you, don't know much about us," said Lynne Ackershoek, the executive director.

She says it matter-of-factly, a mild rebuke to all of us who pay our bills and know where our next meal will come.

We make the occasional donation and hurriedly drop off our old clothes after spring cleaning wanting to spend as little time as possible here with the rough looking people that frankly frighten us a little.

Is it because of the way they look?

Or because of what they represent?

It's hard to reconcile this place with Glens Falls. It doesn't fit our idyllic image.

You might not want to hear this story because you've heard it before.

You understand that there is poverty out there. You understand that people are not making it. That's the way it has always been and, damn it, you're proud that you are not part of it and you're proud that you work hard to provide your family with a nice home, swimming pool and big-screen TV.

And when we notice we have food that is past the expiration date, we know we can drop it off at Community Action.

It is a parade of people this morning. Seniors hunched over on their canes, scruffy looking men who have not shaven and some folks who could just as easily be your next door neighbor. Most are admirably polite and grateful.

"Do you have any diapers in a size one," another young woman asks. When Carroll retrieves a bagful, she thanks him repeatedly. You are surprised at how grateful she is in a world where we routinely complain about the restaurant service or the quality of our cheeseburger.

I am looking at the clock now. I am anxious to leave. I'm uncomfortable here.

Reynolds, who was a waitress for years says this is the best job she has ever had.

"We help people," she says. The others say the same. And it is obvious that they do.

"Some people are working 40 to 60 hours a week and can't make it," said Ackershoek.

"Not on $7.50 an hour and no health benefits. They are one car repair, one broken wrist, one illness away from not making it. Any gains they make can disappear overnight. They live paycheck to paycheck."

When the rent and heat have been paid, sometimes the math does not include money for food.

You are shaking your head right now. You are thinking how terrible this is right here in our neighborhood and few of us have any idea what it could possibly be like.

How could someone get themselves into such a predicament?

But here they are. So many.

Marching through this front door on Maple Street.

And we have dinner waiting for us at home.

P.S.

In January 2021, Community Action in Glens Falls is still providing valuable services to the community and Lynne Ackershoek is still the executive director after 34 years. In her 2019 executive report, Acker-shoek reported that need for services had been dropping through 2019.

DEPLOYED FATHER TO MISS SPECIAL DAY

May 18, 2008

This started with an e-mail just dripping with guilt from halfway around the world.

It was from Jeffrey Trottier, usually of Hadley, more recently from somewhere in Iraq. He was the town supervisor in Hadley who wanted to continue in office even while serving his country overseas. He is now Jeffrey Trottier, master sgt. with the New York Air National Guard's 109th Airlift Wing out of Schenectady and one bummed-out dad.

His daughter, Ashley, graduated from San Marco State in California yesterday and he wasn't there.

There are events in your children's lives - driver's license test, the prom, high school and college graduations - that are big. You don't miss them.

Unfortunately, wars can force exceptions on the people who serve in them.

"A lot of folks over here, a lot of the young people, they don't get to see their kids born," said Jeffrey, trying to say the right thing. "It's a tough time of year any time over here, but especially with my daughter graduating."

It was his granddaughter's first birthday the day we talked on the phone. That was weighing on his mind, too. He had been overseas six months and had been expecting to be back home by now. Now he was about to miss Ashley's graduation.

But like many others, he was needed elsewhere.

The Trottiers know the drill. They are a veteran military family. Jeffrey's son, Justin, has already done two tours of duty in Iraq and is stationed at Camp Pendleton.

"I'm following in his footsteps," said Jeffrey.

"I miss my family, but you know I think I miss the freedom the most. We take a lot for granted. The safety net is a lot different back home than here. I've got an obligation here and I wouldn't trade it for the world. That's the price of freedom."

So Ashley walked across that stage yesterday without him there.

"I said, 'Hey Dad, you are in Iraq. Don't worry about it. No worries,' " said Ashley.

She was also trying to say the right thing.

"She told me that I was more worried than she was," said Jeffrey.

"When I get my master's you will be there for that," Ashley told Jeff.

Sorry Ashley, but I don't think you understand this parents thing. This is mandatory. There is no negotiation when it comes to the first day of school or that first hit in Little League. This is the culmination of those late nights helping with homework, time spent drying those tears and the long talks about everything in your life.

College graduation may really be for the parents.

Those 30 seconds when you glide across that stage with your whole life ahead of you is when your dad gets to stand and cheer what you have become and what you have accomplished. A snapshot and some home movies won't buy that back.

Jeff was talking himself through it the day I talked to him. He was resolute and strong and he was desperately trying to be upbeat, but I didn't buy it for a second.

He told me about the live Webcast that the college was providing.

"It will be fine," said Jeffrey. "As long as there is enough bandwidth and I get to see her walk across that stage, I will be a proud dad."

He was worried a lot about that bandwidth. It was his lifeline to Ashley on her big day.

I have no doubt when that moment happened yesterday, and Ashley was handed that diploma, there was a whoop and a holler that might have woken up an entire base worth of airmen as Jeffrey Trottier made the best of his life in Iraq while wishing he was someplace else.

P.S.

On November 19, 2019, I got an email from Jeff that he had come across this column and he was still in the military. In November 2020, he took over as the top enlisted Airman in the 109th Airlift Wing at Stratton Air National Guard Base in Scotia, N.Y. During his 22 years in the military, he deployed to Iraq, Afghanistan and as an intelligence analyst in Guam.

After graduating from California State University San Marcos, Ashley went to work as an international customer support representative and was engaged in 2009. By January 2021, she had been married 11 years and had two sons.

A DAUGHTER'S DEPLOYMENT

June 15, 2008 - Father's Day

You wonder when it happened.

One day Ashleigh Davidson was a sophomore at Granville Central School, barely 16, playing sports, being a teenager and talking about studying languages at her mom's alma mater Cornell. Then it was nearby Middlebury College.

Then she started talking about West Point and the benefits of a free education and how the U.S. Military Academy was as good a school as any in the Ivy League.

And she's just a kid. What could she possibly know about the world out there? What could she know about where this would lead her?

"My reaction was, 'Oh my goodness,'" said Lisa Davidson, Ashleigh's mom, who is a biology teacher at Granville.

"Oh my goodness," because U.S. troops had invaded Iraq.

"Oh my goodness," because wars are never really in the plans you have for your children.

"I was concerned what would happen and where this road would take her," said Lisa.

That road led to May 31 at Michie Stadium where Ashleigh graduated from West Point as Cadet Capt. Ashleigh Davidson and where Secretary of the Army Pete Geren somberly reminded the 972 graduates that 11 West Point alumni had died overseas in the past year.

"That sends a chill down your spine," said Lisa. "You wonder if one of them, next year, is going to be my child."

Especially when the road leads next to six weeks of training at Fort Benning, Ga., and eventually to a deployment to Iraq in six months or sooner.

Oh my goodness.

Both Lisa and her husband, Joel, talked with great pride of their daughter's accomplishments.

You could hear it in their voices.

"She has always been very tough," Lisa said. "She knows what she wants and she goes after it and she never quits. I have never known her to quit at anything."

But even as those words came out of her mouth, there was something in this mother's voice, something that told you there was regret there, too. Regret that her daughter was that tough, concern over whether that toughness would be enough in a war zone.

Lisa paused and admitted that there were times that she wished her daughter had quit.

You can almost imagine Joel and Lisa watching the evening news each night, knowing that each step their daughter took forward was one step closer to being part of the news, part of that nightmare overseas.

"You have a heightened awareness of the news overseas," said Joel, who is a Vermont State Trooper and spent four years in the Army right out of high school.

"It is not unusual for a female to be killed in Iraq," said Joel. "People may think they are not on the front lines, but they can be put in some very dangerous situations, so I would be crazy if I wasn't concerned."

Ashleigh is home this month, where her mother says she will spoil her. Ashleigh loves languages and hopes to use her expertise in Russian to further her military career.

She is anxious to get her deployment taken care of and is frank about the dangers.

"A guy in one of my friend's companies, he came back a couple weeks ago missing a leg from Iraq," said Ashleigh.

The words are matter of fact. Details from a world most college seniors are not privy to in any real sense.

"That just brought the reality home, big-time," said Ashleigh. "It was someone we all knew. It made it very real that I could get injured or get killed … In the end you just don't think about it."

But I doubt anyone buys that. How could she not think about it? How could her family not think about it?

I ask Joel how his family will get through her deployment.

He hesitates and indicates that is still a long way off even though the reality is that it is very close.

Joel asks me if I have children. He asks if I have a daughter.

"Daughters are quite unique," said Joel. "You tend to be more protective of your daughters."

And that's the dagger.

This time, Ashleigh isn't going on a sleepover, or camp or away to college.

This time, she is going to one of the most dangerous places on Earth.

The time of watching over her, tucking her in and kissing her good night are past. This time, Joel won't be able to protect her.

This time, he cannot keep her safe.

And on this Father's Day, that's got to be his greatest worry of all.

P.S.

After graduation, Ashleigh was stationed in El Paso, Texas and was eventually deployed to Iraq. When she returned home in August 2010, I checked in with her again and wrote a second column.

ADJUSTING TO THE REAL WORLD

November 29, 2010

The question lingers in the dead air of the phone line.

Have you changed?

1st Lt. Ashleigh Davidson considers the question with a long pause. You wonder if she has considered it herself.

"Not too much that I have been told," she finally says.

She says "the real world," the one we all take for granted and gave thanks for this past week, is hard to get used to again after a year in the desert.

The Granville High and West Point graduate says driving a car again was "interesting" and remembering to put gas in it and pay bills were all things that were not part of the daily routine in the Kirkuk region of Iraq where her base was shelled almost daily.

She says there is some "re-adjusting" that has to be done.

When someone slammed a door while Ashleigh was shopping with her mother this week, she was sure that it was a mortar and she waited for the next incoming round.

When she heard a siren in the car, it reminded her of the sirens that went off at her base before a mortar attack. Then she remembered that she is back in the States, back in the "real world."

After all, it has only been a few weeks.

It was just before Thanksgiving a year ago that Lisa and Joel Davidson - Ashleigh's parents - made the trip to Fort Bliss in Texas to say goodbye to their oldest daughter.

There were tears and trepidation and the Thanksgiving that followed had to be bit hollow.

Lisa's hopes had not been realized. When Ashleigh had first enrolled at West Point, Iraq was one of the most dangerous places on the planet.

Lisa bargained that maybe the war would be over by the time she graduated.

While the war had slowed, it had not ended.

Ashleigh had been trained in a variety of fields at Fort Bliss and she was heading to Iraq where she would be in charge of the maintenance of vehicles and later, part of missions to resupply forward operating bases.

How about this for an understatement: "It is a very different lifestyle over there. It is a little bit stressful," Ashleigh said.

She later admitted that her base was one of the most attacked in the country.

"Over time you get used to it," she said.

She also traveled more than 1,000 miles outside "the wire" on resupply missions for forward operating bases for which she was awarded a Combat Action Badge and a Bronze Star.

"Having been outside the wire, you never knew when something could happen," said Ashleigh. "We would drive hours in one direction. It gets a little nerve wrecking. The feeling was that something could happen at any time."

Ashleigh will return to Fort Bliss to begin her captain training. She is halfway through her five-year commitment to the Army and says it is a real possibility another deployment, this time to Afghanistan, could be in her future.

"I'm not thrilled about going," she said. "You have to do what you have to do. I'm not overly worried. The conditions there are a little worse and the region is harder to live in."

Whereever she goes next, you can bet there weren't many Thanksgivings as good as the one at Lisa and Joel Davidson's house this year as Ashleigh visited with family and friends and rode horses with her parents.

"I tried not to tell them the scarier things that happened," said Ashleigh. "My experiences are much less terrifying than many people."

She pauses again to think about the past year.

"I think most of it I have forgotten already."

P.S.

Ashleigh returned to Iraq a second time as a maintenance supervisor and then the maintenance control officer. From June 2011 to May 2015 she had deployments to Afghanistan. When she returned she was stationed in Colorado Springs, Colorado before leaving the military in 2017 to take a management intern position with the Cintas Corporate Fellowship Program.

In 2020, she became a finance executive at J.P. Morgan and lives in Killeen, Texas with her husband who is still active military. Ashleigh maintains a position in the reserves and is attending graduate school at the University of Texas to get her executive MBA.

Lisa Davidson became the president of the Granville Teachers Association and still teaches at Granville. Joel Davidson retired as a Vermont state policeman in 2013.

OUTPOURING OF LOCAL SUPPORT

November 16, 2008

Let's start with this. It is amazing how much goodness we humans can inflict on each other when we want, when we are faced with adversity and times are hard and the stakes are high.

This is what Wendy Single did a while back.

She works in the technology department of the Queensbury School District. Her boss is Matt Hladun. She found out that Matt and Tammy's 2-month-old baby boy had a rare form of aggressive cancer. The prognosis was not good.

She sent out an e-mail to everyone who worked at the school and urged everyone to join her in the school parking lot on a September Sunday.

"I just felt the need to do something," said Wendy.

At 5 p.m., the cars started pulling in off Aviation Road, one after another. People pulled out their lawn chairs and greeted people they hardly knew and met others they had never known. Twenty, 30, 40 until there were more than 50 gathered under a nice shade tree trying to sum up a positive vibe for a baby they had never met.

Near the end, they all stood in a circle and joined hands.

That circle was just the beginning. The word spread, the story grew and the circle got wider.

But first, we have to tell you how Matt and Tammy got to where they are now.

How they were this ordinary little family, building a house, preparing to send 5-year-old Max to kindergarten and 2-year-old Ben to preschool while Tammy took care of their newborn, Will.

Then, on Sept. 12, the world caved in on them.

This is where you shake your fist and ask, "Why?"

Here is where you wonder at what point Matt or Tammy busted down the front door of their local church and demanded an audience with the guy in charge for a detailed explanation.

"People tell us that it happens for a reason," said Matt. "We're not so sure what the reason is yet."

Then you find yourself in C-714 at Albany Medical Center with baby Will conked out on his tummy in a blue onesie and Tammy fawning all over him.

They tell you the story of how this all started with a swollen leg and a trip to the emergency room. They tell you how no one mentioned the word. It was like some hospital code that Matt and Tammy had to figure out.

There was a mass in the baby's leg, a growth in his brain, but no one said the word.

Then Tammy found herself staring at the label on the doctor's white lab coat. She could only stare at the letters that spelled "oncology."

What followed over the past two months has been two brain surgeries, four MRIs and three rounds of chemotherapy. He is four months old now and he is still only 12 pounds.

Matt and Tammy found themselves in a fog in those early days, frightened to death one minute, overwhelmed by gloom the next.

Here's where the circle began to widen again, too.

Matt began writing updates on the Caring Bridge website so relatives and friends would know how Will was doing.

But the first entry didn't feel right. He had more to say. He had to let out his feelings, but he only felt comfortable writing to Will.

Here is Matt's first entry:

"I apologize right away, despite being a little more on the quiet side when speaking, I do tend to be long-winded when I write. I imagine you at 15, looking back at my words and thinking, 'Geez dad, do I have to read all of this?'"

That's the dream that Matt and Tammy hold onto on the best of days. The first days in September were too dark to even consider the possibility.

When Matt was asked to sign "do not resuscitate" forms, he was sure this was for some time far down the road. But it wasn't. It was for that night.

"There are days where everything inside of you says 'Run away, run away!' It is not an option," said Matt.

They got through that night and countless others.

There are more than 60 entries on the Caring Bridge site. Matt has not missed many days, and he has not pulled many punches.

Tammy wrote this entry:

"Daddy felt too exhausted to write last night, and while I don't have the gift to express myself like Daddy, I felt it was my turn to write to you. You had another surgery on Friday to put the port in your chest. I hate seeing it there, but I know it allows the doctors and nurses to help you without having to poke at your little body. I am trying hard to be strong buddy, but seeing what the chemo is doing to your body is hard to watch. You and your Daddy are giving me more strength than you can imagine. Every time you open your eyes I can't help but smile at you despite the way my heart is breaking."

When they got to Albany, Tammy told them a crib would not do. She had to be able to hold Will, kiss his cheek. So she spent her days in the hospital bed next to Will. She refused to leave his side.

"I need physically to be here," she says.

Life slowed for Matt and Tammy. Each day was filled with life-and-death emergencies.

"This is not a two-month ordeal," said Matt. "This is our life."

Then unexpected things began to happen. That circle that Wendy Single helped start in Queensbury led to fundraisers in South Glens Falls and Mechanicville, where Tammy and Matt used to teach, and in Stillwater. The goodwill began to multiply and spread, and this baby seemed to be changing the world for the better without uttering a word.

People began poring over Matt's entries on Caring Bridge. There have been more than 90,000 visits in the past two months. Cards and letters arrived from everywhere, including strangers in faraway countries. One wall of C-714 is covered with them.

People told Matt that people they knew, whom they had not spoken to in years, who simply did not get along, were coming together for them.

And maybe this was the best gift of all. Matt and Tammy overcame their grief and gave into their determination and love.

"Your mom and I decided tonight that we'll be sad for only a little while longer and then we're going to be strong," Matt wrote on Caring Bridge. "We know that everyone who loves, cares, and prays for you will need our strength. We also know that the fight for your life will also require every ounce of strength we have. As your doctor told us tonight, in a couple of weeks, you'll be able to tell us if it's a winnable fight and if it isn't, we're going to make all the right decisions to make sure we cherish every moment we have with you."

"We can be sad and he will still have cancer," says Tammy.

Matt looks at you with the biggest smile, looking like he doesn't have a care in the world.

"I just want to enjoy my son," he says.

Matt and Tammy had reason to be smiling earlier this week. The latest MRI showed nothing was left of the brain tumor.

"Sorry to put you out of business," Matt joked to the neurosurgeon.

It is good news, but not the end of the story. We won't have that for some time. There is still a mass in the leg, and if the chemo doesn't eradicate that, another round of chemo or surgery is an option.

Matt and Tammy still fear the results of each new MRI.

Not too long ago, 5-year-old Ben turned to Tammy and asked, "How do you get to heaven? Do you just walk out the door?"

Tammy lets the story hang in the air. And you wonder if what Matt and Tammy have now, the enjoyment of their little boy today and tomorrow, is their heaven until it's time for Will to walk out that door.

Next week, Matt and Tammy's families will come together for Thanksgiving. This year, it will be in a banquet hall at the hotel across the street from the hospital. They are hoping Will may be able to join in the celebration.

If not, Matt has already told Tammy that he will eat first, then take her place in the hospital room, take his little boy in his arms and drift off into a turkey-induced coma while watching football, and everything will be right with the world for at least another day.

P.S.

Three months after this column was published, baby Will died on February 6, 2009. That November, Matt and Tammy founded the "Brave Will Foundation" to be a driving force in the commitment to pediatric palliative care efforts in the Capital District.

In February 2019, Matt Hladun left his position in the Queensbury School District to become assistant superintendent for teaching and learning at Averill Park Central School. Tammy is a third-grade teacher at Shenendehowa.

IT TAKES A VILLAGE TO BUILD A LIBRARY

December 12, 2008

Christine McDonald leads you out of her office, down the stairs and into her new world.

It is the night before the doors will swing open at the new Crandall Public Library. She stands in the center of the second floor children's room, surveying something that she essentially created, and as she takes it all in, you see it. You see it in the slight upturn at the corners of her mouth, the subtle sparkle in her eyes, and then she turns to look at you to see if you see it too.

"This is a real symbol of hope," she says.

And that's the odd thing about all of this. It is almost 30 years since Christine was named executive director, and you'd think the story of this glorious new building would be the ending, the conclusion to a worthy community project that was the dream of so many.

But that's not Christine McDonald. It is the opposite. This is really the beginning, and if you are going to appreciate this new building in downtown Glens Falls, that's what you have to understand. We're just getting started.

Christine remembers the real beginning clearly.

It was a 25-below-zero day in 1979 when she walked in through the old front door, the marble staircase to her left, the balcony overhead, and she remembers thinking how austere it all looked.

She was a freshly divorced 31-year-old looking for a new job, a new beginning, and she was wondering what she might be getting herself into. She saw a library with potential. It had warm, friendly people and a good reputation.

"It was an open book of possibility," she said.

So she took the job and went to work.

There were lots of things it didn't have.

Year after year, she would knock off another program – films, kids' reading programs, literature groups, folk life – building the reputation and reach for all who entered the building.

But there was more than just those four walls. The real goal was extending that reach beyond the walls, out onto Glen Street and neighboring communities and bringing them all together, making the library the center of the universe for seniors, kids and teenagers.

As the programs grew, she needed a way to fund it. She found out about taxing districts and how several communities could bond together and afford this island in City Park.

The voters bought into it. A taxing district was created in 1992 among Glens Falls, Queensbury and Moreau, and now the library had a funding stream.

It was another beginning, leading to more programs and more growth until she was faced with the grand enchilada of projects – a new library itself.

By 1996, the library was running out of room, and Christine had to know that it would never reach its full potential if it didn't expand.

"It was very hard to go into the children's room," said Christine, "to see how crowded it was. They had no place to even do their homework."

That stuck with her.

But before we go there, I have to take you back again even further, so you understand again about Christine and where all this drive and determination and commitment to community started.

Christine was just out of college, married and working in the Peace Corps in the Patagonia region of South America between Argentina and Chili.

She was building houses – ironic isn't it – in a Habitat for Humanity-type project.

Here she was in this amazingly beautiful, remote place stuck between the Andes and the ocean, and she saw up close what a community can do when it acts as one.

But there was more at work. She suffered from a deprivation of books and film.

She realized the role the books and the words and arts had in her own life and the lives of others, and it stuck with her as she developed her own beliefs about what Crandall Library could be and the meaning it could have.

This was no ordinary librarian.

This one had a cape.

Looking back, you wonder how many people would have stuck with it - would have kept hammering away if they knew this would take 12 years out of their lives without any reward at all.

The first project went before the voters in 2000.

It failed.

When someone offered their condolences and told her she must be devastated, she responded, "You don't learn much by having success all the time, do you?"

That tells you a lot about this woman.

"It was a long, long struggle," she says now.

You ask her what kept her going, what kept her motivated as they looked at different sites and designs and argued over parking and porches and how much of City Park could be taken away.

"When things got bad, I would get up out of my chair and go look at the children's room," she says. "Why wouldn't you want this for the kids? Why wouldn't you want this for the community? They deserved this. It will make a difference in their lives."

And so now we are back here in the children's room that stretches as far as the eye can see, and for the first time you understand where this was all going, what this was all about.

This was about the future. This was about what comes next for this community, this city and those kids that are going to flock through the door.

And you smack the side of your head and say, "Of course! We are just getting started. This is only the beginning."

As you leave, you look up at the second floor. In four of the windows facing Glen Street there is a message for the community: "Thank you very much."

No, thank you Christine.

P.S.

Four years later, Christine McDonald announced that she would retire from her position in the library after 33 years, leaving in August 2012. She had plans to visit friends in Europe and free-lance articles at national film festivals like Sundance. The library continues to be the centerpiece of downtown Glens Falls where the community room is now called the "Christine McDonald Community Room."

When I asked her how things had turned out in February 2021, she responded with a two-page email that could have been an outline for a book. She returned to Sundance as film editor of Multicultural Review, but when the magazine closed, so did her connection for a press pass.

Christine said she found significant joy in the birth of her third godson who she has been caring for weekly since 2017.

In 2013, Christine was asked to join the SPAC Action Council. She was also part of a committee which brought 300 underserved children to the National Museum of Dance for tours. Christine also secured a $1 million grant for a local not for profit.

And travel, boy did she travel. She took a group to Turkey, toured with three friends in and around Paris, did another trip to Vienna and Paris, squeezed in a journey to Iceland, two visits to Spain, a journey to India with her godson's family for a wedding, Sicily, Rome and two weeks in Mexico.

She joined the board of the Glens Falls Medical Mission and went as a translator on her 10th mission in 2014.

In 2016, Christine was asked to be on the selection committee of the NYLibrary Associations Empire Book Awards and got to meet authors such as Toni Morrison, Joyce Carol Oates, Calvin Trillin, Walter Mosley, Russell Banks, Colm Tóibín and many others.

In her spare time, she is part of three book clubs, hikes, skis and hangs out with friends on Zoom, Facebook and WhatsApp.

DOING THE GOOD WORK AT MAUDE'S

February 11, 2009

SOUTH GLENS FALLS - Maude's Kitchen is one of those great little places where the owners are on a first-name basis with their customers and no one minds much if they wander behind the counter to get what they need.

It's commonplace to trade a good-natured barb with the man behind the counter or swap stories between flipping a burger or taking an order.

Squeezed between Abbott's on one end of the block and Jake's Roundup on the other, Maude's is one of those classic family diners.

It has been open for four years. The owners are regular people.

"We're paying the bills, keeping a couple people employed and having one heck of a time," says the man behind the counter.

That's Charlie Granger. Charlie and his wife, Sherry, run the place, but Charlie doesn't want me to use his name for this story. He seems like a straight-shooter who works hard for a living and one of those guys who always lets you know where you stand.

He doesn't want to get his name in the newspaper. Not for doing what comes natural. Not for simply doing the right thing.

That's the thing about this story.

It is really nothing special. It is a snapshot of what life is like in small towns around here, so what's the big deal? So, I hope Charlie forgives me.

Ever since Maude's opened up, Bob and Mary Lou Munger have been meeting friends for coffee two or three times a week. They are regulars and in places like Maude's, that means something more than just dependable business. It also means they are part of an extended family.

The Mungers have been married for 50 years. They have lived in the village most of their lives. They are in their 70s, retired and still quite active.

If you live in South Glens Falls, you've probably run into Mary Lou and Bob before.

Bob says his wife is a "professional volunteer." She has volunteered at the hospital for 15 years or so, served on various community committees and been on the annual Guatemala Medical Mission. She is one of those people that can always be counted on for a good cause. She even got her husband and kids volunteering, too.

"The Mungers do everything for everyone," said Charlie.

Until this past December.

Bob went into Glens Falls Hospital on Dec. 16 for a hip replacement, but there were complications. The next day, Mary Lou, who suffers from osteoporosis, was trying to take some curtains down, took a tumble and broke a vertebra in her back.

The next thing you know, they were celebrating Christmas at Glens Falls Hospital.

By the first of the year, Bob and Mary Lou were back home and friends and family were helping out. But Mary Lou still couldn't get around and Bob couldn't stay on his feet for more than 10 minutes at a time.

So, the folks over at Maude's came up with an idea. There was Beanie Bruce, Bob and Carol Towne, Colleen Wheeler and Charlie and Sherry. They decided to each pick a night of the week, cook up a dinner and bring it over to Bob and Mary Lou. Charlie and Sherry actually did two nights. They would deliver the meal each night, visit for a while and make sure everything was fine.

Of course there were others, too. Folks over in their Jackson Avenue neighborhood helped with the snow removal and looked out for them as well. Since the end of January, folks at the United Methodist Church in South Glens Falls took over the nightly meals.

You've got to love small towns.

"Those people over at Maude's, those are great people," said Bob. "They just treat people nice."

So you are asking Charlie about it again and he doesn't want any part of it.

"Put my wife's name in the paper, she'll like that," he says. I'm thinking he doesn't want people to know he has a soft spot.

Colleen Wheeler is telling you what great people the Mungers are.

"No matter how bad you have it, there is always somebody who has it a little worse," said Charlie. "That's what my father always said and I believe that."

But, more importantly, Charlie and the other folks at Maude's are living it, doing what they can, when they can for those that need it more than they do.

P.S.

Six years later on August 2, 2015, Charlie and Sherry Granger closed Maude's Kitchen with this announcement on Facebook:

"Looking back on our journey eleven years ago, I would never have imagined that after long-standing success we would have developed friends, created memories and established a place where you could sit for hours and have it feel like your own kitchen.

"Now Maude's has had to make a decision. One that has taken some time to come too. But as of 2 o'clock today, Maude's is closed.

"This moment is bittersweet. The eleven-year journey with every-one who has come in is coming to an end, but our friendship will remain. The story is not over, just a new chapter."

There were 43 shares and 82 likes on the post.

In February 2017, Charles suffered a heart attack, was rushed to the hospital for open-heart surgery and recovered.

Robert and Marylou Munger celebrated their 50th wedding anniversary on October 2, 2009 with a dinner at the East Cove Restaurant in Lake George. Robert passed away on March 3, 2016 with Marylou by his side. He was 78.

Bob Towne passed away on November. 22, 2019. He was 81.

George Champion was emblematic of what Hometown, USA was all about. George stood his post as a ticket- taker at the downtown arena for 30 years as an ambassador of all that was good in the city of Glens Falls, N.Y. When the author took his toddler son to his first hockey game, it was through George's door. When he went through the last time, his son could look George in the eye. And when George finally retired, it just wasn't the same. (Photo courtesy of The Post-Star in Glens Falls, N.Y.)

MISSING GEORGE

October 7, 2009

Indulge me for a second, but something has been bugging me since Saturday night, something that didn't sit right about the return of hockey to Glens Falls.

George Champion was not there.

If you've been to the Civic Center any time in the last 30 years, you have probably run into George. He is a gregarious, elderly gentlemen decked out in a red Civic Center jacket while carrying a million-watt personality.

"How you doing tonight?" he would say as he checked your tickets. "Good to see you."

But this wasn't one of those phony "have-a-nice-day" supermarket sing-songs. This was sincere, this was with eye contact and it wasn't long before George knew your face and often your name.

Probably hundreds of us have a tradition of going through George's door to say hello, to wish him happy new year at the Dec. 31 hockey game, to ask him during the state basketball tournament when he is getting out to golf. If the game turned out to be a dog, we often wandered over to kill time with George.

George was not at his door Saturday night. The replacement was nice enough, but it was like showing up at a party where you don't know anyone. George was always the friendly face that welcomed you so you knew you were at the right place.

He did it for 30 years.

He said he missed the Beach Boys concert that opened the Civic Center, and other than the three or four games he missed because of knee surgery a few years ago, he has been there for just about everything else.

He watched me carry my young son into a hockey game 13 years ago and he saw the teenage version look him in the eye last March.

It's not like I didn't know this day was coming.

George told me last March at the basketball tourney that he wouldn't be at the door for the hockey opener. His hip was aching and his knee was hurting and it was just too difficult to work the door anymore.

"I've met a lot of nice people and it has been wonderful," George told me. "Everyone has been so nice to me."

He said it was time to pack it in.

So this is what I hope we can do.

Maybe it is the Phantoms, maybe it is the city, maybe a bunch of individuals like myself who considered themselves part of George's extended family, but we need to get together and make sure that George is at the hockey games.

But not at the door.

Sure we're being selfish, but it just isn't the same without him, and if we want hockey to work, George has to be there.

He should be our guest and have lifetime season tickets in the last row, center ice where we know we can find him. Only now, we can greet him before we find our seats.

There should also be a nameplate on that seat or a plaque in the Civic Center that recognizes what George has meant to this community.

It should read: "George Champion: Ambassador of the Civic Center. He made everyone feel like family."

Until I see George there, it won't be hockey night in Glens Falls.

P.S.

The next December I gathered in the left vestibule of the Glens Falls Civic Center with about 50 other members of the community where they wheeled in George Champion.

Someone else had been reading my column that day and the city fathers had responded. One person after another addressed the assembled - including this writer - and told this humble ticket-taker what his presence meant to them. You could see the tears in George's eyes.

At the end, a green "George Champion's Way" street sign was unveiled near where George used to stand, a testament to three-decades of friendliness. In the annals of arenas, has there ever been an entryway named after a ticket-taker?

It is still there today.

On another December day five years later, George Champion left us for good. The line stretched out the door at the funeral home for his wake.

George Champion was the man who touched so many lives, and his passing left an awful hole.

THE PRICE OF POLITICS

November 4, 2009

Rick Galusha figured his reputation was easily worth $1,550. So he wrote the check.

If you are not from Warrensburg, you probably haven't heard of Galusha. For 26 years he has been doing almost everything for the town - from running parks and recreation, to the water department, to overseeing the landfill and providing maintenance for the buildings and grounds. He is generally considered the "go-to" guy around town if you need something done.

He has worked for five different supervisors and says he always tried to lay low when it came to small-town politics.

"I just follow the rules they make, and I never took sides," Galusha said.

But then his wife called the other day. She asked if he saw the political ad in the Adirondack Journal supporting supervisor candidate Maynard D. Baker and town councilman candidate Bryan Rounds.

The ad said Galusha had neglected maintenance at the water treatment plant, prompting the state to mandate a $500,000 expansion at taxpayers' expense. It also implied he did it for his own gain because he had nearby property that he could sell to the town.

Galusha said none of it was true.

I asked him how mad he was?

"Damn mad," he said. "When I get mad, I get mad all over. Wouldn't you when the whole thing is completely false?"

Galusha, 63, said he had to respond.

"There aren't a lot of people who are willing to put up a response," said Galusha. "I felt this was the right thing to do. This was totally uncalled for when a candidate has to drag an employee into it just in order to win an election."

This is why good people don't run for office.

Galusha went to this newspaper and paid for a full page advertisement on Election Day that addressed the citizens of Warrensburg. His letter ran more than 600 words and was run in type reserved for small headlines. Galusha rebutted the allegations against him and made accusations of his own against Baker.

The most recent edition of the Town of Warrensburg newsletter explains in detail the sewer system updates and the reason why they are needed. It does not say it is state-mandated.

So I asked Baker about his ad that said the state had mandated the expansion of the sewer plant.

"If the state has mandated it, I don't know about that," Baker said.

"Then why does it say it in the ad?" I asked Baker.

"I don't know," Baker said. "I didn't write that stuff up. There was a bunch of us at the beginning of the campaign that wrote stuff up. You have to let it go. It is all part of politics."

Galusha wasn't about to let it go.

"This is my reputation, and every bit of information in that campaign ad is false," said Galusha.

Galusha, who holds an appointed position with the town, wanted voters to hear his side, even though it will cost him his job if Baker is elected.

"I wanted the information out there, and I have been in business before, and I knew that if you want something done, you have to pay for it," Galusha said.

So he paid the $1,550 for the ad and got his message to the voters.

"I wanted to get people's attention," Galusha said. "It was worth every damn penny I paid for it because, win, lose or draw, I can go out with a feeling that I told my side of the story because I can back up my side of the story. If they want these people running the town, so be it, but I've been around this town for 40 years, and I can walk away feeling good about what I have done."

P.S.

By the spring of 2010, Rick Galusha and Maynard Baker had dueling lawsuits in response to their political advertisements. The two eventually settled the lawsuits, then signed a confidentiality clause.

In November 2012, Galusha was dragged into a Town Board discussion because several board members believed his salary was too high. After meeting behind closed doors with the board, Galusha agreed to retire in six months.

Maynard Baker, 83 at the time, ran for supervisor again in 2017 and lost to incumbent Kevin Geraghty. He died on April 19, 2021. He was 91.

MAKING A DIFFERENCE HALF A WORLD AWAY.

November 30, 2010

Sometimes, hope comes from half a world away, unsolicited, in a simple e-mail.

"Right now I'm in the mountains of Afghanistan," the message began. I received it just before Thanksgiving.

The author is 22-year-old Pfc. Bryce Crandall. He is from Lake George, but he is currently serving with a heavy armored division in the Wardak province of Afghanistan.

"I realize this is late in the game, but I just had this idea on guard duty and I wanted to know if you could help me," the message continued.

On guard duty.

The image of some lonely soldier late at night manning his post is a powerful one. It leads you, prematurely in this case, to wonder what we can do for him.

"I'm in the Army and I won't be home for Christmas. That's just my reality," wrote Bryce. "Far worse, however, is the reality that a lot of families in our area are going to have to suffer without during this holiday season. That shouldn't be. I think we should start a charity for needy families this Christmas. I know between myself, friends and family we could come up with a couple thousand dollars, but I'm confident with a legitimate push on your Web site and in your paper we could raise a lot of money to help a lot of people enjoy Christmas in this rough economic climate."

I was a little stunned.

Some kid in the cold mountains of Afghanistan was more worried about families and kids back home than his own hide.

It's enough to kick the "bah, humbug" out of even the most cynical.

It is easy to become disillusioned about our priorities as we see even Thanksgiving, the last bastion of the true family dinner, turned into just another day for big box stores and blowout sales.

Bryce said he had his parents, Chris and Katy, to thank for this idea. He said they have always been "pretty charitable" through the family business, Crandall Excavating, but in a quiet way.

"Pops has the philosophy that a simple thank you note from the actual beneficiary is better than pamphlets, plaques and widespread recognition and all the hoopla that comes with it," wrote Bryce. "That's where I'm coming from."

I called up Chris and Katy and told Katy about my e-mails with Bryce and his idea to help some people back home. Katy wasn't surprised at all. Right then and there, she volunteered to do anything she could to help the cause. Just tell her what needs to be done, she said.

Bryce didn't really have a plan and neither do I. He just wanted to do some good. He suggested we pick a local charity and get the paper to provide a media blitz. Between that, and word of mouth, we could all make the world a little better this holiday season.

Of course, that's what Bryce is already doing, just in Afghanistan.

P.S.

It is not often you get to see your work make a tangible difference, but that was the case after writing this column.

After publishing this column, I reached out to Bryce's mom. She got an account set up at a local bank — "A soldier's wish" — to help families in need at Christmas, and I spread the word with a second column that included Katy Crandall's email from Bryce:

"I gotta be quick 'cause I had to get special permission to use the computer," Bryce wrote from Afghanistan. "Here's what I need you to do. Get a hold of Ken, tell him what's up and that I did get a chance to read his article and it was spot on. Then just pick a local charity of some kind, food, clothes, adopt-a-family, whatever and let him know. See if you can get a sort of Post-Star sponsored charity drive going."

But here's what grabbed me by the throat:

"Go ahead and take $500 from my account to start it off," Bryce told his mom. The second column told readers how they could donate.

After Christmas, I contacted Katy again and she told me that she had received approximately $7,000 from local people and she had donated it to local charities.

That is the power of the press.

SOMETIMES IT RAINS A HURRICANE

February 27, 2011

The day Robin Selinger lost her job, the water tank ruptured and flooded the basement.

That was 20 months ago and the 53-year-old still can't find work.

She has no health insurance. She buys her clothes at a thrift store. She buys day-old bread and dented cans at reduced prices.

When $6,000 in taxes were due, she sold the stock she was saving for a rainy day.

And now it's pouring.

This month alone, she had to replace the alternator on her 10-year-old car, saw the vacuum cleaner burn up, her Netbook stop working and the TV in the kitchen go blank. There is also a leaky ceiling in the family room.

Four weeks from now her unemployment will run out.

"I enjoy a challenge, but this is a bit much," Robin wrote in an e-mail.

Robin was born in Saugerties. Her father worked at IBM and was later transferred to Boca Raton, Fla. With an associate's degree in accounting, Robin went to work in the accounting department of various upscale hotels.

When her father was transferred to California, she stayed in Florida with her life partner of 20 years, David Ford. They settled in western Palm Beach County, a rural area where they could keep their horses. She was working as an assistant controller at a private country club when she got interested in computers.

She went to work at Premier Global Services in 1996 just as the company was expanding overseas. She was part of the international technical support team.

As the company expanded, she traveled to Europe and Asia to set up new offices.

"It was wonderful," she said.

Her pay doubled in 13 years and she was living a good life with an annual salary of $74,000.

"I was blindly going along, enjoying life and buying anything I wanted," Robin said. "I never thought this would happen to me. When we were in Florida we would have dinner parties and have friends over and buy eight or nine lobsters. Now I go to a store where I can get dented cans for 30 cents on the dollar."

In Florida, their rural paradise was being squeezed by suburbia. A series of hurricanes made them question the sanity of staying there.

David had fallen in love with upstate New York during a visit several years earlier and Robin's boss let her move to New York and take her job with her.

They found an 1840s farmhouse in Salem with 35 acres for their horses and eight cats. They added a donkey and some miniature horses to the menagerie and more cats seem to be making the farm home every day.

They moved in 2006 and were happy.

Then came the phone call in June 2009.

"I was told that my job and the jobs of some other people had been eliminated," she said.

The company had been in turmoil for several years. Foreign offices were closed and middle management positions eliminated, but Robin thought she had survived.

"I had been employee of the month several months in a row several times while

I was there," she said. "I have letters of recommendation where one person said, 'I don't think Robin ever sleeps. She is always online.'"

None of that helped.

"I've always been an optimistic person," she said. "I thought this was a chance to do something bigger and better."

She got her first interview that December and was told the starting salary was half what she used to make. She was surprised. She didn't get the job, either.

That same month, David was diagnosed with prostate cancer.

When it rains, sometimes there is a monsoon.

She has had eight interviews since – for both computer and accounting jobs – but no one has made an offer.

One employer told her they had 50 resumes for the job she applied for.

She is online three or four hours a day, checking job services, sending out e-mails, trying to get a lead.

"To put it frankly, being on the dole sucks," wrote Robin in an e-mail. "I want to work."

The good news is that David's last test showed he has beaten cancer.

But now only four weeks of unemployment are left and she hates the thought of her father having to help her again.

"People are out there crying about not getting a raise," she said. "They should be happy they have a job."

Robin is not sure what is next.

"It's constantly like a dark cloud over your head," she said. "You never get used to it and it does affect your self-esteem."

It's a storm far worse than any of the hurricanes she has been through, and her story is just one of thousands.

P.S.

According to Robin's LinkedIn page in January 2021, she has retired to Echo Valley Farm in Salem, N.Y. She finally landed a position as an IT Services Manager and Controller in July 2012 and then the night auditor at a resort in Vermont before finally becoming the senior healthcare supply chain analyst at a local hospital.

DARING TO DO THE RIGHT THING

June 19, 2011

Step back from the issue and consider what we have become.

So many of us are dispirited by the lack of true leaders, the polarization of our communities into blue and red teams that leave no room for negotiation or compromise, and representatives marching lockstep with the orders of party bosses.

Don't we despise that system?

Don't we want political leaders who will be independent, who will find common ground to solve complicated and serious problems in our world?

Step back from the issue a bit further and think about what Roy McDonald did this week.

McDonald has been a staple of the political scene around here for three decades. As Wilton town supervisor for 23 years, he is both revered and despised for making Exit 15 a retail business hub that changed his town forever while holding property taxes at bay. His enemies often said there wasn't a landscape he wouldn't pave.

Some see him as an ambitious self-promoter, a consummate politician and a conservative Republican on the side of big business. He was elected to the state Assembly in 2002, then the state Senate in 2008 when Joe Bruno stepped aside.

Last Election Day, secure in an impending landslide re-election, he spoke passionately of a Legislature that had become a snake pit of downstate vipers. He said he expected more from members of the state Senate beyond serving themselves.

When you are trying to make deals with the guys on the other side of the aisle, questioning their ethics and morality is not the way to win hearts and minds.

But that is Roy McDonald.

This week, he raised the stakes considerably. It is one thing to call out a fellow senator when the cops are at the door, and quite another to stand nearly alone on an issue that many elected officials run from.

Roy McDonald, representing a district where many constituents are so far right they would never make a left turn, announced he was voting for gay marriage.

He did it with classic McDonald flair.

He said he was tired of Republican–Democrat politics. He said they could take this job and shove it if the people didn't like it. He even dropped an exasperated F-bomb.

The most important thing to remember, and the thing that you should consider most, is he said he was trying to do the right thing. In the face of adversity, while breaking ranks with his own party and many of his constituents, he said this was a matter of conscience.

Consider the courage that took.

Consider the ramifications it could have on his political future.

There is no reason for Roy McDonald to break ranks and cast this vote unless he was indeed following his heart.

Perhaps he has been softened by being a grandfather and taking up the fight of autism for two of those grandkids.

Perhaps, at 64, he realizes he is far closer to the end than the beginning and it is time to make a difference.

You can disagree with him on this issue, but no matter how strong your passion, you should not confuse the issue with the man.

We need more people who are willing to change their minds, who are willing to listen to the other side and evolve.

The world changes.

Our culture changes.

We should applaud a leader willing to change with it.

Even if we disagree with him.

P.S.

Five weeks after his vote helped New York make same-sex marriage the law of the state, Roy McDonald came to a meeting with the Glens Falls newspaper's editorial board and said he didn't want to talk about the vote. He proceeded to talk almost exclusively about the vote. He said if they wanted to vote him out of office, fine, he did what was right.

The next year, an ambitious county clerk named Kathleen Marchione forced McDonald to face her in a primary. Two days before the September primary, the two candidates met in Troy for their only debate. Marchione supporters packed the hall and she repeatedly questioned McDonald about his vote to the cheers of her supporters.

"I would ask them, `Do you want me to tell you what you want to hear or do you want me to tell you the truth?'" McDonald told me in 2020. "They didn't want the truth."

When the votes were counted at the end of primary night, Marchione led by 107 votes. Absentee ballots cut the lead to 99 and McDonald dropped out of the race.

"I'm in the party of Abraham Lincoln - I'm very proud of that," McDonald said in a New York Times article before the vote. "I'm not in a party of a bunch of right-wing nitwits. It's Abraham Lincoln. It's everybody included. And I feel that's very important."

A year later, a young woman from Homestead High School in Fort Wayne, Indiana was chosen the winner of the John F. Kennedy Profile in Courage Essay Contest for high school students.

The award recognizes a public official at the local, state or federal level whose actions demonstrate the qualities of politically courageous leadership in the spirit of John F. Kennedy's book "Profiles in Courage."

Jamie Baer's subject was Roy McDonald.

During lunch in the summer of 2020, Roy McDonald told me he was no longer a Republican and that he had quietly went to the town hall where he was once supervisor and changed his affiliation.

"I don't think she even knew who I was," McDonald said.

A THANK YOU FIVE DECADES IN MAKING

September 3, 2019

This letter had a story behind it.

Phil Holcomb had sent it to the newspaper at the end of July. He had been with his dad, James Holcomb, in the emergency room a couple of days earlier. The cancer James had been battling for the past five years had made it to his bones.

He knew he didn't have much time left.

There in the emergency room with Phil and his wife, Lorraine, James sought to tie up some loose ends.

It was his idea to write the letter to the editor.

It was his idea to make sure Stanley Bradley knew how much his actions of 48 years earlier meant to him and his family.

Phil agreed to write the letter for his father.

"James Holcomb has desired that Stanley Bradley be recognized and thanked for saving his son, Phillip, when he was a toddler," the letter started.

This is where I come into the story.

It was an unusual letter to the editor, and I wondered if there was a story here.

I passed it off to one of the reporters, who passed it back to me and suggested it might be a good column. Then I got busy with life, work and family, but I'm pretty sure James would understand.

On the morning of Aug. 14, I saw James' obituary in my newspaper and my heart sank.

James grew up in Granville, was an Air Force veteran and loved to do karaoke at the local nursing home for the residents. Phil said he had a wonderful voice.

"He lived by the rule that a man's job was to take care for his family, no matter what," is what it said in his obituary.

No matter what.

Maybe that's what was weighing on James' mind that day in the emergency room when he got the bad news.

That he had not properly thanked the young hero.

That he had not let him know how it all turned out.

Or maybe he was still stewing over the events from 48 years earlier, when his youngest, Phil, ended up in the bottom of a well at the new house they were building in Hartford.

Stanley Bradley was just 12 years old himself. Stanley ran across a connecting field and pulled Phil from under the water in the well.

"I still don't like water," Phil told me.

Phil, who was 2 at the time, remembered waking up and seeing his mother's face as she performed CPR.

Phil has never met Stanley Bradley. He tried to track him down but couldn't find a phone number or address. He located Stanley's brother, who said he would get word to Stanley about James' last request.

Here's the other part that is important.

Phil is 50 now.

He has spent much of his life working with developmentally disabled adults and children.

Along with his wife, Tammy, he has adopted five children.

When I called him, he was retrieving something the 4-year-old had dropped under the porch.

"James Holcomb extends his heartfelt thanks as well," Phil wrote in the letter to Stanley. "Your quick action saved his youngest son's life."

And impacted so many others.

But maybe most of all, James got to see Phil grow up and live his life.

P.S.

While the column was not published until after James' death, it did show that it was never too late to make things right. After all, James waited nearly 50 years.

LIFE & DEATH

Front-page stories in local newspapers are often tragic accounts of life and death. It is one essential duty of newspapers to report these events, however heart-rending they might be. I believe my columns allowed our readers to better grasp these stories, especially in regard to the heavy toll they so often took on so many. It was an attempt to understand life's human drama.

WHAT WOULD YOU DO?

December 13, 2002

You wake up suddenly in the middle of the night and you know something is terribly, terribly wrong.

You are disoriented. You can smell the acrid smoke choking the life out of you.

You start to cough, fighting for breath.

You make your way out of the bedroom and into the hallway. You can feel the heat. You see the fire.

You can hardly breathe. Your surroundings look strange. You don't know where you are.

Immediately, your thoughts turn to your four children upstairs.

What do you do?

We all know what we think we would do. We'd charge up those stairs, through the smoke, through the flames, and somehow, in the blackness and thick smoke, find those small children - our pride, our joy, our reason for being - and somehow get them out of the house.

Or die trying.

Nothing would stop us. Nothing would get in our way.

Nothing.

That's what we think.

That's what we think we know, and no one is going to convince us otherwise.

Thankfully, we've never had to live that nightmare. Precious few of us have ever had to make that kind of split-second decision of whether to charge up those stairs or rush out the front door for help.

Instantly.

In the blink of an eye, without thought, without consultation, without reservation.

What would we do?

Lesley Ingraham had to make that decision.

A life-or-death decision.

In the black of night, surrounded by the choking smoke and the intense heat from a fully involved fire.

We all know what we would have done.

We know that we would have made it up those stairs and found those children.

We know we would have been willing to give our lives for our kids.

We know that we would have died trying to save them.

But we don't know that.

We don't.

Until you've been there, in the black of night, with your own life on the line, none of us know what we would do. We hope, we pray that we would do the right thing, make the wise decision that would lead to a happy ending, to a verdict that might avert tragedy.

Lesley Ingraham could not make it to her children that terrible morning. She could not get up there to save them.

Nobody knows if the outcome would have been any different if she had made it up those stairs, if she had found the children.

In fact, most likely there would have been just one more fatality.

We all wonder, we all want to believe that love for our children will keep them out of harm's way, that it will help us to be brave and wise and smart in a crisis.

We like to believe that this overwhelming love that we possess will save them.

That isn't necessarily how the story ends in the real world.

Often, it ends in tragedy, such as in this case. Often it ends with the parent dying, too.

So don't judge Lesley Ingraham.

Don't think that you could have done better under the circumstances until you have had to face them.

The woman has lost her four children. She has suffered enough for a lifetime.

P.S.

Lesley Ingraham's four children died in an early morning fire two days before the Thanksgiving in 2002. Afterward, unfounded rumors swirled that Lesley was not home at the time of the fire, and that she had used community donations to take a trip to Disney World.

Letters to the editor that made false accusations were rejected. When I told one caller that we had checked the rumors and they were not true, she did not believe me. This was an early version of distrust in the media. We later learned that town officials had tried to inspect the home the previous summer, but they were not allowed into the home. The story was voted the most newsworthy of the year by our staff and led to a drive to hold absentee landlords accountable.

The gutted home was torn down. In the summer of 2020, the lot was still vacant. The four children are buried in the Union Cemetery nearby. Each of their stones has an image of an angel carved in it.

Lesley and Roger Ingraham relocated to Avon Park, Florida.

HOW COULD SHE NOT KNOW?

May 13, 2008

QUEENSBURY - You couldn't help but wonder how Alicia Lewie spent her Mother's Day on Sunday.

Maybe that's not fair, but it is the obvious question when she is charged with second-degree manslaughter in the death of her 7-month-old son.

After all, it was her roommate and onetime boyfriend, Michael D. Flint Jr., who has admitted to being the monster in the death of 7-month-old Colbi. It was Flint who has admitted to the deep purple bruises and black eyes on the baby's angelic face and the beating that killed him last November.

Lewie is only accused of looking the other way, as she did yesterday when the autopsy photo of Colbi's battered body was again shown in court.

The bruises are deep and purplish and cover both eyes. They glow out from the cheekbones and reach all the way to the earlobes. It is a shocking and sickening photograph.

The horror of this crime is that the victim is a helpless baby. That kind of evil cannot be imagined by anyone with a heart and a conscience. There is no one who will stick up for Michael Flint. There is no one who will come to his defense. Right?

But if you are a parent, if you are a mother, the question is more subtle, perhaps more contentious. How could you not know, as Lewie contended over and over Monday?

It makes you wonder how you spend the Mother's Day after your baby is killed by someone close to you. It was perhaps the only question not asked during the four hours Lewie was on the stand Monday afternoon.

It may have offered the best insight into Lewie's own heart.

Did she spend that beautiful Sunday asking herself over and over again how she could have missed the signs?

Did she spend it blaming herself?

Did she spend it wallowing in the image of that helpless baby's body?

All would seem appropriate responses for a parent.

Dressed in black and carrying a Bible into the courtroom, Lewie answered questions from her lawyer, Michael Keenan, for 49 minutes before District Attorney Kate Hogan began a withering cross-examination, during which Lewie contended over and over that friends, acquaintances and just about everyone else called to testify in this case was mistaken about how they remembered things, especially the question of whether Lewie might have suspected Flint was abusing her child.

But in the end, it was one final exchange between Hogan and Lewie that stuck with me.

"He was wonderful with Colbi," Lewie insisted late into the afternoon.

"Knowing what you know now, was Michael Flint good with Colbi?" Hogan countered.

Lewie paused and stumbled over her words, paused again, before finally saying, "I don't know how to answer that."

How do you not know how to answer that?

How do you not reach into your soul and scream with contempt your feelings for the person that took this life that you created?

Hogan persisted and asked again if Michael Flint was good with Colbi.

"No," Lewie said, staring back.

Even now, six months after the crime, prosecutors still had to drag the admission from her.

P.S.

The next month, Alicia Lewie was convicted of manslaughter in the death of her infant son and sentenced to 7 to 22 years in prison. She did not say anything in court when her sentence was handed down.

Her boyfriend, Michael D. Flint, was sentenced to 22 years to life after pleading guilty to second-degree murder for the death of Lewie's 7-month-old son.

Lewie was released from prison in 2017 after serving nearly 10 years.

She was arrested again in January 2019 as part of an armed robbery of a convenience store. She pleaded guilty to second degree robbery for her role and sentenced to five years in state prison. She must first complete her sentence in the manslaughter case.

She once again said nothing in court.

PARENTS GUILTY

February 15, 2009

They should have known.

No reasonable person can infer otherwise.

Not when there are 20 to 30 young people on your property from early in the evening until way past midnight.

Not when they are drinking beer and smoking dope and making a ruckus around a raging bonfire out in the backyard.

Not when some of them are 16-year-old children, including their own son, who had been in trouble before for this type of behavior.

This is the culture in our communities.

This is what you as parents are up against if you want to keep your sons and daughters alive past the age of 21. Overstated? Well, remember the horrible reality - two 16-year-old girls never made it home from that party.

You know the story.

Dustin St. Andrews, only 16, took his uncle's car without permission and went on a wild joy ride that ended with a tragic crash and the deaths of two girls.

Back at the St. Andrews' property, some kids were passed out. Others were sleeping it off in their cars. And inside the house, Jimmy Joe St. Andrews, 41, and his wife Kellie, 40, say they didn't know what was going on outside their home. This was either the quietest party in the history of recorded time or the St. Andrewses are the deepest sleepers since Snow White. The Putnam couple was on trial this past week for hosting underage drinking parties at their home and providing alcohol to minors.

"This is the party house," Washington County District Attorney Kevin Kortright said in his closing argument Friday. "This is where the kids go to do what they want to do when they want."

Remember this snapshot.

When Schroon Lake Fire Chief Larry Shiel arrived at the St. Andrews home at 3 a.m. on April 21 to tell the St. Andrewses of the accident, he testified that there were beer cans and bottles all over the yard and still a couple of young people around the bonfire.

But don't miss the bigger picture here. Don't get sidetracked by your outrage toward Jimmy Joe and Kellie St. Andrews.

The problem is bigger than them.

There are others just like them who believe underage drinking is no big deal and they would rather have parties under their supervision.

This case paints a picture that raises so many questions about the parenting of so many it should leave us all shaking our heads as we wonder, not only if we can trust our own kids, but if we can we trust the parents of their friends.

If at any point on the night of April 20-21, the St. Andrewses had ventured out into the yard, if they had checked on the group for a minute or two, if they had just shown the least bit of curiosity about what was going on around that bonfire, perhaps two young people would still be alive.

If we can't trust our neighbors to do that, we are truly lost as a culture, a community that is supposed to be watching out for each other.

And the problem is bigger still.

This is just one party in one community. Spring is coming. There will be more bonfires, more drinking and dope smoking.

What do we do about that?

The St. Andrewses were found guilty just before midnight Friday.

But that is not the end of it.

It is just the beginning and figuring out what to do next is the real challenge.

P.S.

Jimmy Joe St. Andrews was found guilty of endangering the welfare of a child, but not guilty of two other endangering charges. Kellie St.

Andrews was found guilty of endangering the welfare of a child and unlawfully dealing with a child. Both were sentenced to 60 days in jail. Jimmy Joe's guilty verdict was thrown out on appeal after serving just seven days in jail.

The couple later separated. In the summer of 2012, Jimmy Joe fired a rifle into a group of people wounding one man. Police believe he was trying to shoot Kellie. His body was later found in a nearby cemetery with a self-inflicted gunshot wound.

Dustin St. Andrews was released in March 2018 and arrested for parole violation less than six weeks later. When he surrendered himself on the parole violation, he was found to be smuggling drugs in his rectal cavity. He was facing another seven years in prison.

A MINUTE IS A LONG TIME

May 18, 2010

SOUTH GLENS FALLS

Lisa Savard steps onto the stage wearing an elegant black jacket and skirt suitable for an evening out at a nice dinner party. Or maybe that's how you dress when the funeral just won't go away.

She gets to the point. She tells the audience the story of her 16-year-old daughter Joelle, killed in a car accident in 2002. She paces back and forth across the stage, steadily, despite her high-heeled shoes and heavy heart. Her voice is without emotion, oddly matter-of-fact.

Her daughter and a friend were out with a boy. They drank some beer and smoked some pot. Out on the road, the driver began drag-racing another car, reaching speeds up to 90 mph and, when he came to a curve in the road, he crashed into a tree.

Lisa stops pacing.

"They told me later Joelle lived for just a minute after the crash," she says. "Sometimes I sit and look at the clock ticking. A minute is a long time."

It is midnight quiet.

She tells everyone about the policeman at the door. She tells them about going to the hospital to identify the body and recognizing one of her rings that Joelle borrowed.

She has lived the nightmare no parent wants to imagine.

When she was done, it was as if all of South Glens Falls was holding its breath.

This was a new tactic for fighting underage drinking. Give Nick Fitzgerald at South Glens Falls High School a lot of credit for not only taking on the fight, but finding a new way to reach the young adults at his school.

Talk to teachers and they will whisper about the drug and alcohol problems in their schools. They will tell you about the students in the parking lot changing their shirts and squirting Visine in their eyes to cover up the signs and smells of marijuana use.

They often must feel like they are losing the battle, especially when there are parents ready to argue that this is just a rite of passage for all young adults.

Fitzgerald, the director of athletics at South Glens Falls and the father of two young children, came up with the idea for South Glens Falls' annual health fair.

He wanted to go beyond the lectures and panel discussions that leave teens rolling their eyes. He wanted something real, something that would linger and remind them that tragedy can be around the next corner.

Fitzgerald conjured up a presentation that was part docudrama and part movie of the week.

He used the resources of the drama club for an opening scene in the auditorium in which a mother talks her husband into letting their daughter have a drinking party at their home so the kids "will be safe."

The party unfolds on stage with 25 or 30 students acting out a Saturday night blowout worthy of a college fraternity party, complete with simulated drinking games.

"When the party scene was going on, the kids were all cheering and chanting," said Fitzgerald about the afternoon performance after the health fair on Friday. "But pretty soon, you could hear a pin drop."

What unfolds is as close to being there as you can get.

Some teens leave the party and a video shows a carload of boys wearing letterman jackets drinking beer, swerving down the road and, finally, hitting a little girl crossing the street to the haunting sounds of a song called, "Too Late to Apologize."

Video produced for this performance shows the teenager being arrested, handcuffed, taken to jail and fingerprinted. John Gray, one of the news anchors at FOX23 News in Albany, cuts into the proceeding to describe the breaking news. Headlines from The Post-Star are shown chronicling the event.

It all seems quite real.

When the action returns to the stage, the partying teens are now at a funeral and a small coffin is carried to the center of the stage.

The combination of re-enactment and reality drives home the possibility of tragedy, leaving those of us that are parents wondering how long we should lock our sons and daughters in the closet.

That's when Lisa Savard takes center stage, telling the story that is still too painful to tell. Yet she has relived it often —at first out of grief, and now to help save souls.

"I put the pain where it is manageable," Lisa tells you about her time on the stage. "But there is a refreshing of pain every time I do it. Seeing her picture on the screen. It is in my throat. I usually cry when I leave."

When she left the stage Friday night, there was not a sound, but hopefully a resolve from a community and a hope that other communities can duplicate the presentation.

When Lisa got home later that night, she cried again.

Her daughter will be gone eight years in June.

P.S.

Between 2002 and 2004, eight teenagers died in underage drinking accidents, including Lisa Savard's daughter. It resulted in an award-winning series called "The Cost of Fun" that chronicled the underage drinking problem in the region and the acceptance of it as a rite of passage. Over two decades, my columns and the newspaper's editorials repeatedly returned to the subject of underage drinking. In 2010, I took my 14-year-old son to this event and heard Lisa Savard speak. He tells me now, he never drank in high school.

Christopher Bliss, the man who was driving at speeds over 90 miles an hour in the accident that killed Lisa Savard's daughter, was sentenced to up to 10 1/2 years in State Prison in 2003.

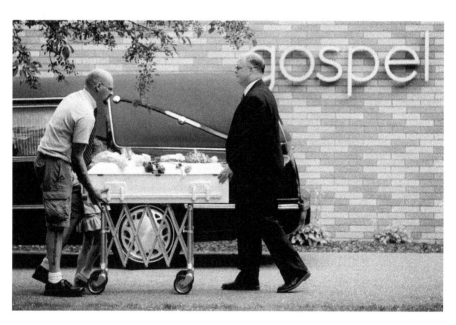

The death of a young child is incomprehensible for any parent, but after an early-morning fire claimed the lives of six children, Carl Smith (left), the children's father, became the personal caretaker of each of their small coffins while the hearts of the community were breaking. (Photo courtesy of The Post-Star in Glens Falls, N.Y.)

COMMUNITY BIDS HEARTBROKEN FAREWELL

July 9, 2010

HUDSON FALLS

At the rear of the Gospel Lighthouse Church in Hudson Falls were class portraits, family photos and certificates of achievement that probably stuck to the family refrigerator of Carl Smith and Samantha Cox.

They were photos like we all have of our kids swimming in the pool, of birthday parties and fun times in the back yard. So many photos, so many memories and smiles from those bright faces and smiling eyes.

They were the kind of photos you share at a family reunion, remembering the "good old days."

Only, in this case, there would only be memories of the six children who died in the Fort Edward fire.

Carl Smith, the father of all six children, somehow mustered the courage to face the filled church and talk about his children and thank the friends and community that have helped them in recent days.

Richard Yancy, the minister at the Faith Baptist Church in Queensbury, told us that "Carl is a little rough around the edges," and the congregation laughed, "but he has a big heart, an enormous heart."

He proved that in church.

He spoke in a strong voice that overshadowed a heavy heart.

"I don't know how I'm going to say goodbye to these children," Carl said, "but I have to."

When the hourlong service had concluded, they called up the pallbearers to the sanctuary in groups of four. One group for each of the six caskets.

Twenty-four of them to take "Car-Car," Mackenzie, Emile, Abbig-ayle, Paige and Hope to their final resting place in Lake George.

The call went out six times.

Each time a group of four would arrive by the side of a casket, and Carl would shake their hands, pat them on the back and thank them for their services. Each time, he would get behind the small coffin and push it to the waiting hearse with the pallbearers on each side.

Each time, another set of pallbearers would wait for Carl to return.

Each time, that big heart had to be breaking a little more.

Samantha's too.

And so many others.

It was as if Carl refused to let those children take another step in their journey without him. It was as if he was trying to make the most of their time left together before that final goodbye.

Nearby, as they were moving away the final coffin, Samantha, the mother of four of the children, was dissolving into tears, her left arm still bandaged from the fire.

And all around her, an entire community's heart was breaking.

P.S.

On an early summer morning in 2010, fire claimed the lives of six children just a mile from where four children died in an early-morning fire eight years earlier in the town of Fort Edward. Four others escaped.

Firemen found a 12-year-old child draped over her siblings in an effort to protect them. The parents were taken to the burn unit in Westchester County and recovered. Their baby was found in their bed.

No working smoke detectors were found in the building. The scope of the tragedy shook communities throughout the region. More than $50,000 was raised community-wide to help the parents with funeral expenses. Carl and Samantha's lawyers later found that $20,000 of the funds were unaccounted for and two of those involved in the fundraising eventually pleaded guilty to petit larceny.

A year after the fire, Carl and Samantha were awarded $485,000 in an insurance settlement. They later separated and on July 29, 2012, Fort Edward police received a call about a man in a car not breathing. It was Carl Smith. He later died at the hospital. He was 37. He is buried with the six children beneath an enormous black granite monument in the northwest corner of Evergreen Cemetery in Lake George.

Over the next two years, various community groups worked diligently to ensure every home had a working smoke detector. In the summer of 2020, a single maple tree occupied the vacant lot where the six children died.

9/11 IS NOW PERSONAL

September 19, 2014

L et's start at the end of the story.

The last day.

The day Tim O'Brien died.

That's what I had to do when I went looking for the name of a Hartwick College basketball star I last talked to 31 years ago. I just wondered how his life turned out.

He worked for Cantor Fitzgerald. You know the story now. He was only 40. He had a wife and three young children and was working on the 105th floor when the first plane hit. It was probably over quickly.

Let's work back from there, because the end may be the least important thing about his life.

He lived on Long Island with his wife and three young children. His dad said he had his dream home with a putting green, tennis courts, pool and basketball court, and he was always out in the yard with the children. He was successful.

"He was the rock of the family," his father, Bernard, said.

Think about that for a second.

How often does the father say that about the son?

"We couldn't have asked for anything more," Bernard told Newsday. "He looked after his family, he looked after his mom and dad, he did very well, he worked hard, but he didn't forget his roots, and he was always there."

O'Brien called his family "the fun family" and would lead the children into spur-of-the-moment mischief and leap into the pool fully clothed, the children following in his wake.

"He taught me not to ever judge people or gossip," his wife, Lisa, told Newsday.

Before moving to Cantor Fitzgerald in 1996, O'Brien worked at Patriot Securities on Wall Street.

His brother Sean told the New York Times in 2001 that when work intruded on his home life, he would tell a visitor, "Stay here. It just gave out a feeling of 'I'm here and I'm going to come back to you.' "

Some people are like that.

One day in 1989, while working at R and J Securities on Wall Street, he interviewed a young woman for a job. It was Lisa.

"I didn't hear a word he said," Lisa O'Brien told Newsday. "I was just thinking, 'OK, this is my husband.' "

And five years later they were married.

Lisa called him "Captain Catholic" because he regularly attended church and refused to curse. He sometimes would spell out the word he wanted to cuss.

His best friend was former New York Jets quarterback and current NFL television analyst Boomer Esiason.

O'Brien talked him into doing a charity golf tournament when Esiason was a second-round draft pick of the Bengals and O'Brien was just a year out of Hartwick.

"The friendship was born in the minute I met him," Esiason told Cincinnati columnist Paul Daugherty.

Later, Esiason asked O'Brien to be one of the founding members for the Boomer Esiason Foundation, which raises money for cystic fibrosis research.

They played golf and basketball together. Their wives were friends.

When Esiason became quarterback of the Jets, O'Brien told him he would always root for him, unless he was playing the Giants. That was a deal breaker.

Nine days after 9/11, 3,000 people attended a memorial service in Rockville Centre, O'Brien's hometown.

Esiason was one of four people to offer up a eulogy. He did it wearing a blue home jersey of the New York Giants.

"Only for my man, Timmy," Esiason said. "Only for my man Timmy."

There are people you meet in your life you do not forget.

I guess that's why I wondered what happened to O'Brien, the All-American I had covered when we were both very young. I guess that's why I searched for his name online.

And for the first time, the loss on 9/11 was personal.

I remember this poised, confident young man who could shoot the lights out from anywhere on the court.

His last game was in the first round of the Division III NCAA Tournament. Hartwick was the underdog against Potsdam State, but it battled all the way and trailed by just a point with seconds left.

And O'Brien had the ball.

He came down the court, was trapped along the sideline by two players and lost the ball.

I remember talking to him in the silent locker room. He was the only one talking. He kept saying over and over, "I just lost the handle on the ball," and that he just wanted to have a chance to take that last shot.

Even now, 31 years later, I know he would have made it.

This past Thursday — on the 13th anniversary of 9/11 — Brian St. Leger, the center on that team, posted a photo on his Facebook page of a baby-faced, shaggy-haired young man holding aloft a trophy with a satisfied smile.

"September 11, 2001 — Always remember Hartwick great Tim O'Brien."

More importantly, remember how he lived.

P.S.

It was a nostalgic piece of curiosity that manifested itself in a Google search in 2014.

For 13 years, I didn't know anyone who died on 9/11. Then, I stumbled on a reference to a basketball player I had covered at Hartwick College in the early 1980s when I was a young sportswriter in

Oneonta, N.Y. He was an All-American guard from a big, boisterous Catholic family on Long Island.

When I searched online for Tim O'Brien's name, the first words that jumped out at me were "Cantor Fitzgerald," and I immediately knew the rest of the story.

When the 9/11 Memorial Plaza opened at Ground Zero, I found Tim's name and ran my fingers across the etching as the water flowed into the footprint of the towers in front of me. Later, when I visited the 9/11 Museum in New York City, I listened to the interviews with his father and sister.

I didn't really know Tim O'Brien that well, but it made the events of that day much more personal. I later heard from Tim O'Brien's father and then a heart-wrenching email from his sister, Kathleen Tighe, that led to another column two years later.

Bernard O'Brien, Tim's father, died in January 2020. He was 87.

'YES, WE ARE LIVING OUR LIVES AGAIN'

September 11, 2016

The email was at the bottom of my mailbox for the past nine months. I could not bring myself to delete it.

Kathy Tighe had written me more than a year after I first wrote about her brother, Tim O'Brien.

It happens that way sometimes.

Your words get passed from one family member to another. In this case, Kathy's mother sent out letters to the family with items of interest: comic strips, recipes and sometimes an article like mine.

Kathy apologized for not knowing when it was written. She said she didn't pay much attention to the news anymore — "Since 9/11, just too painful."

Her brother Tim worked for Cantor Fitzgerald on the 105th floor of Tower One.

Her husband Steve Tighe worked there, too.

"On that day, we lost two fathers of seven children (ages 13 to 6 months)," she wrote back in December. Four of the children were hers.

She said she was glad I had visited the new museum and told me about how she and her father decided to be interviewed for the new museum and how worthwhile it was.

"Because if you listen, you hear a story — a story of a brother, father, husband … ."

But here is why I kept the email.

"Yes, we are living our lives again," Kathy wrote in December. "The 'baby' is a freshman in high school playing soccer like her dad, and basketball like Uncle Tim. My parents continue to attend the games of the grandchildren (24 of them) as they did for Tim and the rest of the brood. Evil tried to destroy our family, but I am happy to say it did not succeed."

Yeah, I know you are tearing up right now, because I did, too.

I stumbled on the email earlier this week while cleaning out my mailbox. Only this time, I decided I had something to say.

I wrote Kathy that her note stayed with me these past nine months, that despite the devastating events all those years ago, it was inspiring to see the hope and passion about life going on, and about her youngest playing ball like her father and uncle.

I told her that I will be thinking of her family this year on the 15th anniversary, and I told her that there are many other people thinking about her family as well, even if they don't know them.

I also told her I hoped my message did not cause further pain, because I don't know how anyone deals with such a tragedy and its aftermath.

A couple hours later, she wrote back.

"It does not cause further pain at all," she wrote. "To the contrary, I find it rather comforting to know that our loved ones are remembered."

She continued:

"This time of year is always anxiety-provoking, but we attend the various services, we keep in mind the devastation brought upon our entire country that day, and make peace with the fact that all the lives lost will live on through the next generation. It is up to us to educate the young and tell the stories of those lost.

"As my wonderful dad says," Kathy continued, "'faith, family, friends — in that order — is all you need to live a happy life.'"

I don't think you can say it much better than that.

P.S.

On each 9/11 anniversary since, I think about the O'Brien family and I think about Kathleen Tighe and I remember that evil did not destroy them that day and that they continue to live their lives, just like all of us.

THEY SHOWED NO HUMANITY

July 31, 2016

It is the dark of night, quiet, just the sound of the wind.

Maybe you are alone in your thoughts, maybe there is quiet conversation after a great day with friends.

Then suddenly, there is something in front of you. It could be a car, a boat, a pedestrian — the details don't really matter — and then you collide.

It happened so fast.

It came out of nowhere.

In the next minute, you either show your humanity or you don't.

That is what is so disturbing about the boat accident that claimed the life of an innocent 8-year-old girl this past week.

We don't know all the details of how the accident occurred. Experienced boaters will tell you that a lake at night, where vehicles do not stay in set lanes, can be disorienting, confusing and dangerous. Drivers are sometimes inexperienced and have little training, boats can appear out of nowhere and accidents do occur.

Imagine that minute afterward, when one boat catapulted over another, tearing off part of its prop and leaving a little girl laying mortally wounded in front of six other family members, perhaps already dead.

Police say the airborne boat briefly stalled after the accident.

There had to be screaming, sounds that carried all across the lake at that late hour.

And not just any type of screaming, but the type of guttural wail you could only hope to someday forget.

There had to be little doubt someone was hurt, that an accident had occurred.

In that moment, the driver of the boat that caused the injuries made a snap judgment that flew in the face of morality and showed his lack of humanity.

He fled the scene. Witnesses said the driver was cursing as he drove away. The navigation lights on the boat were out.

There were four others in the fleeing boat.

Did any of them demand the driver stop?

To turn around and help the injured?

Surely, the four passengers heard the screaming, too.

Surely, one of them had a conscience.

Some morality.

But it gets far worse with one bad decision compounding upon the next.

Witnesses saw the fleeing boat dock at a local motel, and heard someone from the boat telling everyone not to say anything, text anyone or put anything on social media.

One passenger pulled a hoodie tight around his face to hide his identity.

They went into hiding.

The driver turned himself in the next morning.

It had been nearly 12 hours since the accident.

The driver was arrested Friday for leaving the scene. The four passengers were also arrested and face charges of either hindering prosecution or lying to police.

If there was only a charge for not being human.

For selfishness.

These are young people, but not that young. The driver was 24. The others were 27 or 28. They were old enough to know you should stop after an accident, that you try to help people when they are hurt. These aren't just laws, it is what we do as human beings.

I stared at the photo of the five of them handcuffed in Lake George Town Court.

They looked so young, frightened and afraid.

But most of all, they looked small and insignificant.

P.S.

The driver of the boat, Alexander West, was convicted of second-degree manslaughter and is serving 5 to 15 years in prison. In March 2020, Judge John Hall rejected Alexander West's request for a new trial. Three of the four other passengers refused to testify against West.

Two of the passengers, Matthew J. Marry and Kristine C. Tiger, pleaded guilty to misdemeanor hindering prosecution and agreed to serve 45-day sentences. Marry and Tiger were arrested again in May 2017 for drug possession after police seized heroin, Suboxone and hashish from their home. Tiger violated her probation in August 2019 when she was arrested for drunken driving and sentenced to seven months in jail.

Morland C. Keyes, another passenger in the boat who refused to cooperate with police, pleaded guilty in August 2018 to making a punishable false written statement. She agreed to a plea deal that requires her to spend 2 years on probation and complete 100 hours of community service.

Cara Mia Canale, the only one to testify against West, was granted probation.

YOU DON'T WANT TO READ THIS

December 12, 2017

I will warn you right now, you do not want to read this.

It will disturb you.

You will have nightmares, if you can sleep at all.

You will be angry at me for giving you the front seat to unspeakable carnage, for providing images no human should ever conjure up.

You will blame me for sensationalizing the bloodlust and having a liberal agenda.

I will be called a "twinkie," a "lib-tard," and accused of coming for your guns, because I have the gall of speaking of humanity and demanding that this end.

Sorry to disappoint you, but I have given up.

Further gun control is impossible.

I now believe it is not in our nature to be peaceful.

I now believe the monsters in our midst are looking back at us in the mirror.

Consider what happened last Sunday:

"Kelly went aisle by aisle through the pews and shot dying children at point blank range."

That's what a witness who lived told The Associated Press.

Consider those words, and then the image.

We are all culpable.

You should be forced to look at the crime scene photos.

You should be forced to see what an AR-15 will do to the head of a crying baby.

But that won't be allowed.

That would be inhumane, inappropriate for a culture that spills buckets of blood playing authentic-looking video games.

After 20 babies were killed in Newtown, the state of Connecticut passed a law that prohibits the release of photographs, film, video and other visual images showing homicide victims if they can "reasonably be expected to constitute an unwarranted invasion of personal privacy of the victim's surviving family members."

It's to protect the family.

It's not.

It's to protect the gun lobby.

So I offer up these words from one officer who first arrived at the Newtown shooting. I doubt you have heard it before.

"At first glance it did not appear that there were any casualties. To the left of the room as you walk in there was a bathroom in the corner. There was a massive pile of bodies in this room. At the time I did not know that it was a bathroom and wondered how the suspect had the time to kill that many people and stack them in the corner of the room. There appeared to be about 15 bodies in the small room and several bodies, including two adults near the entrance to the room."

Imagine that scene.

Since the killings in Sandy Hook, 49 were killed in a nightclub shooting in Orlando, 58 attending a concert in Las Vegas and another 20 at that church in Texas, and the assailants all used AR-15 weapons.

We have accepted it.

We have condoned it.

So gun manufacturers can make a buck.

Earlier this month, SUNY Adirondack officials armed their security officers to make everyone feel safe.

Police were on the scene during the attack in Las Vegas.

Police arrived at Sandy Hook within minutes.

And even the heroic efforts of an AR-15-toting neighbor near the church in Texas were too late to save those crying babies from execution.

No one is safe.

"All the other bodies were inside the bathroom or in the entrance to the bathroom. An adult victim was lying across the mass of bodies inside the bathroom. … Sgt. Carrio began to lift bodies off of the top of the pile (redacted) and many of the bodies had injuries that were obviously fatal. As. Sgt. Carrio began to empty out the bathroom, it became apparent what had occurred due to how efficiently packed in the bathroom the children were. It appeared as if the teachers in the room immediately upon hearing the gun shots began to pack children into the bathroom. The children that were sitting on the floor of the bathroom were packed in like sardines. One little girl was sitting, crouched in between the toilet and the back corner of the room. I thought that she might have the best chance for survival. As the pile got higher it appeared that there was a mad scramble to get into the bathroom with people stepping on one another and climbing on top of each other. The teachers would not have been able to get into the room even if they wanted to. The teachers appeared to have been shepherding the children into the room and were then probably going to shut the door."

Imagine those final seconds, because we know how this ends for the babies and the teachers entrusted to protect them.

"They did not close and lock the door to the classroom for some reason and were interrupted by the shooter as they attempted to fill the bathroom with children. The shooter then opened fire on the mass of children and adults. As Sgt. Carrio got to the last bodies, it was clear that no one had survived."

These words should leave you shattered.

The image should stay with you, haunt you as it does me.

Maybe sleep will be difficult.

Maybe you will come to the same realization I have come to — none of us will ever be safe.

And we are the monsters because we won't do anything about it.

P.S.

On October 1, 2017, 58 people died in the Las Vegas concert shooting. A month later on November 5, 26 people were murdered in the Sutherland Springs church shooting. I had written about mass shootings before, about common sense gun control and I was stewing over the recent events with the fifth anniversary of the Sandy Hook school shooting coming up when I stumbled on the official report of the killings.

Two months later, 26 were killed at the Parkland, Florida high school spawning another national debate about gun control.

A TEACHING MOMENT

February 25, 2018

I called my cousin Nancy in Connecticut Friday morning. I told her I wanted to talk to her about a column I was writing.

She knew what the subject would be.

Nancy is a second-grade teacher who speaks about "her kids" at every family reunion. She loves "her kids."

She's passionate about teaching.

Nancy is a decade younger than me, and if she stands five feet tall, I would be surprised.

I tried to break the ice by asking what type of weapon she was going to carry to school.

Bad idea.

"You know, I've been getting texts like that from friends the last couple days," she said. "I don't find it funny. It actually infuriates me. That's not my job. It's not why I went to school. You know I love my job, but the day I have to carry a gun is the day I will quit. I will stand in front of a bullet for your child, but I won't shoot a gun."

Nancy told me most of her colleagues felt the same way.

"More guns are not the answer," she said.

This issue is still raw in Connecticut.

Sandy Hook Elementary School in Newtown is just 16 miles from where Nancy teaches.

"Sandy Hook was a game-changer," Nancy said. "We're so close. That hit hard."

She began to tell me about an incident at the school a week or so before the Florida shooting.

"We had a lockdown," she said. "We heard 'Code Red' over the intercom and because it was right at dismissal time, I knew it wasn't a drill."

The second-graders got up from their desks and filed into the bathroom as they had been instructed. Nancy closed the classroom door, locked it, turned out the lights and joined the children in the bathroom.

"We stood there for 10 or 15 minutes," Nancy said. "I didn't know what was going on. I didn't think there was an active shooter because everything was quiet. I just didn't know. I was texting with other teachers and they didn't know either."

Fifteen minutes is a long time to be scared to death.

"I remember kind of praying, 'Don't let this be the day I die,'" Nancy said.

Finally, an assistant principal arrived to let Nancy know everything was alright.

There had been a home invasion nearby and the police asked for a lockdown.

"It was scary," Nancy said, "but I was happy my kids knew what to do. How sad it is that they have to do it, that they live in a world like that, but none of them were upset, they were good."

She bought them doughnuts the next day.

Nancy says she doesn't worry about school shootings.

"You can't live your life that way," she said.

But there are reminders.

Every day when she takes her kids out to the playground, she finds herself face-to-face with a little red-headed girl named Catherine Hubbard.

After the shootings at Sandy Hook, Nancy's school was one of 26 that received new playground equipment from a group of New Jersey firefighters.

Catherine Hubbard was just 6 when she was murdered at Sandy Hook.

"Every day that we play on that playground I see that beautiful little red-head girl," Nancy said.

Nancy was quiet for a second, then continued.

"I can't believe we can't get our government to get assault weapons off the street," Nancy said. "I don't know what the answer is, but that would be a good place to start."

P.S.

After Parkland, there was talk about arming teachers. But it never gained much serious traction, probably because of teachers like my younger cousin Nancy. A month later, 10 people were killed in a school shooting in Santa Fe, New Mexico. In October, 11 were killed in a Pittsburgh synagogue. And in November, another 12 were killed in a mass shooting in Thousand Oaks, California.

TIME STANDS STILL FOR PARENTS

June 23, 2018

This is the reality for Christine and Richard Taras.

Their lives ended that day, too.

Time stopped.

Every day they are back there again rehashing the conversations, remembering the last time they talked with 13-year-old Jacobe, trying to piece together the puzzle of what they missed and what they could have done differently to pull that sweet little boy back from the abyss.

They are stuck.

Each day is the second Monday in April three years ago, and they are trying to stop it all over again.

Trying to find the silver lining in a shotgun blast.

"We found out about our son being bullied in a suicide note," Christine tells you bluntly. "It was too late to do anything then."

That anger comes through repeatedly.

Christine and Richard jump in and out of their lawsuit they filed against the South Glens Falls school district, telling you who they think lied, why the school was at fault and the need for a cultural change to address bullying by notifying parents when it happens.

Richard leans forward in his chair and tells about being talked down to by legislators playing political games, instead of trying to do something good to save lives.

They say it is for the greater good, but it is obvious the sadness still envelops them both.

"Every day I wake up and say to myself, 'You're one more day closer to seeing your son again,'" Christine says.

"It's a hollow feeling," Richard tells you. "It's a little anger, little bit of guilt. We're doing something good in my son's honor. He showed me that I have a long way to go."

Just last week, the two were having dinner in Lake George. Abruptly, Christine was back there again. The young man taking their order was Jacobe's age and Christine tried to imagine Jacobe if he lived.

"I kept wondering if he would have been one of those polite waiters," Christine said.

The anger only dissipates when they are asked about their son, about the memories they had with him.

"He was a very loving kid," Christine says.

She tells a story about him playing soccer in elementary school and stopping to help up one of the opposing players who had fallen.

"Jacobe was the type of kid that if there was a new kid in school, he would be the first one to invite him over to join the group," Christine said.

After Jacobe's death, the school put together a book of memories from his classmates. One girl wrote, "Jacobe was nice to people who weren't nice to him."

The stories paint a picture of a child who was cherished and cared for, but the stories always lead back to April three years ago.

They had just returned from a vacation in Florida. On Monday morning, Richard got Jacobe up for school and made him breakfast. Afterward, Jacobe laid down on the couch for 10 minutes before the school bus came.

"I remember kissing him on the forehead and telling him it was time to go to school," Richard said.

You know they have told these stories before.

You know they have rehashed it in their minds, looking for something, searching for answers.

What did they miss?

What could they have done differently?

When Jacobe came home from school that day, Christine asked him about his day. Jacobe said it was fine.

"I joked with him that the girls must have liked his tan," Christine said. "He kind of smirked. I had some errands to run and I asked him if he wanted to go. He said he didn't."

"I came home with a puzzle," Christine said. "We loved doing puzzles together."

Chris found him.

And time stopped.

They have not had closure. They have not moved on.

"My wife is still on day one," Richard says. "I'm a little farther down the road."

Richard admits there are things he still can't bring himself to do, things he used to find enjoyment in, things that he shared with Jacobe.

"There was so much good in him," Richard says. "How come there was that much despair. I just can't contemplate that darkness."

Then the guilt bubbles up.

"I would tell him this moment would pass," Christine said. "He showed us that moment sometimes doesn't pass."

"I will own it," Richard said. "I would tell him that sometimes you just have to suck it up. I'm partly a failure. I didn't protect him. Even though I talked to him, did I talk to him?"

Last month, the jury said the South Glens Falls school district was negligent in Jacobe's death, but awarded no damages.

Christine and Richard are appealing the decision.

Earlier this week, a bill requiring school officials to notify parents if their children are being bullied in school was voted down in committee in the Assembly.

Christine and Richard say they will continue the fight.

They are still back there, but they do hope for a better future.

"I'd like to get back to living my life," Richard says. "That's why I'm building a cabin in the woods."

"At some point I hope to start having enjoyment out of my life," Christine says, but she is quickly back there again relating a conversation she often had with her son.

It was their thing.

"Jacobe?" Christine would call out.

"Yes, Mom."

"I love you."

And Jacobe would roll his eyes.

"I know, Mom."

For a fleeting instant, Christine seems to smile.

P.S.

In January 2020, a New York State appeals court denied an appeal by Richard and Christine for a retrial of the original lawsuit and ratified the jury's verdict that the school was "negligent, but not to the point that damages were warranted."

The court wrote: "The conduct of defendant's employees was not blameless during this period. Indeed, it appears that several minor incidents involving decedent provided missed opportunities for them to uncover what was going on. But the fact remains that the trial proof neither established the degree of the bullying that decedent received at school nor showed that defendant could have anticipated its impact upon him."

SPORTS

My newspaper career was divided into two parts. My first 20 years were in sports and my next 22 were in news. But in many ways, I never left sports. I jumped at the chance to fill in at the state basketball tourney in Glens Falls and continually was drawn back to my roots.

RED WINGS WIN THE CALDER CUP

May 17, 1989

Bill Dineen looked like had been caught in a rain shower. Sam. St. Laurent was his usual quiet self, albeit a smiling self. Joe Murphy puffed on a big cigar, blowing big round rings like the proud father of twins. Murray Eaves just wanted to sit down. He was tired.

The Adirondack Red Wings were Calder Cup champions for the third time in a decade, going out with a dazzling offensive spectacle that kept the largest crowd ever to attend an American Hockey League game in Glens Falls in delirious celebration with a 17-goal shootout worth of Wayne Gretzky. The Wings scored 10 of them.

The defensive effort was a circus, but of course that was appropriate and maybe even a little expected after an eight-day layoff. And as defenseman Dave Korol said, "Who's going to remember that anyway?"

So when Brent Fedyk scored on a breakaway with 3:38 to play and Murray Eaves added an empty-netter with 30 seconds on the clock, a red wave of euphoria spread across the Glens Falls Civic Center and a solitary fan held up a simple brown cardboard sign:

"Who needs Albany?"

Indeed.

The crowd roared its approval.

If they were seeing red over recent rumors about a move to Albany, it was put on the back burner for the time being. Championship teams are few and should be appreciated.

"You could see the momentum when we took the ice," Korol remembered. "I think we need that after the eight-day layoff, it gave us a lift."

And each time the Wings scored, the pandemonium spread.

Korol, one of three players for the 1986 championship team, tied the score 1-1.

Then came Fedyk twice. The Wings had scored three times in 28 seconds — a new team record.

And when the Wings scored again to make it 4-1, it was over — or was it?

The game turned out to be a microcosm of the entire Wings' season. Although the team showed brilliant offensive execution, at times last night, its defensive play was painful.

And that reflected the past season.

"At the beginning of the year, I thought we were going to be a team that had a hard time scoring goals," Glenn Merkosky said, champagne dripping down his face. "As things turned out, we were an offensive powerhouse."

And with the brilliant play of goaltender Sam St. Laurent filling the final piece of the puzzle, the Wings were not going to be denied the Cup.

"Sammy just played great," Korol said. "We certainly didn't help him at all."

That was not the case at the offensive end.

The New Haven Nighthawks closed to within one, 8-7, but the Wings were not going to be denied with Fedyk and Eaves providing the final two tallies.

At 10:49 p.m. Glens Falls time, the Calder Cup was in possession of captain Eaves.

And the Wings began the parade around the ice, handing the Cup from player to player, each taking part in the victory procession.

"It was a lot sweeter this time around," Korol said. "Last time, I didn't play that much that year and I didn't really know what to do."

"Nothing you can say can ever compare with it," Merkosky said.

"They get a little bit better as you get older," smiled coach Dineen after his champagne shower. The mild-mannered Dineen plans on celebrating his win by catching up on his paperwork.

"This one is a lot sweeter," Eaves said.

As the Wings completed their victory lap, Eaves carried the Cup over to the corner of the rink and held it aloft, pointing to a group of people seated above.

"This was for the wives," Eaves said.

"Bill (Dineen) said at the beginning of the playoffs that the wives had the players for 80 games, but for the playoffs, we're his.

"The hockey wife is a very special individual," Eaves said.

"I think I'm going to sit down now," Eaves said.

Eaves and the rest of the Wings deserve the break.

P.S.

I had been sports editor in Glens Falls for only eight months when I was plunged into one of the biggest sports events in the city's history. The Adirondack Red Wings, the city's American Hockey League team, were in their prime and in the Calder Cup finals. It was Game 5 and the Red Wings were up 3 games to 1 and hoping to clinch the Calder Cup at home that night.

The problem was that the one weak spot on my sports resume was hockey. I hadn't covered the team all year when I decided to write a column on deadline for the biggest game of the year. I couldn't even get a seat in the press box.

With no seat in the press box, I remember finding a chair outside Heritage Hall where I started scrawling in long hand - we did not have laptop computers in those days - the outline of the column. It was the first of many hockey columns in the years to come.

Coach Bill Dineen retired after the Calder Cup-winning season, but was later called out of retirement to coach the Philadelphia Flyers in 1992 and 1993. He had a record of 60-60-20 over two years before being fired by the Flyers after the 1993 season. Three of his sons - Gordon, Peter and Kevin - all played in the NHL. Bill Dineen died on December 10, 2016 in Queensbury, N.Y. He was 84.

THEY NEVER BELIEVED THEY COULD LOSE

May 30, 1992

ST. JOHN'S, Newfoundland — Truth is, these Adirondack Red Wings never did believe they would lose.

Not really.

Not in New Haven.

Not in Springfield.

Not in Rochester, pushed up against the wall by a 7,000-fan firing squad.

And especially not in the Calder Cup finals way out in the Atlantic in a hockey-crazed hunk of rock called St. John's in the province of Newfoundland.

Win four on the road? If that's what it takes.

The power of positive thinking.

That's what Adirondack coach Barry Melrose was selling. It was the foundation of these Calder Cup champions, that and going to the body.

"If you have the mind, the body will follow," Melrose had preached.

The Red Wings bought into that little bit of psychology and it may never have been as important as when the Wings were hit with a double minor at the outset of the third period Friday night in the deciding Game 7, trailing 2-1.

"The whole thing Barry taught was to believe in ourselves," said Chris Tancill. "It was never over in our minds. We just needed one good bounce, one good break. We were down one goal and that's minimal. We knew it was just a matter of getting to (goalie Felix) Potvin. Sooner or later, the bubble would burst."

Optimistic?

This team was confident almost to the point of cocky. Of course this team killed the double minor penalty.

Then the Wings tied the game when Keith Primeau knocked the defenseman off the puck in the St. John's end and the hard-luck Tancill waltzed in for the unassisted goal.

One good break for Adirondack, please. Tancill capitalized.

That set the stage for Sheldon Kennedy's game-winning tap-in.

"We worked too hard for this to get away," Gary Shuchuk said. "We had 20 guys who worked hard all year."

Of course this team would win. Four times it scored in the final period to win 5-2 before another sold-out crowd at Memorial Stadium.

Off it went with the Cup.

Captain Chris Luongo passed the silver trophy to Shuchuk, then to Lonnie Loach. All of them got to hold it once. This was what the last two months had been all about.

Now, they were champions.

"We grew as a team, we jelled, we came together," Luongo said, still carrying around that Instamatic camera he had used a day earlier on the plane. "There were a lot of one and two-goal games at the end of the season that we won that we wouldn't have won earlier."

And you know what? Those hockey crazies up in Newfoundland, they stayed for the whole thing, politely applauding a job well done. Why not? They were the only fans who got to see Adirondack at its best or at its "Bester" — as the signs in the Civic Center might say.

The Adirondack Red Wings were the best in the American Hockey League.

That was all that Melrose wanted all along.

"Barry was a prophet as far as that was concerned," Luongo said. "He wanted us to be the best team going into the playoffs and that's what we were."

At the end, too.

That was the goal.

That was the realization.

These guys weren't like the front-runners in 1989. This team came out of the purgatory of mediocrity just to finish second. The defense didn't come around until almost March when Bobby Dollas climbed on board from Detroit. Goalie Allan Bester never settled in as the goaltender until the final weeks of the season.

The one constant was a physical, punishing playing style and a ton of penalty minutes.

"I won this thing when I was 25 with Sherbrooke," Dollas said quietly. "I had come off a lot of winning teams and you kind of take it for granted. This one was a lot sweeter. Both these teams were road warriors. It was a great battle."

That's from a guy who when he first arrived would have much rather stayed with the big club.

"You know, maybe it was all for the best," he said. "There's a lot of people who have come to me since and said, 'You're one good defenseman.' So maybe I proved something to some people."

Of course, that was what this team was all about all year, proving things to people, proving things to themselves.

Melrose was the architect of this team. It was a team built not specifically on size, but rather size with speed.

In professional hockey, speed doesn't kill without size, and when the playoffs came around, the Wings threw their weight around.

The rule of thumb was that no team would be able to stay with the Red Wings over a long seven-game series.

The St. John's Maple Leafs took them the distance, right up until the final 15 minutes.

The Red Wings did it the hard way — as usual.

In the locker room, the champagne flowed and the tired Red Wings soaked up all of it.

Gary Shuchuk sat exhausted on a bench. Another player poured champagne over his head. This was the second ring for Shuchuk. He won an NCAA national championship ring at Wisconsin.

"This one is better," Shuchuk said. "Because this was a seven-game battle. And in the NCAA, they didn't let us have champagne in the locker room."

With that, a shower of champagne came from every corner of the room.

Shuchuk loved every second of it.

P.S.

Unlike the 1989 Calder Cup champs, I covered this team regularly. It is hard to forget the final trip to Newfoundland aboard the Detroit Red Wings' private jet — Red Wing One — and flying in over the icebergs on the way into St. John's. The game was special too, with the Red Wings coming from a goal down in the third period to win.

Because of the time difference and the private jet, we were all back in Glens Falls by 11 p.m. where the sportswriters and team all spent the rest of the night at Dango's, the local watering hole, where we sipped beer out of the Calder Cup and watched the sun rise.

Coach Barry Melrose parlayed the championship into a head coaching job with the Los Angeles Kings of the NHL the next year and then took them all the way the NHL finals with Gary Shuchuk providing a game-winning goal in one game. Melrose was still coach when the Kings acquired legend Wayne Gretzky.

Melrose was eventually fired in his third season after a 13-21-7 start during the 1994-95 season. He was hired the next year as a hockey commentator by ESPN where he remains to this day. Melrose still resides in Glens Falls.

The Adirondack Red Wings left after the 1998-99 season and the city struggled to keep the hockey franchise viable. In 2004, Melrose and fellow ESPN commentator Steve Levy purchased the Adirondack Frostbite of the United Hockey League.

Melrose got the itch to coach again and was hired by the Tampa Bay Lightning in 2008 but lasted just 16 games and was fired a month into the season. He returned to ESPN in 2009.

Many of the players went on to have notable NHL careers. Keith Primeau played 909 games in the NHL and scored 266 goals. Defensemen Bobby Dallas and Chris Luongo both had excellent NHL careers with Dollas playing 646 games in the NHL and Luongo 218. He is currently the head hockey coach at Michigan State. Gary Shuchuk played 142 games in the NHL and Chris Tancill 134.

CROSIER'S WORLD TURNED UPSIDE DOWN

November 17, 1996

HUDSON FALLS — You look at him, this slightly built young man in the Cambridge football uniform, and wonder how he could be this strong.

Not physically.

Not that kind of strength.

This is about inner fortitude, muscle of the soul, a silent composure you don't often see in someone just 18 years old.

In the last 24 hours, Scott Crosier's world turned upside down.

After football practice Friday, he went to his job at the Burger Den in Cambridge where he is a cook. That's when he got the news.

His father Randy, a truck driver for a company in Troy, had gone to the doctor for a bad headache.

They found a brain tumor.

Randy was taken to Albany Medical Center.

That's where Scott Crosier, Cambridge's star running back, spent Friday evening.

The tumor was large, but it was on the outside of the brain. The doctors scheduled surgery for Monday.

Scott Crosier left the hospital at 3:30 a.m.

He went to bed at 4:30.

But sleep was not an easy companion.

He skipped the team's usual game-day breakfast to try to rest. The Cambridge team was told about Scott's father.

"We talked to the team about it but Scott was always going to play," Cambridge coach Al Rapp said. "The last thing his Dad said to him was, 'Go win the ballgame.'"

You put yourself in his place and you can't imagine how anyone could do it.

How could he concentrate at all?

On the play?

On the snap count?

How could he be here with his body and somewhere else with his mind and still perform so admirably in a game that meant so much?

But that's what Scott Crosier did Saturday against Tupper Lake in the state quarterfinals.

It was simple.

Get the ball.

Run.

He escaped into his exceptional talent only to find, ultimately, there was no escape there either.

"You want to forget everything," Crosier said. "But I couldn't. Actually, I thought about it the whole time."

On Cambridge's first play from scrimmage, Crosier was handed the ball. He cut into the line, turned it outside and raced 45 yards down the left sideline for the first touchdown of the game.

Just as he has done all season long.

Get the ball.

Run.

That's what he did the entire game.

He scored three touchdowns.

He rushed for 145 yards.

He hurled his body with reckless abandon on defense.

But after each play his thoughts returned to his father.

To the hospital.

To the surgery on Monday and his hopes that everything will be OK.

"My father is the most important thing," Crosier said just moments after being named the offensive co-MVP for the game with teammate Don Record.

He speaks calmly, seriously, but without an obvious emotion. He looks around at his teammates who are smiling and yelling and whooping it up after moving within one victory of a berth in the state championship game and a trip to the Carrier Dome.

"But this is important too." Crosier continues. "This is important to these guys and they depend on me."

Late in the second half, Crosier was hit hard.

"I thought I got knocked out," Crosier said.

The referee made him leave the field until his head was clear.

He disputed this decision with the referee.

When Cambridge scored a touchdown on the next play, Crosier raced back onto the field to take his usual position for the extra point. The Cambridge coaches caught him and took him out again.

"I just didn't want to stop," Crosier says haltingly. "I wanted to keep going. I wanted to keep playing."

Get the ball.

Run.

It was the worst part of the day for the young man.

There on the sideline.

There was no need to run anymore.

There was no reason to score another touchdown, not with a 35-0 lead.

There was nothing more Cambridge could ask of him.

There was nothing more he could ask of himself and that was the moment when it all caved in on young Scott Crosier. When it finally hit him as he knelt on the sideline and quietly sobbed.

P.S.

I had forgotten about this column until 2014 when I got an email from a woman who told me I had written a column about her husband when he was playing high school football for Cambridge. She wanted to surprise him with the column and wondered if I could send her a copy.

She gave me the date it was published. When I saw the column, I remembered the game and the athlete clearly. Telling those inspirational stories was one of the things I enjoyed most about sports.

Checking back from nearly 25 years later, I found Scott Crosier's father Randy was still with us.

Scott's Facebook page showed that he had moved to Florida, served in the U.S. Army and had a job as an X-ray field service engineer. By the look of the photo on his Facebook page, it looked like Crosier and his wife Jamie had a couple boys of their own. I hope they get to read the column about their dad someday.

20-YEAR LOVE AFFAIR NEARS END

February 27, 1999

We all knew that the Adirondack Red Wings might someday leave town. We weren't naive about that. We knew that professional sport was a business and while the American Hockey League was growing into bigger and bigger markets, Adirondack's own market seemed to be shrinking and its fan base wandering away, so when the word came Thursday night that the Red Wings days were numbered, we knew it was nothing personal.

That's the reasonable and logical response.

But sports is not about reason and logic. Sports is about real people who adopt real teams, who treat the players as heroes and idols and, sometimes, under the best of circumstances, these teams creep into our lives in ways we never expected and before long they have captured our hearts.

The sight of the team colors, the team's logo, past players and coaches all become part of the local fabric, part of personality of the community, a piece of who we are and how we define ourselves.

That's what happened here in Glens Falls.

It has been a love affair for 20 seasons. From the time Ned Harkness convinced every man, woman and child from Albany to Warrensburg that they could not live without professional hockey, this army of hockey novices has been a loyal and adoring family of fans. Only now, 20 years later, they are hockey aficionados about to be orphaned.

Over the past two decades, Saturday night became hockey night in Glens Falls. Anyone who was anyone came to the Red Wings games. It was more than just a hockey game, more than just an athletic contest, it became a meeting place, a rare destination where folks could pry themselves away from the television set for a night to go out and interact in a social situation whether it was 30 below in December or a balmy 70 during the playoffs.

This wasn't a success story, it was a love story.

Sure, it's lost some of that along the way. Folks drifted away, the franchise was taken for granted and the American Hockey League began to grow in ways that no one ever expected as it gradually abandoned its small-town roots, leaving beyond other brokenhearted communities in Binghamton and Utica.

But Glens Falls is different.

The Adirondack Red Wings were once considered one of the greatest success stories in professional hockey. Now they are near the bottom of the league in attendance. The team might be the worst in the history of the franchise and people are making jokes about them. It is a fairy tale story that unfortunately has an unhappy ending.

But at its core, the Adirondack Red Wings still own the hearts of the people of this region.

We've all heard the rumors of the Red Wings demise for years. One day they were going to Flint, Mich., the next day Norfolk, Va. Anywhere anyone had a spruced up new arena was a potential moving site for the Red Wings. But it never happened.

That gave me hope.

The Red Wings are owned by Mike and Marian Ilitch, the wealthy founders of the Little Caesars pizza chain. Sure the Adirondack Red Wings lost money. But that was the price of developing players that led Detroit to two Stanley Cup championships.

None of us here in Glens Falls know the Ilitchs and that's what gave us hope.

In my wildest dreams, I hoped that Mr. and Mrs. Ilitch were small-town people too. Folks with big hearts who visited our town and fell in love with it the way so many of their coaches and players did.

People like Bill Dineen, Barry Melrose, Greg Joly, Glenn Merkosky, Joe Paterson, Claude Legris and Peter Mahovlich, who came here to play some hockey, and somewhere along the way they lost their hearts too and never left.

They chose to raise their families here, not in Detroit or a dozen other hockey stops in the United States and Canada. They chose to stay in Glens Falls. So why couldn't that happen to the Ilitchs?

In my dreams I kept seeing some up-and-coming executive in the Detroit Red Wings front office punching out the numbers and showing the Ilitchs how they could make so much more money in some other locale with a larger market, a better economy and a more lucrative deal. And always, Mr. Ilitch would shake his head to this young person, smiling wisely, then responding that they just didn't get it, that Glens Falls was about more than dollars and cents, that it was about a community that had adopted this business venture, that had fallen madly in love with it and even if it cost him some money, that was a fair price to pay for what he got in return.

But the news Thursday night shattered that image.

Maybe it never, ever existed. Maybe only in my own fantasy world.

I think of all the people I have met over the years at Red Wings games, the people that I can greet by their first name from George Champion at the door to Jack Cushing behind the goal, to any of dozens of season ticket holders.

I think of not having those Saturday nights anymore. Even right now as I type this, my 3-year-old is sitting in my lap asking me what I am writing about and I stare back at him unable to give him an answer that he would understand.

I'm thinking about New Year's Eve and how that has become a tradition for my family to go to the Red Wings game as our way to celebrate the new year. I always figured that my little boy would grow up at Red Wings games, that it would be that bond between father and son from toddler to adulthood, the one thing we could always have in common like I had with my Dad and the Yankees.

And now I realize that won't happen. And that leaves this empty spot in my chest and all of a sudden it is hitting me, right now as I type this, oh my gosh, somewhere along the way, no matter how much I'm supposed to be objective as a newspaper writer, this team, these players over a decade of season, these fans have captured my heart too. Boy, they gave us some thrills.

I was there when Bill Dineen won that second Calder Cup and I swore the roof of the Civic Center might be blown off by the noise. I was also one of the few out there in Newfoundland to witness Barry Melrose's championship and that joyous flight home on Red Wing One.

I was there for the retiring of Glenn Merkosky's number and his hiring as coach and the gradual decline over the past few years as the talent dried up and the Civic Center became this hockey desert...

This is what the people in the Detroit front office don't realize.

This is a community that has given its heart and soul to something, it has given it from father and mother to son and daughter. They are ripping out a part of us that is so dear. Can any price be worth that?

Even now, the fact that this news has leaked out is probably seen as just some bad public relations for the Detroit front office. We see it as so much more. It is a death in the family.

P.S.

By 1999, I was from Glens Falls and I was pretty sure I would never leave. The Civic Center was my second home and over a decade of hockey I had grown to understand the special relationship between this community, this region really, and the Adirondack Red Wings.

It was a love affair. They were family.

When word came that the Red Wings were leaving after 20 years, it was a blow to the community, and quite frankly the hockey nights have never quite been the same.

Professional hockey did return to Glens Falls in several different incarnations, but it has been a struggle to support all the teams. The Adirondack Thunder, part of the ECHL, cut their season short in 2020 and then suspended play for the 2020-21 season because of the pandemic. They expect to be back in 2021-22.

ANDY DRISCOLL'S LONGEST DAY

March 4, 1999 ·

GLENS FALLS — How can I tell you about Andy Driscoll, this teenager I barely know, this waif of a player on the Glens Falls basketball team?

How do I convey to you what he went through Wednesday when a celebration of basketball turned into the longest day of this young man's life?

How can any of us even begin to understand the loss he felt when he was pulled out of a second-period class Wednesday morning to be told that his Mom, Donna Driscoll, had died from breast cancer at the shockingly young age of 45?

So here is this young man, just 12 hours after learning about the death of his mother, standing before me in the glare of the television camera light and talking about his loss.

"They pulled me out of school around 9:30 or 10 o'clock and told me that my Mom had passed away," Andy Driscoll said. "I knew I was going to play. One of her favorite things was to watch Glens Falls play basketball. It meant so much to her."

Donna Driscoll, a registered nurse at Glens Falls Hospital for 20 years, had been fighting this disease for five years. Her two children, Sarah and Andy had spent most of their teenage years living with their Mom's battle.

Andy said his Mom was not much of a sports fan, but somewhere along the way she fell in love with this group of kids that played for Glens Falls High School.

She had watched Dan Hall and Matt Monahan play with her son Andy since they were in grade school. She watched them grow up. And she had watched it all come together this year, watching every regular season game in one of the greatest basketball seasons in the history of Glens Falls sports. All these Glens Falls kids had become part of the family.

"She was like my second mom," said Monahan.

"I grew up with Andy," Hall said. "I was always at his house. My mind was on her all day. All of us seniors were pretty close to her."

But when Glens Falls started play in the Section II Boys Basketball Tournament last week, Donna Driscoll was not there. She couldn't make it to Hudson Valley Community College Saturday for the quarterfinal win against Albany Academy either.

Time was getting short.

"My Dad (Dan) spent the night with her last night," Andy said. "She told him that she wanted me to play."

The word spread quickly through Glens Falls High School Wednesday morning. Andy Driscoll is a good student, a quiet kid, and popular among the student body. Anyone who ever saw him play basketball would have to love him.

Physically, he has no business being on the varsity. But he finds a way to get the job done with a scrappy defensive style and a refusal to back down ever. He is a coach's dream.

"I don't know how he does it," Monahan said. "He's so tough."

"The hardest part was waiting the whole day," Andy said. The entire Glens Falls team tried to compose itself, to get its mind on basketball, even if only briefly, to address the challenge at hand and try to get to the championship game of the sectional tournament.

"We tried to stay as focused as we could," Monahan said. "But it was hard."

Glens Falls trotted out onto the court with a 20-2 record and a hastily attached black strip of tape across each of the players shoulder straps.

Joe and Mike Romeo carried an obviously distracted group of young men in that opening quarter and, gradually, the team began to settle into place. At the start of the second period, some students began to unfurl an enormous 50 to 60-foot banner along the bottom row of the stands at one end of the Civic Center.

"Get after it Indians. This is for Drza — from all of us." It was a message of support for Andy Driscoll.

At almost the exact moment when that banner became fully unfurled, Glens Falls stole the ball and Andy Driscoll found himself alone in the open court streaking toward the basket — and that enormous banner in front of him — and leaping high over the La Salle player for a score that may have been the most emotional two points Glens Falls has scored all season as a spontaneous standing ovation broke out from all around the arena.

"I'm 30 years old and I couldn't put myself in that situation," LaSalle coach Brian Fruscio said. "He's going to be real successful in life if he's this tough already."

That was nothing.

This was not the same Glens Falls team fans that Donna Driscoll had seen win all those games. Their minds were elsewhere. Glens Falls struggled to hold onto its lead in the final minute and with 41 seconds to go and leading by just four, Andy Driscoll was fouled.

He stepped to the line and dropped the first shot perfectly through the net, then instinctively thrust his right arm into the air and pointed skyward. He did the same thing with his second opportunity and repeated the feat twice more with 13 seconds on the clock. He was a perfect 4-for-4 to seal the victory.

"She was looking down over me tonight," Driscoll said in the glare of that TV light.

Sitting on the bench, Matt Monahan, Andy Driscoll's best friend, watched in amazement as he calmly sank those foul shots.

How could he do it, Monahan was asked?

Just a teen-ager and thousands of people looking down in that arena as that one action unleashed a day's worth of grief.

How could he find the concentration, the fortitude to hit those free throws with all that had gone on this day? How was it possible?

Monahan didn't hesitate. He gave a half smile, pointed meekly up the heavens with his own right index finger and slowly dissolved into tears.

P.S.

I had been out of sports for three months when the annual Section II Basketball Tournament convened at the Glens Falls Civic Center. I volunteered my services to Sports Editor Greg Brownell to cover some games. I was glad I did.

On the morning of the semifinals, Glens Falls basketball player Andy Driscoll was told his mom had died from breast cancer. What followed that evening is why we watch sports. This waif of a teenager decided to play because there was nothing his mother enjoyed more than watching Glens Falls play basketball. What followed — on the court and off — was as much heartbreaking as it was inspirational. Just thinking back, I have tears in my eyes all over again.

A couple of years later, I saw Andy working at one of the retail outlet stores nearby. He recognized me and introduced himself. Even then, I still wanted to give him a hug.

I ran the column again as part of a "flashback" series in the weeks before I retired. I received an email from Andy's former guidance counselor. He said Andy had applied to Colgate University, but the school was a little bit of a reach for him. The counselor said he included my column as part of his recommendation to the school and followed up with a phone call and Andy was accepted.

Andy graduated from Colgate, got his MBA at Michigan and is now working in the financial sector in Chicago.

A TRUE OLYMPIAN

February 8, 2002

SALT LAKE CITY

Amy Peterson lives in this private little hell that none of us could ever imagine.

You sit with her and ask about her day and there is nothing really to talk about, nothing very interesting anyway. She doesn't have a job so her friends call her on the phone and ask her what she does.

"Grocery shopping," she says.

"I clean the house," she adds.

On a good day, Bodean, her golden retriever mix, gets a day in the park chasing a ball.

When she is pressed, she comes clean with the truth.

"I try and get through the day," Peterson said this past summer from her home in Ballston Spa.

That's what it's like when you have Chronic Fatigue Syndrome.

You sleep 12, sometimes 14 hours a day and you wake up like you've just finished an all night New Year's Eve celebration.

Now throw that little wrench into the middle of your training for the Olympics and see how you do.

That's what happened to Amy Peterson back in 1996. Here was the best short track speedskater in the United States, coming off a two-medal performance at the Lillehammer Olympics and suddenly she had nothing.

Her tank was empty.

Her best friend and training partner, Andy Gable, was all over her. She was goofing off, she wasn't working hard enough. She didn't want it bad enough.

Peterson knew differently.

The doctors couldn't find anything wrong. Gabel told her to work harder. Peterson did. The harder she worked, often the worst she did. Sometimes she would just burst into tears, frustrated and confused by what was happening to her body, unable to explain why she had suddenly gone from best to bust.

Finally, Dr. Roger Kruse of Toledo, Ohio, diagnosed Peterson with Chronic Fatigue Syndrome. There was relief, but no cure. She had to live with it.

Peterson hooked up with Pat Maxwell, the coach of the Saratoga Winter Club, to design a special training regimen. She regained her form. She made the 1998 Olympic team and finished fourth in the 1000 meters in Nagano.

Her greatest accomplishment, she said.

Until now.

Tonight, Amy Peterson will lead the United States team into the opening ceremonies of the Winter Olympic Games, holding the stars and stripes high. Her fellow Olympians have voted her the honor of carrying the American flag.

That's what makes the Olympic Games so special.

That's what makes the Olympic Games one of the last vestiges of pure and unadulterated sport.

Amy Peterson has spent her hours over the past few years in a small, rented house on a dead end street in Ballston Spa, getting through each and every day, one at a time.

She often couldn't even train with her Saratoga Winter Club teammates. Their workouts were too early in the morning for her, or too late at night when she was already in bed.

So she would work out on her own.

Sleep when she had to.

Play with Bodean when she could.

This is what makes the Olympic Games so special. There's something so pure and special about someone so dedicated, that they dedicate four years for four days of competition. And even if she does not win a medal, she will have been rewarded.

I don't want to be naive.

The United States Olympic Committee is paying $25,000 for each gold medal this time around.

Some of the richest millionaires in the NHL will also be marching into that stadium tonight, but they will have to take a backseat to Amy Peterson.

Even if you don't know the luge from the halfpipe, you should tune into the opening ceremonies tonight, tune in to see Amy Peterson holding that flag as high as can be. Tune in to see a true sportsman.

During the Olympic Trials, Peterson didn't want to conduct interviews with the press. She couldn't. It was too draining. She would lose her focus. She couldn't afford to waste that energy.

After she had won her ninth national title in the past 10 years, her father Howard found her near the medal platform. He couldn't speak, his emotions spilling out over all his daughter had been through.

He hasn't seen anything yet.

Amy Peterson has devoted her life to short track speedskating. She is 30 and in some ways hasn't even started her life yet.

When Amy Peterson walks through that portal tonight, holding that American flag to the heavens, she will have emerged from that hell into a wonderful slice of heaven. And it will all have been worth it.

Don't miss it.

P.S.

Amy Peterson failed to medal in the 2005 Olympics. It was the last of her five Olympics. She was inducted into the U.S. Speedskating Hall of Fame in 2006. She took up coaching after the 2002 Olympics and was named the USS Northern Regional Coach and was named coach of the year in 2005 before returning to skating that year and qualifying for the 2006 World Team, but she failed to qualify for the Olympics. Peterson married, has four boys who also skate and coaches at the Saratoga Winter Club in Saratoga Springs, NY.

JACK SHEA WAS THERE, FOR SURE

February 21, 2002

PARK CITY, Utah

Whether you're an atheist, an agnostic or a devout follower of an organized religion, whether you believe there is life ever after or spirits just floating in some great beyond, how could you not believe that the newly departed Jack Shea wouldn't hang around for the greatest athletic show of them all.

And when his grandson Jimmy was nearing the finish line Wednesday morning within one-hundredth of a second of a gold medal, it's even easier to believe that Jack was there providing just the slightest of tailwinds to get Jimmy across the finish line in first place.

These are the sports stories that give us all hope.

These are the stories that make us believe that there is something better beyond this world.

These are the moments when good guys from small towns like Lake Placid stand in the warmth of Olympic glory, even if it is snowing.

At first, the story all seemed so unfair.

Jack Shea, a 91-year-old past Olympian who had been a defender of the Olympic ideal his whole life, was booked to watch his grandson Jimmy complete a family trifecta in the Olympics. Then Jack's car collided with another vehicle on Jan. 22 and within two hours Jack was dead and the driver was charged with drunk driving.

"A lot of people ask me if there is a lot of anger towards the drunk driver," said Jack's grandson Jim Shea Jr. "No, I don't have any anger toward the guy. The guy didn't set out to it. I'm very confident and sure that he did not set out to hurt my grandfather."

In of the most touching moments in Olympic history, Jim Shea Sr. and Jim Shea Jr. (Jack's son and grandson) carried the Olympic torch in the opening ceremonies. They both swear that Jack was there with them.

Before the competition on Wednesday, Jimmy revealed he had a leg injury that could hurt his chances of winning the gold.

Then Jimmy posted the fastest first run of the day to guarantee he will be the last racer of the competition.

You couldn't write a story with any more tension and drama or one with a better ending.

Jimmy Shea trailed halfway through the final run by the tiniest of fractions and in the final burst across the finish line, the world held its breath. And then a split second later, exploded with a roar of approval.

Jim Shea Jr. had won the gold.

He reached into the lining of his helmet and showed the photo of Jack he carried with him. He fingered the speedskating medal hanging from his neck that Jack won in 1921.

"Now that I have won the gold medal, it is not what is important. It is the friendships," said Jim Shea Jr.

An hour later, his father stood outside the interview room and told reporters he's not much with words.

"You don't have to win a medal," said Jim Shea Sr. "I'm a true believer, like my Dad, in the pure Olympic ideal. This is just icing on the cake. These kids will never forget walking into the stadium in the opening ceremonies and the hair standing up on the back of their neck."

Most of the rest of us won't forget Jimmy Shea sliding across that finish line a micro-second ahead for the gold medal and the hair standing up on the back our necks, our eyes moist with tears and a smile on the face of a nation.

How could you not be happy for Jimmy Shea?

How could you not be happy for his family?

Jim Shea Sr. is asked if he is angry that is father did not live to see this?

"Sure I'm angry," said Shea Sr. "But he lived to be 91 years old and he had a spectacular life and he was sharp right up until the last two hours before he died. I have a lot to be thankful for.

"The people of this country and my community in Lake Placid are so kind," said Shea Sr. "We're from a little town and it is very touching how people reached out to us. People of this earth should be kind and they should be peaceful. That was one of my father's Olympic ideals."

And maybe right there is a good reason all this happened in the first place.

"My Dad was a plain, simple guy from a small town," said Shea Sr. "We weren't about the glory."

So why would the spirit of Jack Shea care about the gold medal at all?

Maybe because his grandson and his son and Jack himself were the real thing, the real McCoy of what sport should be all about and maybe we all needed to hear about that again and forget about the French judge.

There is still good in the Olympics.

There is still good in sport.

So if you ask me, Jack Shea was front row and center at that finish line yesterday. And when that sled approached, with the brightest of smiles, he gave young Jimmy's sled the tiniest of pushes because that's something we all needed.

Thanks Jack.

P.S.

On the front page of the Salt Lake City Tribune is a photo of Jimmy Shea that runs the length of the page, his arms raised above his head in triumph, his mouth agape as he swallows the fact that he has just won the Gold Medal and tucked away in the bottom left corner back in the crowd is a middle-aged writer with a can't-believe-it smile - me.

Shea never competed in the Olympics again. He founded the Shea Family Foundation to raise money for kids in sports and serves on the Utah Board of Economic Development. He retired from skeleton sledding in 2005. He currently lives in Park City, Utah and has two daughters and a son.

SMALL-TOWN BOY DELIVERED BIG TIME

January 15, 2008

Each winter, I would go to the small house off Dixon Road in Queensbury and visit with Johnny Podres.

Joan would answer the door and show me into the living room, where John had his feet up on the easy chair, reading a copy of *The Racing Form* next to the roaring fireplace.

Joan would usually excuse herself to a different part of the house or go walk their basset hound.

"She really loves that dog," John would say.

Then we'd talk baseball.

He was pitching coach of the Philadelphia Phillies then, and he would talk about the pitching prospects and going to spring training and, if pressed, he might tell a few stories about the old days.

I loved it when he told the old stories.

I was too young to have ever seen Johnny Podres pitch, but I knew my baseball history. I knew the story of how he delivered a Game 7 World Series victory and lifted the entire borough of Brooklyn to the top of the world.

It always came back to 1955 when it came to Johnny Podres.

Always.

It had to.

Here was this 23-year-old, baby-faced pitcher from Witherbee, a little mining town just up the Northway from Glens Falls, thrust onto the greatest sports stage in the world. And he delivered.

Over the years, I must have asked him the question a dozen times in a dozen different ways: How did he do it, and what was it like?

He often answered the questions with more questions.

"How did I do it?" he would begin, and you would wait for him to bring his full expertise of nearly five decades in Major League Baseball, only to hear him conclude: "Maybe I just got lucky."

It was almost as if John didn't understand it himself.

He knew how to pitch. He knew he had talent, but the enormity of what happened in 1955 always seemed to be elusive for him. At least when speaking on the record.

When Ken Burns came out with his documentary "Baseball," a full five minutes was devoted to Game 7 in 1955.

I can remember asking John for his reaction.

What was it like to know his performance on that October day in 1955 put him at the crossroads in this golden era of baseball?

What was it like to know that it still meant so much to so many people, and it always would?

When Podres beat the Yankees, it was like Bucky Dent beating the Red Sox.

Nothing he did before and nothing he did after would ever matter quite as much.

The reality was that he was a better pitcher afterward. He won 18 games with the Los Angeles Dodgers in 1961 and was selected for four different all-star games after 1955.

When his career ended, he became a pitching coach, taught Frank Viola a change-up and predicted great things for a young Phillies pitcher named Curt Schilling.

The young pitchers loved him, and I think he took great delight when they discovered that he had beaten the mighty Yankees in Game 7 and came to him to know what that was like.

But they had to go to him. He never volunteered the information.

While Podres was legend, he was certainly imperfect off the field.

He was a chain smoker, battled alcoholism, loved to gamble and struggled to put two sentences together without at least one expletive.

That was Johnny. Rough, gruff and fun to be around.

He struggled with his health for years and had heart bypass surgery four different times. That eventually forced him off the baseball diamond and into retirement to fish for bass at Lincoln Pond and winners at OTB.

I last saw John in Cooperstown this past summer. That seems appropriate now.

He was with some of the baseball old-timers, players like himself who had been there in 1955 and knew what he had done. He was signing autographs for a price and seemed to be enjoying himself.

In Cooperstown, he will always be a fresh-faced 23-year-old with a live left arm, and it will be Oct. 4, 1955, every day of the year.

Godspeed to Johnny Podres. He was one of a kind.

P.S.

Just before retiring in 2020, I ran my tribute to Johnny Podres in a "Flashback" series of my past columns. I received an email from Johnny's daughter-in-law showing Johnny's grandson at the Baseball Hall of Fame in Cooperstown besides a life-sized bronze statue of Johnny pitching in the 1955 World Series.

Johnny is a legend and it is the way we all should remember him.

On December 8, 2010, every seat in the downtown arena in Glens Falls, N.Y. was filled as fans gathered to watch Jimmer Fredette (Number 32) and his Brigham Young teammates play the University of Vermont. Residents remember it simply as "The Jimmer Game." This was a town hall meeting for 10 kids in shorts, part church social, part Fourth of July picnic. It was another chance for all of us to come together to celebrate the good fortune of Fredette. He would be named college basketball's player of the year in the spring and then a first round draft choice in the NBA. But on this night he belonged to Glens Falls. (Photos courtesy of The Post- Star, in Glens Falls, N.Y.)

GAME BROUGHT US TOGETHER

December 9, 2010

In the end, this had little to do with basketball.

Really.

This was a town hall meeting surrounding 10 kids in shorts. This was part church social, part Fourth of July picnic, part high school reunion.

It was all around you right from the start as each person made their way through the crowded concourse at the Glens Falls Civic Center.

The going was slow because of all the hugs and handshakes.

Neighbor meeting neighbor, old friends finding each other, connecting again after years, and each one of them saying to the other: "Isn't this great?" "It is," came the response over and over again.

These were Christmas-morning smiles.

The old building was filled like it rarely is anymore and the reasons had little to do with a great basketball team or the expectations of a taut back-and-forth game.

The reasons were as varied and personal as the number of people in attendance.

Turn around and the guy behind you told the story about the time he and his friends — all around 30 — took Jimmer on their team in a pickup game at Crandall Park and he was the best player there — at the age of 12.

The people next to you mention they are cousins.

In front of you are a couple of people that followed Jimmer all through high school and next to them is a guy who played basketball with his father at the YMCA.

Everyone had a story, a connection, and a reason to be there. These were 7,000 friends touching base with their nephew home from college. The basketball was really an afterthought.

His introduction — never had one person needed something less — might have been enough for most people. He was the first player of the night and the standing ovation said it all.

The message was clear that those in attendance approve of the path he has carved in the real world and we can't wait to see where it will lead him next.

He stood tall on the court with one hand raised in appreciation of our appreciation just as he had done so many times as a teenager.

He seemed to know instinctively what he meant to this community, but more importantly, he seemed to understand that he wouldn't be the person he is today without so many of the people in that building last night.

That's pretty darn rare.

"Isn't this great?"

You heard it again and again as this little drama played out over two hours where his play on the court did not disappoint.

He scored the first seven points for Brigham Young.

He dazzled everyone with a behind-the-back pass in the second half that led to a BYU lay-up.

The players around him are bigger than in high school, but his presence is the same, his game as smooth and effortless as ever. As hard as it is to believe, he has gotten better.

As BYU pulled away late in the game, all that was left was the final curtain call.

The place rose again in unison and the game stopped as Jimmer walked slowly to the BYU bench appreciating every second of the ovation.

Even the players still playing seemed to be looking on in awe of the romance between native son and community.

They took it all in and from somewhere around you, you heard it again from one of the spectators:

"Isn't this great?"

P.S.

Four years earlier, I would excuse myself after dinner and head down to the Glens Falls High School gymnasium to see Jimmer Fredette play. I was there for every home game.

Glens Falls went all the way to the state championship that year, Jimmer became the all-time leading scorer in New York State history and my wife told me I loved Jimmer more than her.

Jimmer got a full scholarship to Brigham Young and by his junior year had established himself as a Division I college basketball star.

BYU thought so much of Jimmer, it gave up one of its home games in Provo so his hometown fans could see him play one more time.

When the tickets went on sale that summer, the line curled out from the box office at the Glens Falls Civic Center, down Glen Street and around the back of the arena. Whatever it took to get inside in December for the "Jimmer Game", I was ready. I showed up more than an hour before the box office opened to be sure I was there. I took my son and two friends and bought them all BYU T-shirts.

THE JIMMER COMET

April 10, 2011

GLENS FALLS -- The Fredette house is just around the corner from Sanford Street School.

It is part of a typical Glens Falls neighborhood with little more than a body's length separating each home. It is a place where neighbors are family and you raise each other's kids. You could call the blue house nondescript, maybe modest is a better word, but essentially what we are saying here is that it is tiny. It's hard to believe that Al and Kay Fredette raised three kids there.

The house may someday be a basketball log cabin where crazed fans come to see where it all started.

Laugh, if you like, but few thought Jimmer Fredette would ever be a basketball comet - not even his parents - and now Al and Kay have to figure out how to share their youngest child with the rest of the world.

"It is overwhelming," said Al from the small living room where some sort of Jimmer memorabilia is never far from being tripped over.

"I worry about him," said Kay. "I'm always texting him that this is not what life is all about. But he is a pretty level-headed kid. But I don't think he is very comfortable with it."

Sure, this all comes from an uncanny ability to shoot a basketball into a basket from amazingly long distances, but really, it's something more than that, and, of course, many have their theories.

It's the small-town upbringing. It's the fact that he is a kid of fairly normal height that seems to be able to do things that far more athletic and talented athletes cannot. He works hard and makes these ridiculously long shots routine.

"We've had people contact us from Italy, Germany, Aruba, from all over the world," said Al. "People tell us that they are not even basketball fans, but they watch Jimmer play."

The basketball community here in Glens Falls has known this for some time, but this year Jimmer Fredette went from being a very good college player to a great college player.

If you ask Al and Kay when they realized it, when it finally dawned on them that they were in the middle of a media-fueled, fan-crazed tornado that was swirling around their son, they have a hard time putting their finger on it.

Al says it was the Utah game on Jan. 11 when Jimmer scored 47 points. Kay says that was the start, but it was the string of games after that when 40 points became routine. What happened over the next two months was a blur, a frenzy of one unbelievable event after another.

BYU rose as high as third in the national rankings. After Jimmer dropped 43 on San Diego State, NBA star Kevin Durant tweeted that Jimmer was the best scorer in basketball. Period.

President Obama mentioned Jimmer when picking his tourney bracket.

Larry Bird marveled at his ability in a Sports Illustrated interview and in back-to-back weeks he was on the cover of Sports Illustrated.

"When he first started his college career, I vowed that I was going to print out everything that was written about him," said Kay. "I thought it would be a nice memento. Somewhere along the line, I just gave up."

Who could blame her?

The whole basketball world went "Ga-Ga" over Jimmer.

When the season started, Jimmer used to come out to the court in Provo after games and sign autographs for 20 or 30 people.

By the end of the season, hundreds were waiting for him, and they were of all ages.

"One night he signed for two and a half hours," said Al. "Finally, the coach came out and said he had to leave to get something to eat."

One time, Al and Kay were walking to the game when they saw a fan with a life-sized cutout of Jimmer coming toward them. "Look," said Al to Kay. "Here comes your son."

The success has slowed Al and Kay down, too.

"Everywhere you go, you have to be patient," said Al, "because everyone wants to talk about Jimmer. You kind of have to build it into your schedule."

Since the end of the season, Jimmer has been named an All-American and has claimed almost every national player of the year award. Back in Provo, he has become such a rock star that school officials asked him to stop attending classes because his presence was a disruption.

"I asked him what he does on campus when he goes out," said Al. "He said he wears a hoodie and tries not to make eye contact."

Up to 30 different agents have been pursuing Jimmer as a client.

"It has been an amazing experience," said Kay. "It's like a dream, but it has taken on a life of its own."

The family is in the final stages of hiring an agent as Jimmer readies for the NBA draft on June 23. It will be a big payday that could set Jimmer for life.

Al, a financial planner, says he will be handling Jimmer's money in the future. He doesn't expect Jimmer will ever have to worry about making a living after the end of his basketball career.

If Jimmer flourishes in the NBA, Al envisions the whole family being involved in Jimmer's career as the family business, or perhaps with a foundation that would do good things for people.

"If we work it out right, it will allow us all to spend time together and that's what it is all about," said Al.

In recent weeks, Jimmer was offered $20,000 to make an appearance at a corporate event.

"This is kind of crazy," Al thought. Jimmer decided not to go.

A businessman in Utah, offered to give him 6 percent of the gross sales if he would lend his name to a restaurant called "Jimmer's Place." He turned him down.

"You have to stay grounded," said Al. "And stay close to family."

It doesn't appear that Al and Kay have too much to worry about.

They related how, in the middle of the frenzy of the NCAA tournament with Jimmer and his BYU teammates preparing to play Florida in New Orleans, they got a text from Jimmer.

"Is it true they are closing the Sanford Street School?" he asked. "That's too bad."

Sometimes late at night, Kay will hear her phone beep and there will be text from Jimmer:

"Good night, Mom. Love Jimmer."

From the Fredette living room, you could hear a basketball bouncing in the backyard.

After all these years, the Fredettes probably didn't even notice.

"Yeah, sometimes kids from the neighborhood come over and shoot baskets," said Al.

Maybe they are hoping for lightning to strike again, maybe they are hoping for a little bit of Jimmer magic to run off on them. Hey, why not.

P.S.

On June 23, 2011, a couple thousand people got together to watch television at the Glens Falls Civic Center. It was called "Jimmer Jam".

Jimmer Fredette, one of their own, was about to be drafted by the NBA. They put up the basketball court that Jimmer once played on, constructed a big screen TV behind one of the baskets and nearly 2,000 people showed up to watch the NBA draft.

In Heritage Hall, a room below the main concourse at the Civic Center, there was a Jimmer museum exhibit where you could look closely at Jimmer's John Wooden Award for being named National College Player of the Year. The Milwaukee Bucks drafted Jimmer 10th and then immediately traded him to the Sacramento Kings.

Unfortunately, the NBA never worked out for Jimmer. He played just 241 games in the NBA for five teams over six seasons.

In 2011, Jimmer announced his engagement to BYU cheerleader Whitney Wonnacott and they were married on June 1, 2012 in Denver. They have two children, a daughter and a son.

He later made millions playing for Shanghai in the Chinese Basketball League where he was a star. He was playing his third season there in January 2021.

REMEMBER GLENS FALLS AS 'HALLOWED GROUND'

March 14, 2016

GLENS FALLS — The story starts with a letter, so it should not be surprising that the letter-writer was a mailman.

It was early in state tourney week when I received this note from James Bergman of White Plains:

"Just a note to (tournament director) Doug Kenyon and his staff, all the volunteers and the city of Glens Falls for making the New York State high school boys basketball tourney the great event it was for 36 years. As someone who has been to all 36 years of this tourney, I can say thank you all, it will be missed in Glens Falls."

Imagine, a mailman from Westchester County taking the time to say thank you.

It tells you something.

And Bergman was hardly alone. He said there used to be 15 or so of his friends who came to the tourney together, now it is down to seven or eight.

It was just the beginning of an emotional week that was equal parts nostalgia, sweet memories, and by the time the final horn sounded at 4:49 Sunday afternoon, bittersweet goodbyes, with just a touch of bitterness for how the bidding process was rigged.

Dan Conley, who has been a tournament volunteer for 22 years, was waiting for me, when I arrived at the tourney Friday morning.

He handed me a half-dozen thank you notes, you know, the kind of formal handwritten correspondence polite people used to send to acknowledge a nice present or good deed.

Apparently, they are still sent to tourney volunteers.

"You know a lot of people are talking about losing the tournament and what they remember," Conley said. "But this is what I am going to remember — these letters."

Each of them rehashes a small act of kindness by Conley or one of the volunteers that made the tournament so special to the visitor, they had to write.

And Conley is just one volunteer.

By Sunday afternoon, Conley was wearing a bright yellow T-shirt someone had given him. The message was to "Boycott Binghamton."

Yes, there are some hard feelings.

"I can tell you that on Sunday afternoon when I am driving down the Northway, I am going to have a tear in my eye," said Bergman. "Glens Falls and the New York State Basketball Tournament will always be my special place.

"I fell in love with the way Glens Falls runs the tourney, the way the city embraces the tournament," Bergman said.

It was a theme repeated over and over by volunteers, spectators and participants alike.

Fresh off a semifinal victory, Troy coach Rich Hurley said, "I used to come here as a kid when I was in elementary school. I saw those great teams from Mount Vernon and Archbishop Molloy, so I know something about the tourney."

"I'm sad to see it leave," said Bishop Grimes coach Bob McKenney, who has won five state titles here. "It was always a very special place to come and play."

Conley pointed up into the stands.

"Those people are from Fort Ann, and they come here every year," he said. "See those folks over there? They have been coming here since their son was in diapers. He's now on the high school team in Ogdensburg."

I've got one of those pictures, too. It shows my 1-year-old son sitting on my lap on press row. He's in his second year of college now.

By Sunday's final, the crowds had thinned. Just 1,381 came out to see the last game.

At halftime, public address announcer Bill Wetherbee asked the state tourney volunteers to gather at center court.

There had to be more than 100 of them. It took a while to line them all up for a group photo as Wetherbee read an acknowledgement from the New York State Public High School Athletic Association for the role the volunteers had in making the tourney so special.

Front and center presenting a plaque to Tournament Director Doug Kenyon was Executive Director Robert Zayas, the man responsible for moving the tournament to Binghamton.

His presence didn't sit well with some people.

When Wetherbee was done, he raced to center court to get into the photo.

Unfortunately, only a handful of people got on their feet and applauded.

It should have been more.

Aquinas won the final game in a rout and attendance was average for the weekend. The games were mostly one-sided, although some of the shooting was the best we had ever seen. Just when the players learned how to shoot in the Civic Center, the tourney is leaving.

Wetherbee signed off after the final game, saying this was not only the end of the 2016 tournament, but the end of three and a half decades in Glens Falls.

"Bittersweet," Kenyon said at the conclusion.

But I'd much rather reach back to Friday morning with the Civic Center rocking and Moriah coming back from 16 points down to stun little Panama Central School.

Panama is located in the farthest southwestern corner of upstate New York. It's closer to most of Ohio than it is to Glens Falls.

Here's what their coach Ed Nelson said about Glens Falls: "It's hallowed ground up here."

P.S.

Putt LaMay, the athletic director at Glens Falls High School, brought the New York State Basketball Tournament to the new Glens Falls Civic Center in 1980 because no one else wanted it.

Over the next 36 years, "The Road to Glens Falls" became the goal of high school basketball teams across the state. At one point, the boys' tournament was at the Civic Center and the girls tournament was at nearby Queensbury High School.

Personally, there was nothing more exhilarating for me each year. As sports editor, I would often show the movie "Hoosiers" at my house the night before the tournament began.

So even though I had been out of sports for 17 years, I relished the chance to cover one more tournament in 2016 - the last one - and give it the sendoff it deserved.

Over the next three years, I did not go to any of the state tournament games in Binghamton, even when Glens Falls High was playing for the state championship. We still had the federation state tournament, but the private schools from around the state rarely created the same energy or buzz.

So when Glens Falls High won the state title in Binghamton in 2019, it meant that Glens Falls would return to the Civic Center for a chance at the overall state title.

It was just like the old days with the Civic Center filled to capacity. Glens Falls won both games.

After three years in Binghamton, the New York State Public High School Athletic Association voted to bring the tournament back to Glens Falls in 2020 for another three-year run. The pandemic canceled the tournament in both 2020 and 2021.

WELCOMING BACK STATE CHAMPS

March 20, 2019

The video is 13 seconds long.

I've watched it a few times since Saturday.

Shot from press row at the arena in Binghamton, it shows Joseph Girard III gliding past one defender, catching the ball and effortlessly banking in a layup at the buzzer to give Glens Falls the state basketball championship.

To make history.

To make a region smile.

I suspect hundreds had their phones trained on the court with the settings set to "video" as history unfolded and the celebration ensued.

Through the miracle of social media I've watched that 13 seconds a multitude of times from a multitude of angles in the Binghamton arena.

Every time the ending is the same.

Every time it is even more satisfying.

Every time I smile.

There is one video shot from up high.

Another from the other end of the court that gives a wonderful vantage point to view the hysteria of the Glens Falls cheering section.

Someone shared the video to ESPN, which made it one of its top 10 moments on Saturday.

I guess I've become a bit of a fan.

I've been a regular at Glens Falls games the past few years.

I like live sporting events and the up-tempo ball this team plays. And of course, the Girard kid is special.

A few years back, I described Jimmer Fredette as the type of high school player you see once in a generation, but this is Glens Falls where the DNA tends to replicate when it comes to basketball.

Thirteen times I saw Glens Falls play this year.

But I wasn't in Binghamton on Saturday.

Instead, I found myself in a line on Monday morning. At 10 a.m. I was 30 or so back when the tickets for the Federation state tournament went on sale.

For all of New York's illogic in having a second state tournament — public high school teams play the private schools this weekend for an overall state title — it serves our purposes this year.

Glens Falls gets to come home and we get to celebrate the state championship.

I was thinking back to the last time I stood in line at the Civic Center. It was Fredette's senior year at Brigham Young and BYU agreed to schedule a game against Vermont at the Glens Falls Civic Center. The line stretched around the block that time.

But what a special night that was.

When the public high school state basketball tournament was moved to Binghamton four years ago, one of my first thoughts was that JG3 and his Glens Falls teammates would not have the chance to play in the state tournament here.

But I forgot about the Federation tournament.

Suddenly, the Federation tourney is the hottest ticket in town.

More tickets were sold in the past couple of days than during the entire weekend some years.

They said there were 6,000 on hand for the Section II championship game earlier this year.

I suspect there might be more on Saturday in the Class B semifinals.

I got my tickets Monday morning.

I will be there Saturday afternoon to thank these young men for the thrills they have given us, and making my life just a little bit more fun.

P.S.

Ever since Jimmer Fredette had played for Glens Falls a decade earlier, I had been attending Glens Falls High School games. I believed I missed one game in the previous four years when Joe Girard III was playing. Like Fredette, he was a special player.

New York's Federation State Basketball Tournament pits the public high school champions against the private schools, mostly from New York City. Following Glens Falls' state title the week before in Binghamton, Glens Falls returned home to knock off South Bronx Prep 77-70 in overtime with Joe Girard III scoring 42 points. Glens Falls Civic Center was filled with over 6,000 people.

The next day in the championship game, Glens Falls knocked off Cardinal O'Hara 88-79 with the Syracuse-bound Girard scoring 43 points and his cousin Trent Girard 21. His future coach at Syracuse, Jim Boeheim, was in the house to see it all as well.

So was I and a few thousand of his family and friends.

COACH TAUGHT MORE THAN PLAYERS

March 1, 2020

It wasn't too long ago that I heard from a former Oneonta State soccer player I had met when covering the team 35 years ago.

Mike Kopp lives up here now, and had coached the Schuylerville girls team for a few years when he recognized my name in the newspaper.

We talked a little bit about those Oneonta State teams, and frankly, I was surprised at the number of player names I remembered. We finally got around to talking about Coach Garth Stam.

He was the kind of guy you don't forget.

I guess I would call him stoic, maybe a bit of an enigma.

He had to be at least 6 feet, 6 inches tall, thin as a rail, and he looked far more like a basketball coach. In a day and age when coaches raged along the sidelines, he rarely said a word.

Mike told me the old coach still lived in Oneonta, but spent part of the year in Florida.

I heard from Mike again Wednesday.

The old coach had died. He was 88.

"As we've discussed, he was a true gentleman," Mike wrote in an email. "A man who turned high school graduates into fine young men. And for me, that's his legacy."

We all should live lives of such meaning.

I thought about Coach Stam a on Wednesday. I remember him as being a man of few words, which made it difficult for me when I wrote about the team and how they had played.

In sportswriter parlance, he was a bad quote.

I sensed animosity in his silence.

I remember being frustrated and finally confronting him about what was wrong.

I don't remember his exact words, but essentially, he believed I knew absolutely nothing about soccer and even less about how game stories should be written.

He didn't believe he should have to provide an in-depth analysis in detailed quotes to me after the games. He believed I should just watch the games and write what I saw. He explained that was how they did it in other countries.

The old coach made some good points.

I was 25 years old and had never played or watched soccer at all. I was flying by the seat of my pants and I knew it. So I asked him for his help. I asked him how they wrote about soccer in other countries. He explained there was little if any concern for statistics such as shots on goal or saves. It was about the flow of the game, the tactics and the skills of the players. When a goal was scored, he told me to describe it in great detail.

He told me the worst place to watch the game was from the sideline, advising me to find the highest spot on the bleachers so I could see attacks as they developed.

I struck a bargain with the old coach, who was in his 50s and twice my age.

I asked him to help me.

I asked him to help me understand the tactics and explain to me what he was seeing on the field, and I would try using fewer quotes from him.

I guess you could say I became his student.

Eventually, my stories depended less on statistics and more on description. And while the quotes from the old coach never got much better, I believed we reached a mutual respect. Over the years, I tutored more than one young sportswriter about how to cover soccer, often using the words of the old coach.

In the fall of 1985, Oneonta State qualified for the SUNYAC tournament in Buffalo. I remember riding along with Coach Stam in his car. The team won both games that weekend and claimed the conference championship.

It was the last conference championship for Coach Stam.

Over the years, he coached six All-Americans and 18 of his players were drafted into professional soccer.

And he helped one young sportswriter as well.

P.S.

Not long after the column ran in The Post-Star, I got a call from the sports editor at The Daily Star in Oneonta – my old job – who told me he did not know much about the old coach and asked if he could run my column in the Oneonta newspaper.

THE WORLD

The world often affects our lives in unexpected ways, whether it is through the past or in the present. My travels as an editor and tourist often led to stories that I believed my readers would appreciate.

DREAMING OF OTHER WORLDS

April 23, 2004

In the dying sunlight of one of those great-to-be-alive April evenings earlier this week, I found myself sipping a glass of white wine on a terrace on the crest of a hill where Arlington, Va., overlooks the Potomac River and downtown Washington. It was a view even God himself would have stopped to admire. I'm not sure about the wine.

I fell in love with this city when I was in eighth grade and I've never looked back. No place can compare to Washington.

Over this past week at a national meeting of editors, I've seen President Bush wing a speech on the state of the nation that even he seemed bored with, Sen. Hillary Clinton criticize all things Republican and Secretary of Defense Donald Rumsfeld almost convince me that things are going to be OK in Iraq.

It was a whirlwind of information and activity.

And as always when things are so busy, time to compress and relax is needed.

I was sitting with John Humenik editor of the Quad City Times in Davenport, Iowa, finishing up a beer at a small Irish pub across from Union Station, when a man sat down next to me at the bar and ordered an Irish coffee.

We made small talk.

He was vague and evasive about what he did.

I told him how I just took my son to the new air and space museum outside Dulles Airport and had seen the SR-71 spy plane.

That got him talking. He talked in great detail about it. I talked about some of the other aircraft and spacecraft he had seen.

His name was Ken Szalai. He used to work for NASA. In fact, he used to be the head guy at the Dryden Flight Research Center at

Edwards Air Force Base in California. It was there that they perfected space shuttle landings. It was there that he helped develop experimental aircraft.

I'd like to say we talked about the shuttle and space program and outer space, but the reality was that he tutored us.

We asked him what happened with Columbia. He told us to go back and read the report - that there were life lessons for all of us. He said there were people at NASA who suggested they maneuver a spy satellite into position to check the shuttle wing, but the evidence was not strong enough.

"Having a feeling isn't enough at NASA," he said. "You have to have data."

He scribbled drawings of the Challenger and the O rings and what happened there.

He filled another cocktail napkin with the wing of Columbia. He talked about physics and Newton and Neil Armstrong visiting his house.

He said he knew Commander Rick Husband of Columbia. He said he knew Commander Dick Scobee of Challenger.

"What was it like to lose a shuttle crew?" I asked.

He stared back sternly and didn't hesitate.

"Has anyone ever called to tell you that your wife is dead?" he said loudly and directly. "And you can come down to identify her body, which is in about 23 pieces. That's what it was like."

He explained how NASA had some of the greatest minds in the world. But they were also human.

He explained the problems with the Hubble Telescope. He said focusing the telescope in space was like looking at a line of 100 cars coming at you with their lights on and in the 100th car is someone holding a candle. The candle is the star you want to focus on. He said that NASA had solved that problem by adapting software used by doctors in mammograms.

Szalai retired in 1998. His biography seems to have every honor one could possibly have from the aerospace industry. Last year he was asked to head a panel that would look at the feasibility of using the Apollo command module for future space flight.

And maybe a return trip to the moon.

"Why would you want to go back to the moon?" he was asked.

"We're out of practice," Szalai said. "We haven't been there in 30 years."

We talked about what it would take for a manned flight to Mars.

He explained it would take nine months to get to Mars with current technology. A nuclear reactor the size of the beer cooler in front of us would have to be built. The Mars astronauts would have to wait another year before the planets were in the right position to head back again.

"By then, they would be returning with the first Martians," Szalai said with a big smile. Obviously, this would be a co-ed trip.

The bar was almost empty. Four hours had elapsed without any of us ordering another drink since Szalai first ordered the Irish coffee. We were all getting tired. We exchanged business cards.

"You know," Szalai said. "Somewhere in America, right now, a mother is tucking in the first person to land on Mars."

He smiled and let it sink in.

At the end of a long week of speeches from this world, it was good to know there are still those who dream about other worlds.

P.S.

John Humenik eventually became my boss at Lee Enterprises - owners of the Glens Falls newspaper - as the vice president for news. At various editor conferences and meetings over the years, we often retold the story of meeting the NASA guy in the pub across the street from Union Station.

PAYING RESPECTS TO A PRESIDENT

January 3, 2007

WASHINGTON, D.C.

We staked out a spot in the bushes along a makeshift fence on the Capitol grounds, only to be chased away a few minutes later by a policeman with a flashlight.

For the next 90 minutes, several hundred of us waited across the street on top of a marble wall in front of the Cannon House Office Building for President Ford's flag-draped casket to arrive.

Why were we there?

Even now, I'm not sure of the answer.

The people were young and old. Some remembered him as President, others did not.

We stood silently, saying little, holding a vigil for a man none of us ever met. Those who did talk whispered in muffled tones. There was no laughter.

I drove over 400 miles the day before to be there, to be part of the moment and witness the spectacle of a President lying in state.

As a president, I had no strong feeling about Gerald Ford. When Jimmy Carter challenged Ford for president in 1976, I voted for Carter. It was my first presidential election. It was a long time ago.

Shortly before 7 p.m., they played "Hail to the Chief." And somewhere over on the Capitol grounds, cannons rumbled a 21-gun salute.

None of us said a thing.

And then the casket began its slow ascent between two perfect rows of the military honor guard. I could see it through the zoom lens of my camera. I don't think my son could see much at all.

It was over in a few minutes and we all quietly dispersed.

On New Year's Eve, while most people prepared for parties, my son and I lined up for the public viewing of President Ford. We met an older woman in line whose husband was in the Navy and stationed in Washington. She told us that the number of people in line was nothing compared to that of President Reagan. She stood in line seven hours that time.

It took us just an hour to get to the entrance of the Capitol rotunda.

Inside, it was startling how perfect the honor guard appeared, like mannequins or wax figures frozen at attention.

The colors of the flag seemed vibrant in the bright light. The rotunda seemed small in the presence of a President lying in state. It seemed to shrink up for the occasion, the casket resting on the same bier that carried the coffins of Abraham Lincoln, John Kennedy and Ronald Reagan.

It did not seem to matter at this moment whether he was a Republican or a Democrat, just that he was an American and that at one time he was our President and our leader. Politics seemed to shrink away.

We were there less than a minute.

We were the people, offering up our respect as citizens of a great county.

I was honored and grateful to be there.

P.S.

When George Herbert Walker Bush died on November 30, 2018, my son and I briefly considered reprising our visit to Washington. My son was finishing up his first semester of graduate school so we had to take a pass because of his final exams.

When the Capitol was overrun by protesters on January 6, 2021, it was even more personal for us because of our experience paying respects to a former president.

IT WAS ORADOUR WE WILL REMEMBER

September 13, 2011

We sat on the stone wall overlooking the Dog Green Sector of Omaha Beach.

Below us, families set up their beach chairs and children splashed in the surf on a beautiful sunny day. It could have been Million Dollar Beach in Lake George in August.

The tour guide said it was here that 66 American soldiers were killed in 8 1/2 minutes on D-Day. It was the portion of the beach portrayed in "Saving Private Ryan."

This was hell on Earth on June 6, 1944.

It was a big reason I was in France earlier this month. I wanted to see the beaches. I wanted to see where the paratroopers landed at Sainte-Mère-Église. And I wanted to see the American cemetery.

But what I came home with was the story of Oradour.

Oradour-sur-Glane is a little village in central France a long way from the landing beaches of Normandy.

In the days after the Allied invasion began, the French Resistance began to fight back. The Germans were alerted that an officer in the 2nd SS Panzer Reconnaissance Battalion had been captured by the resistance near Oradour. He was never heard from again.

The Germans responded. They suspected people in Oradour had been involved.

On June 10, four days after the invasion began, the Germans surrounded the small but vibrant town of Oradour and sealed it off. They ordered everyone into the village square. They herded the women and children into the town church. The men were led to six different barns where the Germans had already set up machine guns.

The Germans looted the town and set it on fire.

When you walk through the gates into Oradour today, you are transported back in time to 1944. Most of the stone walls to each building are still intact, although they continue to crumble.

There is a trolly line that runs down the main road and the electrical wires are there. Those around you whisper until you get to the first sign that tells you this is where a group of French men were massacred.

It is one of the six barns.

People stop and they look. They stare at the walls looking for bullet holes, maybe expecting to hear the screams from a half-century ago.

Down the road a little ways, there is a butcher's shop and then a garage with a burned-out 1940s car.

Then there is another sign about a massacre.

And then another.

And another.

The longer you walk on the main street, the quieter it gets. You hear people's footsteps. You feel the quiet.

When you get to the church, you debate whether you should go in at all. The roof is gone, but it is otherwise intact. It was here that 247 women and 205 children were gathered when the Germans began lobbing in grenades.

The space is not that large, and you can't imagine the terror.

The church caught fire, and when the wounded tried to escape through windows and doors, they were gunned down.

In all, 642 people of Oradour died on June 10, 1944.

There is a monument in the nearby cemetery with two small caskets with glass lids. Inside the caskets are dried flowers and bone fragments.

Around you are crypts with family photographs of those who were killed. The victims were as old as 90 and as young as one week.

I was told the story is well known in France, but I had never heard it before.

Many of those responsible for the massacre were killed fighting off the Allies in the weeks and months that followed. But no one was ever brought to trial. There was never any justice.

After the war, General Charles de Gaulle decided the village would never be rebuilt. It would be a memorial to the cruelty of Nazi occupation.

Driving back to my cousin's home that evening, there was little talk.

I thought about Omaha Beach again, and the reason for the sacrifices there was never more clear.

P.S.

My son was 15 in 2011 and a colossal history nerd. While my wife and I had always wanted to see Paris, the goal was to show our son the beaches at Normandy.

One of our first stops was Omaha Beach where my son filled a couple of small plastic containers with sand. Later at the American cemetery, one of the officials gave my son American and French flags to bring home with him.

But the true horror of the war did not hit home for another week when my cousin, Paul Sally, took us to Oradour.

It showed the true horror of war and why Americans needed to sacrifice their lives.

THIS BAND OF BROTHERS

January 11, 2011

On Monday, a day when there was so much talk of mourning, there was little, if any, talk about the death of Dick Winters.

Considering his humble nature, maybe that's as it should be.

Dick Winters was the central character, first in Stephen Ambrose's World War II book "Band of Brothers," and later in the HBO mini-series of the same name produced by Stephen Spielberg and Tom Hanks in 2002. The book and movie chronicled the exploits of 101st Airborne's Easy Company from D-Day to the Battle of the Bulge.

Several years ago, the father of a friend of mine passed away. At the funeral, my brother and I compared notes and admitted that both of us were shocked that this soft-spoken man that we did not know well had been a Marine with a resume of Pacific battles that we had only read about in history books.

"He was the real deal," my brother said.

The "Band of Brothers" mini-series brought the type of film realism to the small screen that had earlier been realized only with "Saving Private Ryan" on the big screen. It was a blood-gushing, bomb-blasting war movie that was filled with action, but what moved you was the camaraderie and humanity of this group of men trying to survive. Dick Winter's leadership and his relationship with his men is the centerpiece of the story.

"He was the first one out there, yelling, 'Follow me!'" fellow Easy Company veteran Bill Guarnere told The New York Times.

Easy Company parachuted behind enemy lines on D-Day. Most of the command was killed when one of the planes was shot down, and Winters was left in charge of the company. In the first day of action, he led 13 men on an assault that destroyed a battery of German howitzers that were shelling the roads leading off Utah Beach. Winters and his men took out the position and also discovered a map that laid out the German defensive positions. The attack was such a textbook maneuver, it is still taught at West Point.

For his efforts, Winters was honored with the Distinguished Service Cross, the second-highest honor awarded by the U.S. military.

Winters once told his co-author of "Beyond Band of Brothers" that "war does not make men great, but sometimes, war brings out the greatness in men."

What stays with you is not his actions with his rifle, but the way he led men in battle.

Each of the 10 episodes of the mini-series was book-ended by an interview with the aging surviving members of Easy Company who would quietly, often fighting back tears, remember the things they had seen and the men they fought with. One of those men interviewed was the real Dick Winters.

Those interviews hit home. You could see the anguish in each of them, and it made their sacrifice raw and all the more touching.

"Like most veterans who have shared the hardship of combat, I live with flashbacks," Winters wrote in "Beyond Band of Brothers," his memoir of his war experiences. "... distant memories of an attack on a battery of German artillery on D-Day, an assault on Carentan, a bayonet attack on a dike in Holland, the cold of Bastogne. The dark memories do not recede; you live with them and they become a part of you. Each man must conquer fear in himself."

Dick Winters was the "real deal."

Tom Hanks released this statement on Monday:

"When our days run their course and a man like Dick Winters leaves us, time and providence remind us that human beings can do giant things."

The "Band of Brothers" book and mini-series brought Winters a certain amount of fame and opportunity in his later years, yet the CNN website reported that he did not make any money off his memoirs or speeches. He gave the money to a variety of organizations near his Hershey, Pa. home.

In the forward to his book "Beyond Band of Brothers," Winters writes this:

"In the twilight of my own memory, my thoughts always return to Easy Company, to happier times when a group of young men joined together to fight for freedom and to liberate a world from tyranny."

Dick Winters, 92, died on Jan. 2 of complications from Parkinson's Disease. Among his final wishes was that the news of his death not be released to the public until after his funeral. Apparently, he didn't want the fuss.

Someday soon, my son and I will make a pilgrimage to Pennsylvania, and we will seek out Dick Winters' final resting place and pay our own respects. We regret we never had the chance to meet him and thank him in person.

That's what I am mourning today.

P.S.

During our 2011 trip to the Normandy beaches in France, we toured the battlefields with a company called "Band of Brothers Tours." The English guide tailored many of our stops with events chronicled in the HBO mini-series, including the site where Winters took out German guns shelling Utah Beach on D-Day.

In the van, we talked in length about the service of Dick Winters - the protagonist and hero of the miniseries - and his actions after D-Day with Easy Company.

HONORING THE 'REAL DEAL'

April 9, 2013

EPHRATA, Pa.

The cemetery at the Bergstrasse Evangelical Lutheran Church outside Ephrata in rural Lancaster County is not hard to find.

It is bordered on two sides by busy county routes and you will not find any more tranquility there than if you were doing errands around town.

For me, this had been a destination since I first heard of the death of Dick Winters two years ago.

Winters, who died at 92 in January 2011, became a reluctant celebrity war hero when the story of Easy Company was told in the Emmy-award-winning miniseries "Band of Brothers."

The moral core of "Band of Brothers" centers on Winters' humble leadership and his commitment to the men in his command. It struck a chord with me, and I suspect many others.

Winters' story was not about being a war hero, it was about setting an example that the men in his command would respect and follow. It apparently lasted a lifetime.

When Winters passed away from complications from Parkinson's disease, he knew it would get a lot of attention, so he left instructions that his death not be revealed to the public until after his funeral.

When he was buried, there were just seven members of his immediate family present.

I suspect that Dick Winters figured it would end there, that he would slip away quietly. But that has not been the case.

There have been others like me and my son.

They have continued to come five or six each week, leaving mementoes and flags around the simple granite marker. They have come to pay their respects. I suspect Winters, and I'm sure he would detest this, has become the figurehead for an entire generation of World War II sacrifice.

There are no signs, no markers that tell you that Dick Winters is buried here, which is also no surprise, but his final resting place is not hard to find.

As we walked down the hill from the Lutheran church, one spot in the cemetery stood out above the others. From 50 yards away there was a clump of small American flags. Dick Winters is buried there in a family plot with his father and mother. His wife, Ethel, who died just a year after he did, is also here.

The marker does not tell about parachuting into Normandy on D-Day or taking out the guns at Brécourt Manor to save hundreds of lives on Utah Beach. It doesn't speak to the quiet eloquence and the extraordinary respect he commanded from his men or the HBO miniseries that made him famous.

There were 13 small American flags fluttering robustly on this blustery April afternoon. The number changes because random visitors keep leaving them. The marker simply says:

Richard D. Winters
WW II - 101st Airborne
1918-2011

My son and I offered up a moment of silence as we paid our respects to someone we both admired, but had never met.

When we visited the Normandy beaches two years ago, our tour took us to Brécourt Manor where Winters led a small group of soldiers in taking out a German artillery position that was shelling Utah Beach. Winters was later honored with the Distinguished Service Cross for the lives he saved that day.

Before leaving on our trip to Pennsylvania, we had packed a small plastic container with some sand we had gathered from the beaches in Normandy.

At the base of Winters' headstone, my son leaned over and poured some of the sand on the grave.

This was for the men he saved that day.

It was our way of saying thanks.

As we were about to leave, my son took a letter from his pocket and put it behind one of flags on the grave.

I don't know what it said, but my son told me later he wanted to say thanks. Others have done the same and I suspect will continue to do so.

P.S.

It had been two years since Dick Winters passed away. During my son's junior year of high school, we planned a trip to the Gettysburg Civil War battlefield in Pennsylvania.

Lancaster County, where Winters was buried, was not far from Gettysburg. My son later earned an internship at the Gettysburg battlefield and worked there for three summers.

TEACHING BELFAST'S LESSONS

May 20, 2015

While the trip to Belfast was billed as a vacation, it also had a purpose in exposing my son to his heritage in Northern Ireland, and a world once described simply as "The Troubles."

My cousin John was giving the tour. We turned left down a narrow street lined with row houses on each side and stopped at 32 St. James Place. It was here my mother grew up in a Catholic neighborhood with two brothers and three sisters, and here where I spent an entire summer in 1964.

We got out of the car and posed for photographs next to the hedge in front of the tiny garden area. It was on this stoop my father and several of his shipmates serenaded my mother with "My Wild Irish Rose" at an hour well past when a respectable young lass should be receiving company.

My grandmother — fearing what the neighbors would think — invited the slightly intoxicated sailors into her sitting room. It was probably the only way they would stop singing.

It was here, too, that my cousin John told us about those days during the 1970s when Northern Ireland was at war.

I didn't want to pry. I didn't want to bring up bad memories, but as we drove I asked him about those times, while my son listened in the back seat.

John told about a routine that included being searched by British soldiers three, sometimes four times a day on his way to and from school and warnings from his father not to cause any trouble.

It was just down the road that a bomb exploded one day and my aunt found two British soldiers mortally wounded.

Northern Ireland was occupied. The Irish Republican Army members were terrorists.

We drove down the Falls Road and you could still see the steep walls topped with barbed wire that separates the Protestant and Catholic neighborhoods, although they are not needed any longer.

Our guide pointed to a gate that is now open to traffic between the two neighborhoods, only to be closed again after dark. He believed it was out of habit.

We stopped at a "Peace Wall" where several men were working on a mural.

"It's really sort of a tourist attraction now," John said.

That night the clan gathered at John's house. My cousin Linda remembered when my parents visited in 1973 at the height of the Troubles.

"That was when your Daddy was arrested," Linda said.

"Detained," I corrected.

My father had been using his new movie camera to take pictures. He wanted to show the armored vehicles in the street and the military presence. When he was seen taking pictures of the local "police station," the soldiers asked him to come with them.

They questioned him and took his film.

This was a time when bomb threats were real and searches were regular.

Later that night, my 19-year-old and his three 21-year-old Irish cousins talked about what life was like at their respective schools. They did not sound so different.

There was no hint of the troubled past.

I asked John about the future, and would the peace last. An entire generation of children had grown up with no memory of the bad times while mixing with children of different neighborhoods where religion did not seem to be the issue of the past.

Belfast is again a bustling hub where business is good and cruise ships dot the harbor, depositing tourists on its streets. A new Titanic museum opened recently.

The children know nothing else, and that gives me hope the peace will hold and my son will always be able to visit where it all started.

P.S.

By 2015, my son had one year of college under his belt and I wanted to complete his family education with a trip to Belfast. My cousin, John Flynn, toured us around the city, showing the walls between the Catholic and Protestant parts of town that were Ground Zero for "The Troubles" during the 1970s.

We stopped at Belfast City Hall and showed the spot where my mom and dad first met and took the obligatory photos.

We headed down the Falls Road, then turned onto St. James Place where we stood outside a row house and I told the story of three slightly intoxicated American sailors standing on the stoop singing "My Wild Irish Rose" one night in the 1950s. My grandmother quickly brought them all inside, afraid of what the neighbors would think.

It was in this neighborhood that I spent the summer of 1964 as a 7-year-old. That night we sat around drinking beer, my son getting acquainted with his college-aged cousins and all of us thinking of absent friends.

TO THE READERS:
YOU DON'T HEAR ABOUT THE HARASSMENT

June 30, 2018

*W*hen the Capital Gazette in Annapolis - a newspaper much like my own - was attacked and four people killed, I addressed our readers on the front page.

Newspaper folks are different.

I've tried to impart that to you, dear readers, at different times and different ways over the 29 years we have known each other.

We demand high standards from ourselves and each other while trying to make a positive impact on our community. We are not perfect, but we try to be whenever possible. And we are always trying to be better.

That made Thursday's horrific attack on the *Capital Gazette* in Annapolis, Maryland, very personal to all of us here at *The Post-Star.* I know our publisher Rob Forcey feels the same way.

As we learned about the victims, I was struck at how similar their lives and careers were to people who work here right now.

One of the editors was exactly my age, graduated from college the same year I did and crafted a long career in community journalism.

Another victim was a community editor, someone who writes about nonprofits and the accomplishments of people's kids.

The *Capital Gazette* is a newspaper with a mission much like ours. It covers town meetings, high school sports and community events that are rarely controversial.

Their editor, Jimmy DeButts, tweeted out this yesterday: "Just know @capgaznews reporters & editors give all they have every day. There are no 40-hour weeks, no big paydays — just a passion for telling stories from our community."

That's not only us, but that is true of the vast majority of daily newspapers across the country.

That makes the people special. And they give up too much for too little.

Those of you who know people who work here probably know that already. We live our lives here, raise families, coach teams, play basketball at the YMCA and participate in life here.

What you don't know is the ugly other side.

The accused killer had a long-running beef with the newspaper. Many of you will conclude he was a lone psychopath. But I want you to know that his fixation with the newspaper is not unusual.

As our staff talked yesterday, we recounted dozens of instances of relentless harassment by someone who felt they had been done wrong by the newspaper.

The behavior that preceded Thursday's shooting in Maryland is also commonplace here in this community.

We've had death threats, been told people were going to "get us" and, earlier this year, someone left our newspaper on the porch rolled up in dog feces.

Consider that type of harassment for a second.

The harassment got so bad for one of our reporters six years ago, we filed charges and that person went to jail.

I had one person leave me critical voicemail messages daily for nearly a year.

Last month, I received an anonymous threatening letter, telling me not to write about a certain subject or else.

The accused killer had a beef with a newspaper that is a community institution. And he finally acted.

I was shocked but not surprised by yesterday's murders.

I knew it was only a matter of time, considering the written and verbal attacks on journalists.

But yesterday morning, everyone in my newsroom showed up to work, talking about their kids, what they planned to do this weekend and what stories they were working on. They were ready to go back on the front lines.

They put up with a lot to do an important job they love and one that brings them great satisfaction.

I'm proud of each and every one of them.

Ken Tingley
Editor

P.S.

During the summer of 2019, pro-Trump demonstrators began assembling in downtown Glens Falls and confronting anti-Trump demonstrators. After one of the first rallies, I wrote that things could get "violent".

By the fall of 2019, the newspaper was regularly being verbally attacked by the protesters. During one rally, a protester said they were coming for us at The Post-Star.

When the Capitol was overrun in January 2021, I was shocked, but not surprised because we had seen the beginnings of the behavior right here in Hometown, USA.

CHURCH SCANDAL HAPPENED EVERYWHERE

August 22, 2018

The document is remarkable for its humanity.

That may sound strange to you. After all, it was a two-year grand jury investigation into the widespread sexual abuse of children in the Catholic Church in Pennsylvania.

Consider how it begins: "We, the members of this grand jury, need you to hear this."

It is a plea for help.

It is a call to action for all of us.

It should not be ignored.

"We know some of you have heard some of it before," the report continues. "There have been other reports about child sex abuse within the Catholic Church. But never on this scale. For many of us, those earlier stories happened someplace else, someplace away. Now we know the truth: It happened everywhere."

Consider that conclusion.

Our community should know that better than most, because we know it happened here as well.

The story sounds like something you have heard before, and you may want to look away, but you should not. The Pennsylvania report contains the profiles of more than 300 clergy members charged with abuse. Sixteen years earlier, *the Boston Globe* identified 150 to 250 priests in Boston.

But this is not old news. Rather, this is an attempt to confront the past, the misdeeds of the church leadership and bring justice to the victims once and for all. That has still not been done.

"We have been exposed to, buried in, unspeakable crimes committed against countless children," the authors write. "Now we need something to show for it. Courtesy of the long years of cover-up, we can't charge most of the culprits. What we can do is tell our fellow citizens what happened and try to get something done about it."

So I ask you to listen as well, whether you are Catholic or atheist, to consider the atrocities committed and how they were covered up by senior church officials, and if you are equally outraged, demand change from our leaders in the state Legislature.

The grand jury identified over 1,000 child victims from over 500,000 documents subpoenaed from the church. They believe the actual number is thousands more.

"We are sick over all the crimes that will go unpunished and uncompensated," the grand jurors wrote. "This report is our only recourse. We are going to name their names, and describe what they did — both the sex offenders and those who concealed them. We are going to shine a light on their conduct, because this is what the victims deserve."

The investigation found a distinct pattern among diocesan leaders across the state, "not to help children, but to avoid scandal."

Those exact words appear over and over in church documents.

Abuse complaints were kept locked up in a "secret archive" as stipulated in the church "Code of Canon Law." Only the bishop was allowed a key.

Special agents from the Federal Bureau of Investigation identified a series of practices the grand jurors called "a playbook for concealing the truth."

The grand jurors concluded this: "Despite some institutional reform, individual leaders of the church have largely escaped public accountability. Priests were raping little boys and girls, and the men of God who were responsible for them not only did nothing, they hid it all. For decades. Monsignors, auxiliary bishops, bishops, archbishops, cardinals have mostly been protected; many including some named in this report have been promoted. Until that changes, we think it is too early to close the book on the Catholic Church sex scandal."

The investigations found that the victims were "brushed aside, in every part of the state, by church leaders who preferred to protect the abusers and their institutions above all."

And when Pope Francis spoke out on Monday, he provided no course of action going forward.

The grand jury could only bring charges against two priests because of the statute of limitations, but other investigations continue.

You should download the Pennsylvania report because it happened "everywhere."

You should read the 12-page introduction and the seven pages of recommended changes. There are hundreds of pages of documents chronicling acts too horrendous and too numerous to include here.

They are reaching out, not as grand jurors charged with prosecuting crimes, but as human beings needing to fix the system and find a way to protect children while getting peace of mind for the abused.

"Grand jurors are just regular people who are randomly selected for service," the grand jurors wrote. "We don't get paid much, the hours are bad, and the work can be heartbreaking. What makes it worthwhile is knowing we can do some kind of justice. We spent 24 months dredging up the most depraved behavior, only to find that the laws protect most of its perpetrators, and leave its victims with nothing. We say that laws that do that need to change."

That's why New York needs to pass the Child Victims Act.

That's why you should contact your state representative immediately.

P.S.

New York State passed the Child Victims Act in January 2019. It allowed victims of child abuse to sue for damages even if the statute of limitations had expired. We had followed the debate over the issue for years. There were several former priests in the community who had been accused of abuse.

MAYBE A CHILD SHOULD LEAD US

December 23, 2018

You need to know about 15-year-old Greta Thunberg.

It will make your day, I promise. I first learned about her from one of our letter-writers — Bernice Mennis — who told me to watch the extraordinary speech she gave at the United Nations climate change summit in Poland earlier this month.

Thunberg, a pig-tailed wisp of a girl, looks even younger than 15, but sounds much older.

Last September, Thunberg walked out of class to protest the lack of debate over climate change leading up to the Swedish elections. She said she got the idea from the Parkland kids in Florida.

For three weeks, Thunberg boycotted school and sat on the steps of the Riksdag in Stockholm with a sign reading "Skolstrejk för klimatet" — School strike for climate.

After the election, she went back to school four days a week, but each Friday she returned to the steps of parliament as her protest gradually gained international acclaim. Other protests were organized in The Netherlands, Germany, Finland and Denmark.

Thunberg appeared in the "Rise for Climate" demonstration in Brussels and the "Declaration of Rebellion" in London.

I never heard about any of these protests, just as I had never heard of Thunberg.

Thunberg inspired thousands of students in Australia to walk out of school, despite Prime Minister Scott Morrison's warning of "more learning in schools and less activism."

It was another example of a politician who got it all wrong.

But I don't recall seeing any protests around here, or anywhere in the United States for that matter.

It's clear we are not concerned.

At the same conference where Thunberg spoke, a United States delegation made a presentation in support of coal.

It was greeted with mocking laughter.

As the only country in the civilized world not to support the fight against climate change, we deserve the mockery.

Thunberg spoke at the same conference.

Nobody laughed when she said, "You are not mature enough to tell it like is. Even that burden you leave to us children. But I don't care about being popular. I care about climate justice and the living planet."

The pig-tailed sprite was poised and deliberate as she called the adults of the world onto the carpet.

"Our biosphere is being sacrificed so that rich people in countries like mine can live in luxury," Thunberg said in a strong, even voice. "It is the sufferings of the many which pay for the luxuries of the few.

"The year 2078, I will celebrate my 75th birthday. If I have children, maybe they will spend that day with me. Maybe they will ask me about you. Maybe they will ask why you didn't do anything while there still was time to act.

"You say you love your children above all else, and yet you are stealing their future in front of their very eyes."

Thunberg and her family also walk the walk.

She has stopped eating meat, and flying on airplanes, and her parents have followed suit. The family installed solar batteries, started growing their own vegetables and have an electric car.

To make an appointment with a journalist for an interview this fall, they rode a half-hour on their bikes.

Her words grew stronger as her speech proceeded in Poland.

"Until you start focusing on what needs to be done rather than what is politically possible, there is no hope. We cannot solve a crisis without treating it as a crisis.

"We need to keep the fossil fuels in the ground, and we need to focus on equity. And if solutions within the system are so impossible to find, maybe we should change the system itself.

"We have not come here to beg world leaders to care. You have ignored us in the past and you will ignore us again.

"We have run out of excuses and we are running out of time.

"We have come here to let you know that change is coming, whether you like it or not. "The real power belongs to the people."

The applause was polite at best.

The climate talks resulted in nearly 200 nations agreeing to a set of rules to limit warming of the planet that they all knew did not go far enough.

The United States was not one of them.

What we need is the leadership of a 15-year-old girl instead of what we have now.

P.S.

Greta Thunberg's activism was just beginning. In January 2019, she addressed the World Economic Forum and declared, "Our house is on fire." She met with Pope Francis, was boycotted by right-wing politicians and supported by 224 academics who signed a letter of support, saying they were inspired by her actions. German Chancellor Angela Merkel said that young activists like Thunberg had forced her government to act faster on climate change.

In August 2019, she sailed across the Atlantic on a sailboat to dramatize carbon-neutral travel. It took 15 days and afterward she addressed the United Nations.

Time Magazine named her their 2019 Person of the Year. President Donald Trump mocked her choice by tweeting, "So ridiculous. Greta must work on her Anger Management problem, then go to a good old fashioned movie with a friend! Chill Greta, Chill!"

Greta responded by changing her Twitter biography to: "A teenager working on her anger management problem. Currently chilling and watching a good old fashioned movie with a friend."

Greta was nominated for the Nobel Peace Prize in both 2019 and 2020.

Dachau was the first Nazi concentration camp in Germany. The author visited there in the spring of 2019 on an appropriately gray, drizzly day. It should always be raining at Dachau. (Photo by Ken Tingley).

IT SHOULD ALWAYS BE RAINING AT DACHAU

May 19, 2019

It had been raining for most of the day, and for the first time you could really hear the birds chirping.

It's what stood out for me at the time.

The birds were so loud, and it didn't seem right.

We hesitated outside the nondescript brick building. There were hedges and a lovely green garden that you only seem to find in Europe. The surrounding tree-lined grounds were park-like, an irony considering what happened all those years ago.

I wanted the birds to shut up.

Didn't they know?

When you turn right off the path at the entrance to Dachau Concentration Camp, you are face to face with the swinging wrought-iron gate and the words of advice for all Nazi political prisoners at the time — Work shall set you free.

Dachau was the first concentration camp.

This was where it started, with Nazi political prisoners doing forced labor, and where the first of the Jews were brought, where torture was perfected and medical experiments begun.

This was starting point of the Holocaust.

Ground zero.

When you pass through the gate — as all visitors do now — you can be overwhelmed by the scope of the grounds that stretch on endlessly, with only the outlines of the foundations for the prisoners' barracks and distant guard towers that have been rebuilt.

Appropriately, the skies were gray with a steady drizzle the day I visited.

It should always be raining at Dachau.

Located a short train ride from the Bavarian capital of Munich, Dachau was established weeks after Adolf Hitler took power in 1933.

The Munich police chief — Heinrich Himmler — designed the camp as a place where German political prisoners were initially housed, then male Jewish citizens.

Torture and murder followed.

What I learned was that rule of law still existed in Germany in 1933, and that the horrors didn't happen all at once, but gradually and over time.

Three weeks after the camp opened, four young prisoners were shot and killed. It was said they were trying to escape.

A young German prosecutor was sent to investigate the case, along with a regional medical examiner. Autopsies were done on the victims. The wounds suffered by the victims did not match the guards' accounts.

The prisoners had been murdered.

The prosecutor persisted in pressing the case, despite political pressure, and eventually filed arrest warrants against "unknown perpetrators."

But the indictment papers were intercepted before they could be delivered.

Himmler, a rising lieutenant to Adolph Hitler, had been alerted to the work of the young prosecutor, and Adolph Hitler stepped in and ordered the warrants shelved.

In a display case at the Dachau museum, it says simply that the brave prosecutor was dismissed in 1934 and his replacement closed the investigation.

It is just a footnote to what happened at Dachau.

The fact that there was once rule of law at Dachau is overwhelmed by the monstrosity of the crimes that happened later.

It is estimated some 206,000 prisoners spent time in Dachau. Another 30,000 died there.

The stories tell of torture, medical experiments, rampant disease and a prison population of over 60,000 when the camp was liberated in 1945.

It is all a nightmare, yet it is all too real with the rain coming down.

Through the gate and to the right is a building where the prisoners were brought, stripped of their clothes and possessions. In the beginning, their possessions were catalogued and their money put away for safe-keeping.

Early on, some were even released, but soon there was a saying around Munich: "Dear God, make me silent, that I may not come to Dachau."

We go on to visit the barracks, the religious memorials on the grounds, stepping around the puddles.

And it is quiet.

Few of the visitors are saying anything.

Then we turn toward the brick building on the other side of the fence, where the rain has stopped and birds are chirping madly.

There is a sizeable chimney coming from the roof of the brick building.

I approach a doorway inside, where over the archway of a swinging metal door, is written a single word — Brausebad.

It means showers.

There is total silence in this room, and I notice I can no longer hear the birds.

It's hard to imagine they ever chirped here.

It's hard to imagine why they would now.

P.S.

During a tour of Austria and Germany that exposed us all to an amazing array of vistas, the one memory that stood out was our visit to Germany's first concentration camp. We took photos of ourselves there that day, but we were not smiling.

DEATH OF NEWSEUM

January 2, 2020

They shut down the most important museum in Washington, D.C. Tuesday.

The death of the Newseum has not been widely reported.

Nor has its loss been mourned properly.

It is another indication of how we have lost part of our moral center, a bit of our soul.

It's an indication how little we appreciate the importance of a free press in protecting our other freedoms, while living in a world where 9 out of 10 people cannot write a letter to the editor or depend on a trustworthy source of information.

Consider that for a second.

Just 13 percent of the world's people live in a place with a free press.

So, I had to say goodbye.

I knew that within those Newseum walls, I would find inspiration about a profession that is in trouble, which is being belittled at a time when it should be celebrated.

When I arrived at the Newseum Sunday morning, it was appropriately raining.

The line started at the main entrance on Pennsylvania Avenue, wrapped around the side of the building down Sixth Street and around the back onto C Street.

They all couldn't be in the news business.

Over its lifespan, the Newseum, despite a $25 admission fee, drew nearly 10 million visitors, but its operating costs were formidable. And once donations from the big media companies dried up, it became apparent that the museum could not be sustained in a city where other world-class museums are free.

"The Newseum was immersive and interactive, challenging younger visitors in particular to understand that our nation's history has been driven by courageous people determined to make this a `more perfect union' by using the rights of free expression," wrote Ken Paulsen, one of its early directors, in USA Today earlier this year. "Sometimes, those heroes were journalists; more often, journalists were there to chronicle the courage of others. An attentive student could walk into the Newseum as a high-schooler and walk out a better citizen."

Those students learned about murdered investigative reporters like Don Bolles and Chauncey Bailey; the photographer whose last frame of film showed the World Trade Center crashing down upon him; and how crusading newspaper editors made a difference in the Civil Rights movement.

I found this engraved into one of the Newseum's walls:

Free press is a cornerstone of democracy.
People have a need to know.
Journalists have a right to tell.
Freedom includes the right to be outrageous.
Responsibility includes the duty to be fair.
News is history in the making.
Journalists provide the first draft of history.
A free press, at its best, reveals the truth.

It's what so few don't understand.

Up on the sixth floor was a collection of newspapers from the Revolutionary War through the murder of five Capital Gazette reporters a year ago.

Each year contained multiple important news stories. Many, I had forgotten about. This building was not just about the First Amendment, but how stories, events unfolded, how we saw it then, and how they remain a part of our history.

Consider this again: The Capital Gazette published a newspaper the day five of its journalists were killed.

There on the wall of the Newseum was the nearly blank editorial page it published that day:

Today we are speechless.
This page is intentionally left blank today to commemorate victims of Thursday's shooting at our offices.
Tomorrow, this page will return to its steady purpose of offering our readers informed opinion about the world around them, that they might be better citizens.

That was written from the back of a pickup truck. The Capital Gazette newsroom was a crime scene at the time.

I spent six hours and 10 minutes at the Newseum Sunday, reveling in our nation's history and the greatest moments of journalism.

The Newseum building was bought by Johns Hopkins University earlier this year.

The 12 sections of the Berlin Wall and the three-story guard tower from Checkpoint Charlie will go into storage.

While there are some traveling exhibits, there are no current plans to replicate the exhibits someplace else.

That is a loss for all of us in so many ways.

It was dark out and still raining when I finally finished looking at the collection of Pulitzer Prize-winning photography.

The Newseum gift store had run out of merchandise and the staff was asking everyone to leave.

I was sad, and a little angry.

This was American history.

This was the celebration of the unique American, idea envisioned by the Founding Fathers, of a free press.

That ideal of showing how a free press covers its community and sometimes changes the world is going into storage.

That was not right.

Where were our leaders? Why was this museum not being preserved?

I think my friend and colleague Ken Paulsen said it perfectly:

"Unless we understand and embrace the vital role a free press plays in our democracy, we encourage politicians of all stripes to denigrate and dismiss the journalists who daily keep a check on corruption and government abuse."

Too many of us are OK with that.

P.S.

Our trip to Washington included a tour of the Supreme Court, the Library of Congress and witnessing a #metoo protest outside the Capitol across the street. My son and I walked over to the Capitol and took some photos before heading back to the hotel. The city was mostly deserted. A year later, the Capitol would be attacked by a mob that would have been better served touring the now defunct Newseum.

DOCTOR DOES THE RIGHT THING

March 29, 2020

You want fearless, this is what it looks like.

You want hope, this will give it to you.

Dr. Colleen Smith, an emergency room doctor at Elmhurst Hospital in Queens where 13 patients died of the coronavirus on one day last week, had seen enough.

Things had been bleak, essential supplies were short, so Dr. Smith did something about it.

She brought two reporters from the New York Times — Robin Stein and Caroline Kim — into the emergency room — The HIPAA privacy law be damned—to not only show them what the conditions were like, but let them shoot video as well.

She broke the rules.

She talked to reporters about things she wasn't supposed to talk about because the public needed to know.

Her colleagues needed to be protected.

Consider the reporters for a second, too.

They take a lot of guff, especially when you work for the New York Times. But how many of us would visit ground zero of a contagion without a cure?

Not many, but the story Dr. Smith had to tell was critical.

She told the world about her daily reality.

"The frustrating thing about all this is that it feels like it is too little, too late, like we knew, we knew it was coming," Smith says in the video. "Leaders in various offices (in the New York City medical community) are saying, 'We're gonna be fine, everything's fine.' And from our perspective, everything is not fine. I don't have the support that I need.

Even the materials I need to physically take care of my patients. This is America and we are supposed to be a first-world country."

It was a warning to the rest of us that management isn't always on top of things.

Smith talked about an emergency department that is now seeing 400 patients a day instead of 200.

She talks about the refrigerated tractor trailer that is parked outside, just in case.

She talked about her colleagues who are now becoming ill.

This is important for us to know as well.

I'm hoping the carnage we are seeing in New York City will be a wake-up call for those of us in this community that we need to do more to prepare.

We need to be staying home all the time.

Our contact with outside world needs to be non-existent to slow this virus down.

But this past week, there were plenty of cars on the road. The convenience stores appeared to be doing a brisk business, and I wondered how serious we were taking this.

We've heard from local hospital workers that they are concerned about whether they have enough protection while doing their daily jobs.

They don't understand why some masks are being saved for a later date.

There is justified fear and angst among them. Back in Queens, Dr. Smith must make do with one N-95 mask all day.

"The anxiety of this situation is really overwhelming," Dr. Smith said. "We get exposed over and over again and we don't have the protective equipment that we should have.

"What is scary now is that the patients we are getting are much sicker," Dr. Smith said. "Many of the young people who are getting sick don't smoke, they are healthy. They are just young regular people between the ages of 30 and 50 who you would not expect to get this sick."

You need to see the video for yourself.

You need to listen to this young doctor and take this more seriously.

"I don't care if I get in trouble for speaking to the media," Dr. Smith finally says.

That's bravery.

That's a real heroine.

There are so few people who stand up for the greater good. Dr. Smith did that here. That may be what is most inspiring.

"I want people to know this is bad. People are dying," Dr. Smith says. "We don't have the tools that we need in the emergency department and in the hospital to take care of them.

"And...," she says, starting to choke up. "It is really hard."

P.S.

This column was my last regular column for The Post-Star. The next week I began three months of family leave before announcing my retirement. By January 2021, nearly 400,000 Americans had died of Covid 19 and hospitalizations were at an all-time high.

New York had seen more than 1.2 million cases of the virus and more than 40,000 deaths.

MY LIFE

Over my 32 years at The Post-Star, my column often touched on my family, friends and experiences. These columns often resonated with readers more than any others because they were regular stories about life, death, living and growing up. In 1988 I moved to Glens Falls, N.Y. as sports editor of the daily newspaper. Gillian and I had a son, Joseph, in 1996 and I became managing editor of the newspaper in 1999. While working in Glens Falls, I wrote approximately 3,000 columns.

Over the course of his 30 years writing columns for The Post-Star in Glens Falls N.Y., the author's family was often the subject of his columns. In many ways, his readers became part of the family as well, following the ups and downs that all families experience. Thankfully, his wife, Gillian and son, Joseph, never complained about the loss of their privacy. (Photo by Ken Tingley).

ONCE UPON A TIME...

October 15, 1996

When the Yankees won their first American League pennant in 15 years Sunday night, it reminded one old-time Yankee fan of another era of baseball, of another time when Chris Chambliss hit a fairy tale of a home run. It was a reminder of what baseball had been and what it could be again in the future.

For the last few hours I have tried to make sense of it all.

Evening has turned to night and one by one the lights at my home have gone dark, leaving me to figure this all out in the quiet of midnight.

Trying to come to terms with my emotions.

Trying to figure out what it all means.

Just a few hours earlier, the New York Yankees won the American League pennant for the first time in 15 years.

My team.

My sport.

At least it used to be.

Then came the Pete Rose scandal, Bart Giamatti's death, the strike, the cancellation of the World Series and my own private alienation from the game.

The game that used to mean so much to me now meant so very little.

It was all quite puzzling.

Especially this evening as the Yankees put away the Baltimore Orioles and I switched back and forth between the football game and, unbelievable as it sounds, the baseball game.

Seeing the Yankees storm the field in celebration.

Seeing the tears in manager Joe Torre's eyes.

And the champagne flowing in the Yankees' locker room.

Gosh darn it, I'll admit it, I'm sitting here right now with a little smile on my face.

Because I've been there before.

There is an entire generation out there that has not.

They were experiencing this for the first time.

All over the region.

Kids and young folks leaping around in their living rooms Sunday night with can't-quit smiles you may never see again.

Their team.

Their time.

Not mine.

My time was 1976.

The Yankees had not played in a World Series in 12 years then.

I was 19.

Working in a grocery store.

No girlfriend.

Just starting college without any idea what I wanted to do with my life.

And nothing meant more to me than baseball.

Yankee baseball.

There were times in those years when my Dad got up and walked away from a Yankee game on the television set; passed completely on a trip to the Stadium to take care of his duties as a father, husband or homeowner.

I vowed then that I would never share that type of adult ambivalence toward this sport for which I had so much passion.

That was 20 years ago.

What a jarring realization that so much time had passed.

In fact, Monday was the 20th anniversary of Chris Chambliss' home run.

I need no videotape. That memory is still so sweet, so fresh.

It was a high fastball from Kansas City reliever Mark Littell that Chambliss ripped high into the dark night, climbing higher and higher until it caromed off the wall in right-center just short of the right field bleachers, Chambliss' arms raised high over his head in a touchdown signal, his fists and teeth clenched in defiant rage.

What a moment.

My father and I leapt into each other's arms and danced about the living room in a pure innocent and utterly spontaneous celebration that would never again be repeated in our household.

A year and a half later I left for my last two years of college. I never lived in my father's house again.

That bottom-of-the-ninth piece of history, for me, will forever be the single most exhilarating moment in sports.

My team.

My moment.

Looking back this night, I realize that for the first time.

Not because there won't be sporting theatrics of equal or greater value, but because of where I was at that point in my young and oh so impressionable young life.

It was my time and no sporting event will ever be that great again.

That home run may have a great deal to do with why I still write about sports.

Why I hold the people and the games so dear.

Why I think I understand their importance to us all.

So much has changed since 1976.

Ken Burns said in his baseball documentary that *the game* would go on forever because it was *the game* that was important, not the players, not the owners, not the greed.

Six years after the Chambliss home run I got married and honeymooned in California where my bride consented to two baseball games. She has been by my side at a half-dozen other ballparks across the country, but we have never been to a Yankee game in 14 years and the Yankees have never been to a World Series since we were married.

This past February, on a cold winter morning on the day pitchers and catchers were due to report for spring training, she gave me a son.

Nearly 40 years ago, I was born on an April evening during a baseball season in which the New York Yankees played the Milwaukee Braves in the World Series. This year, these Yankees could play the Braves again in the Series. For me, there is a certain symmetry to that.

Will the game pass from father to son?

Will I someday take my son Joseph by the hand and walk him through that once-in-a-lifetime portal at Yankee Stadium?

It is a decision that has to be made.

Last year, I vowed never to watch baseball again.

Baseball's numerous problems made that easy: the labor unrest; the unceasing supply of home runs; the greed; and the spitting incident.

Where does it all end?

Perhaps the better question is where does it begin again?

Maybe that's what I'm looking for.

There is this 8 X 10 black and white framed photograph on the wall near my desk at home.

I've had it for nearly 10 years, but this past spring I finally had it framed and hung on the wall. The timing is purely accidental and obviously ironic.

It is the instant when Chris Chambliss hit that home run in 1976. Twenty years ago. The ball just leaving the bat and beginning its climb into history.

It is an instant that I will lovingly cherish in the bosom of my soul until the day I take my last breath, as much for what it meant to me as a young fan as for the memory of leaping into my father's arms to share that moment of pure spontaneous joy.

I'm looking at the photograph right now and remembering exactly how I felt 20 years ago. It is very clear what I have to do.

Joseph, son, wake up, I have a story that I have to tell you.

Once upon a time in a Yankee Stadium far, far away...

P.S.

I do my best thinking alone in the house late at night. That was the case here. I had grudgingly watched the final innings as the New York Yankees won the American League pennant for the first time in 15 years.

I had vowed to never watch baseball again after the 1994 strike that cost baseball the World Series.

But there was a baby in the house now, and an obligation as a father. I had promised myself I would not be one of those writers who wrote about their kid all the time. But this was different. This was father and son and baseball. Surely, it would be OK just this one time.

My son's life and what I hoped for him came up many more times over the years. In some ways, Joseph was a child of *The Post-Star,* sometimes spending time literally under my desk, and running around the newsroom. I always felt the readers were an extended family of aunts and uncles.

It all started that night in 1996. Eight years later, I took that baby to his first game at the old Yankee Stadium. In 2009, I took him and my brother, Dave, to the new Yankee Stadium for Game 2 of the World Series. The Yankees won, too.

JOB LOSS LEADS TO FEAR FOR A FRIEND

June 27, 2003

My best friend was fired this week, and I don't know what to say to him.

We've known each other since we were 11, playing Pop Warner football together.

We survived junior high as a couple of uncool kids. We played football and basketball in high school, double dated when we finally discovered girls and had our first drink together.

The day after we graduated from high school, we drove off to North Carolina and spent a week on the beach as high school graduates ready to conquer the world.

He was the only friend to visit me when I went off to college in Kentucky.

I was in his wedding; he was in mine.

I was the godfather to his daughter. He was the godfather to my son.

We graduated together in 1975 and departed on separate paths, yet, for some reason, we have remained friends and in touch. He is the only person I can say that about from my hometown. He may be the one person in the world I trust the most.

He just turned 46. He has one son in college, a daughter will start in the fall. His youngest son suffers from a rare condition that has affected his development. His boy has special needs and is a handful at home, so his wife doesn't work.

He was fired a couple weeks ago, but I just heard about it.

He works in the computer field. He had two years of computer training and worked nights for years to finally earn his degree.

He worked his way up in his company until he was running a department. Recently, he went back to school to start work on a master's degree. He said something about trying to keep up with all the kids coming out of college.

My friend is angry.

You can hear that over the phone.

He joked that he was considering a career as a gigolo.

He joked that it was time for his wife to go back to work and he would stay home and vacuum.

I can hear his wife saying in the background that they are going to move to Glens Falls and she is going to become the Zamboni driver at the Civic Center.

We all laugh, but the jokes aren't funny.

I told him that I thought it was terrible. He had worked for the company for over 20 years and they discarded him.

We hear about these stories all the time. We hear about employees being fired, about companies downsizing, about companies shutting down. We read about it in this newspaper weekly. But this one hit close to home.

Like your health, a good job that supports your family is sometimes taken for granted. When it is gone, it is frightening.

My friend called me after 11 the other night to talk.

I told him that this might be the best thing that ever happened to him. I told him that maybe he will start down another career path and find an even better job. Maybe he will decide on a different job and find work that is even more rewarding and fulfilling.

I don't think he believed me.

I told him I was there for him if I can help him in any way, but to be honest, I don't know what that possibly could be.

He has severance pay. He has almost a year to get another job. He has good qualifications.

But for the first time in his adult life, he is not the breadwinner. His future is clouded and I know he's scared.

To be honest, I'm scared for him.

Or maybe I'm scared because I know it could happen to any of us.

P.S.

There was an economic recession during 2001–02 and my best friend lost his job as a department head. He had just turned 46. He survived over the next couple of years doing freelance work for other companies. He often had to spend weeks on the road away from his wife and three children.

His story was not unique. In 2005, he finally landed a position with a big company in New York City, but it required commuting by train from his home in Connecticut two hours each way. The days were long and I don't know how he did it.

In 2011, he was diagnosed with Parkinson's Disease which made the commute even more difficult and the future cloudy, but he continued to work and make the long commute. In 2019, he went on short-term disability, returned to work for nine months, then went on long-term disability.

WHITE HOUSE BECKONS, NATURE CALLS

January 9, 2004

When my 7-year-old son said he wanted to visit the Air and Space Museum in Washington, D.C., this past fall, I was thrilled.

I love Washington. It is my favorite city and I couldn't wait to share it with my son. Inevitably, the first thing I do in Washington is head down Pennsylvania Avenue and take a walk around the White House. I'm drawn to it as a symbol of power and a place of history. I've done this at least a couple dozen times.

From in front of the South Lawn, I find myself peering through the fence, up to the mansion, trying to find the windows to the Oval Office in the West Wing or evidence in the residence that the president might be home.

On this particular weekend, the White House Garden Tour was scheduled. Twice a year, the public is allowed to walk onto the grounds of the White House, stand in the shadow of the Truman balcony, check out the Rose Garden and be just 20 yards from the Oval Office. This was a dream come true.

After finally clearing the metal detectors and slowly walking up the driveway toward the Truman Balcony, my son tugged on my jacket and temporarily stopped my monologue on the history of the United States.

"Daddy, I have to go," the little guy said.

No way, I thought. I probably didn't hear him right.

"Daddy, I really have to go," he said again. The dance was starting.

They have this tour twice a year, or exactly 92 times since I've been alive, I thought. I had waited 45 years for this opportunity and a chance to see something I never would again.

"I'm sorry, you'll have to wait," I said and walked off to show him the Truman Balcony when he would have preferred the Truman washroom.

I took some more photos and approached the Rose Garden.

The tug came a little harder this time.

"Daddy, I really, really have to go," he said. Did I hear right? Yes, he was whimpering.

OK, I've been there. I know the feeling. I scanned the pristine grounds of the President's house. Surely, a government as organized and bureaucratic as ours would have a plan in place for every possible emergency when it came to the president, his home and its security.

I approached a man in a dark suit, sunglasses and an earpiece who stood in the path of a ground level doorway to the White House.

"Excuse me," I said. "My little boy really has to go to the bathroom and I wanted to know if you could give me some advice about that."

Looking through me, apparently enthralled with some aspect of the Washington Monument, he said matter-of-factly, "There are no facilities available on the grounds."

I wanted to push the lad forward and say, "Tell that to HIM!" But I didn't.

I knelt down and in my best "Father Knows Best" voice told him, "The mean man with the machine gun under his coat says you are going to have to wait." Again, that's what I wanted to say.

The little boy nodded and agreed to hold out a little longer.

The president's dog was out frolicking in the Rose Garden as people took photographs. And there was the Oval Office, right there. I point all this out to the dancing boy.

"Are you almost done, Dad?" he asked.

I knew he was in terrible discomfort, but this was a once-in-a-lifetime opportunity, I thought to myself. We walked farther down the path to where there was a small wooded area and bushes.

The dancing boy looked up at me for an answer to his pain.

Hey, why couldn't I let my son do what the entire Democratic Party had been doing to the president for the past three years?

What could happen?

Thoughts raced through my head.

Would the Secret Service really surround him as he trotted off into the bushes and demand that he come out with his hands up?

Would that extra little moisture at the base of a tree short-circuit some device that is sensitive to incoming heat-seeking missiles and imperil the safety of the president?

Could the little guy really kill off a tree that was planted byDolley Madison? Or worse?

My son might receive a blot on his record that would lead to an annual audit of his taxes for the rest of his life.

"Son, you've got to hold it," I said sternly. "This is the White House and you can't do that here."

Even if everyone else has, I thought.

This past week, I put up the new calendar my brother gave me for Christmas.

"Hey, that's the White House," my son said, pointing to the January photograph.

"Do you remember visiting there?" I asked.

"I sure do," he said. "I really had to go to the bathroom."

P.S.

After the birth of my son in 1996, I began featuring him ever more frequently in my columns. For the most part, it was a means to an end, a way for me to make a point subtly. But sometimes the stories were just routine slices of life that anyone who had been a parent could relate.

To his credit, I never heard Joseph complain about the sometimes embarrassing predicaments I described in my columns. At age 24, he related one conversation with a high school teacher who mentioned a story about him in my column.

"I'm probably the only kid in school who has to say to his dad, `Hey, this is off the record,'" Joseph told the teacher.

WHY DID HE CHOOSE ME?

May 12, 2004

What made this kid pick me?

Did I look like I was born yesterday, an easy mark, a sucker right off the plane from Palookaville?

Was it just that I was in a hurry, dressed nicely and looked like somebody who would readily part with some dead presidents without breaking stride?

We were standing in the middle of the casino at the MGM Grande in Las Vegas last week.

He said he was a college kid. He said he had just graduated from the University of Pittsburgh and was in Vegas on a job interview for Dupont. Somehow he had missed his plane. He didn't leave himself enough time to get through security and the airline couldn't get him another flight for another day.

He said he was a good kid.

He said he got the job with DuPont.

He said I looked like a nice guy, the kind of guy who would want a stranger to help his kid if he ever got into trouble in a strange city.

I was late for dinner and the kid sounded like a telemarketer.

He showed me his driver's license, his plane ticket and his letter from DuPont.

He needed a hotel room. He didn't have any money.

What about credit cards?

Didn't have any?

What about family?

His parents had both died three years ago.

What about the nice folks over at DuPont?

He had left a message, but no one had gotten back to him.

He didn't have money, but he had answers.

Here's the thing: There was this part of me that really wanted to help him, bail him out, come to his rescue and give him a story for the rest of his life about the nice guy in Vegas who saved his butt. The story sounded so crazy, so ludicrous that it might just be true. And he was right, I wanted to think that there are other good people in the world who would step up and take care of a good kid in trouble. I could afford the $129 and he did seem like a good kid.

"You know how bad this sounds," I said to him.

He said he knew.

"Especially in this city."

He said he just needed $129 for a hotel room. He seemed so desperate.

I asked him if he had tried the Motel 6 across the street. He said they were booked solid.

I asked if he had tried some of the other older hotels downtown that were cheaper. He said there was some sort of Internet convention in town and there were no hotel rooms.

I found my hand digging deeper into my pocket to guard my wallet. There are hotels in Las Vegas that can accommodate more people than there are in Glens Falls so I found it hard to believe that Las Vegas suddenly had a no vacancy sign out front.

I was being scammed, but I wanted to make sure.

I told him that I really had to make it to an important dinner, but if he would like to meet me back at the front desk in an hour, I would make sure that I got him a hotel room, but I was not going to give him any money.

He said he didn't want me to go to all that trouble.

"I'm not going to give you any money," I said again.

He didn't say anything and I walked away.

I've thought a lot about that kid on the way back home and why he was hustling me. I thought too about how he really had me believing him for a few minutes.

Part of it made me mad, part of it made me sad and part of it made me glad that I lived in a place where if a total stranger walked up to someone in the street and asked for help, you didn't have to worry if they were telling the truth.

P.S.

I had been managing editor at my newspaper for five years when Publisher Jim Marshall asked me to represent the newspaper at Lee Enterprises' annual meeting in Las Vegas. But this was one story I did not believe needed to stay in Vegas.

A TOUGH GOODBYE

August 30, 2006

It was supposed to be a reunion, a chance for the nine grandchildren of Joe and Ruth Tingley to catch up, reconnect and celebrate the heritage that we all have in common as cousins. Instead, it turned into a farewell.

Two days before the reunion, my cousin Dawn announced she and her husband, Chris, had sold their home at 46 Prindle Avenue in Ansonia, Conn. The house was old and needed work, and the yard was much too big for a busy mom and dad with three kids. It made perfect sense, except that this was our grandparents' home.

This was the last connection to our heritage, the last connection to Joe and Ruth and their four children - Phyllis, Edward, William and Robert. They were all gone now, and we really only had the house and our annual gatherings. But with our families spread across the Northeast, most of us had not been there in years.

Back in the 1930s, Joe Tingley and his brother Ed bought a piece of farm land and built two-story houses side by side with big front porches and stone foundations meant to last forever.

There was a small barn where my father raised a goat during the Depression. There were two chicken coops for eggs and poultry and a garden that once covered most of the three acres of property during World War II. It was now just a small vegetable garden that my cousin Kevin - the youngest of the cousins - maintained more out of habit and tradition than any real need.

In the back corner of the lot, my grandfather had built a horseshoe court, where his brothers gathered on summer Sundays to pass away the time.

I can remember as a small boy sitting in lawn chairs, sipping lemonade with the women and hearing the clang of metal shoes in the distance, punctuated by rousing cheers and laughter after a big score by one of the teams. It always seemed to be dark before the men came back with big smiles on their faces to gulp lemonade and recount the competition from the court.

It was a unique place, a fascinating place for kids to run around and explore while our parents visited with the folks.

It was really surprising the house had not been sold sooner. When my grandmother died, my Uncle Bob moved his family into the house. When he passed away, his family stayed, and later his daughter Dawn and her husband moved in with their family. It seemed like it would stay in the family forever.

The house is showing its 70 years of age and looks smaller than when we were all kids.

On Friday night, my brother, my cousin Kevin and I wandered through the weeds in the overgrown horseshoe court in the gathering dusk. We stood there for 10 or 15 minutes, looking, listening as if we expected to hear those wonderful sounds of summer again and knowing it was the end of an era, knowing we would never see this place again.

Each spot in the yard, each room in the house was a trigger, setting off a flood of memories for all of us, some the same, some different.

The kitchen table was still right by the window where my grandmother Ruth used to hold court. She always sat in the chair on the left farthest from the door looking out at her bird feeder. As a teenager, I mowed her lawn, and I can remember countless hours of conversation about the family, about her life and my own hopes and dreams.

The living room, which no longer smelled like pine needles, still triggered memories of a long ago Christmas when my Uncle Bill carried my cousin Gail and I around the room. And it was over against that wall where I said good-bye to her a few weeks before she died. Can it really be 24 years ago?

One after the other, the memories returned with such clarity. Each of us having a different experience.

One by one, we took our kids by the hand to the entryway to the front porch. There, at the base of the stairs, was something to which we all could relate. Crafted into the hardwood floors in brown wood was the family name – TINGLEY. It was permanent, the legacy of the family for the future, the one thing that would not change.

Dawn told me she made the new owners promise that they would not remove the name from the floor. They agreed, saying that it was part of the history of the house. That made us all feel good.

Dawn told me she cried herself to sleep that night after seeing us come home, after seeing us recount countless memories from our childhood. It was also the first time in several years that all nine cousins made it to the reunion.

There was one more thing I had to show my son. In the basement bathroom, long covered with layer after layer of white paint, you could still see the jagged outline where someone had carved the initials "ET" with a small pocket knife.

I explained to my son Joseph, that my father, Edward Tingley, had carved his initials there as a boy and had gotten in a whole heap of trouble. My father had showed me the initials years ago when I was just a boy.

Joseph nodded and walked away, unimpressed. I took a photo of the wall with the initials in the dark and damp basement. Then, with the cousins calling for a group photo of all 28 of us upstairs in the living room, I ran my fingers slowly, gently over the initials one last time.

P.S.

I asked my cousin Dawn if she could salvage the initials my father had carved into the bathroom wall in my grandmother's old house, but it never happened.

The cousins continued to meet annually for a number of years in upstate New York, New Hampshire, Cape Code and Canada. We later learned that the buyers of the Prindle Avenue property had not kept their word. The "Tingley" name that had been inlaid in the hardwood floor in the entry to the house had been removed.

"I wish they would have asked, because I would have paid to have it taken out so we could keep it." Dawn told me in January 2021. I think we all would have chipped in for that.

TWISTS AND TURNS ON THE WAY TO NORMAL

April 29, 2012

For a while, I was counting the trips to Burlington ... 8, 9, 10 ... as they piled up over the past six months. Then one Friday, I began focusing on the last trip.

That was Friday.

The first trip was in September. The doctor there confirmed my wife, Gillian, had ovarian cancer. She is only 53. That was a Tuesday. They did the surgery Thursday.

The doctor removed a grapefruit-sized tumor and four days later she was released from the hospital. Chemotherapy began a few weeks later and we began our ritual.

Two weeks on, then three weeks off.

Then repeat.

It was how we began many of our weekends.

It is a beautiful drive through the Vermont countryside to get to Burlington. It takes two hours if you don't get stuck behind a farm tractor or a slow-moving tractor-trailer. The treatment takes about six hours, sometimes longer, and we often did not get home until after dark.

After the dread of that first trip, the drive became routine. After a few weeks, I started looking forward to the trip, which I thought a bit odd. The two hours in the car became our time. Sometimes, we hardly said a word. Often, we talked continuously. It was a time for us that had slipped away over the years, but maybe more importantly, it was an acknowledgement we were in this together.

When I am stuck for an idea to write a column, I ask myself a simple question: What is bothering you; what are you thinking about? Over the past six months, it was often the trip to Burlington, or more specifically, the aftermath, which often left Gillian weak and very sick. I knew she would not want me to write about it, that she would not be comfortable as the heroine of another story about the life-and-death battle with cancer.

So six months later, the darkness of that September surgery has lifted. Upon reflection, it is odd how quickly the battle becomes part of the routine, part of the regular rhythms of life. It was as if those trips to Burlington were trips for groceries.

So as we prepared for that last trip, I knew what I wanted to write about.

It was Gillian and what she had done for me and our 16-year-old son Joseph over the past six months.

She made it seem easy. She made it seem normal, so ho-hum what she was going through, and that allowed us to go on with our lives. That was a great gift.

Gillian is a pediatric nurse at Albany Medical Center. She often handles chemotherapy treatments for kids. Over the past six months, she earned instant credibility with the kids. She had an in with them, a connection — she didn't have any hair, either.

She could relate to their symptoms, and, I'm sure, their fears. They could compare the ports buried beneath their skin where they pour in the drugs.

Often, there were back-to-back 12-hour shifts at the hospital, followed by another trip to Burlington.

Somehow she did it.

Last week, before the last trip to Burlington, we decided to run out and buy a new lawn sprinkler. It was one of those perfect spring evenings and as I backed the car out of the garage, Gillian realized she did not have the hat she usually wears to cover up what's left of her hair.

I told her I would wait for her to get it.

She paused a second and said she didn't need it.

A few minutes later, in the beautiful twilight of that spring evening, we walked hand-in-hand into the big-box store.

This is who she is now.

This is who we are.

P.S.

After what we hoped would be the final chemo treatment in 2012, the cancer came back again four and a half years later, and the trips to Burlington returned. The routine, the ordinariness of the drive through Vermont countryside returned as well.

There were also college visits, high school and college graduations, birthdays, swim meets, Christmas decorating and family trips to all the places we always wanted to see. We lived. We took that very seriously.

Along the way, we both lost our mothers. After Gillian's mother passed, we were going through her things and found a neatly folded newspaper clipping tucked into her wallet for ready display. It was this column. I don't remember Mavis saying much about my columns over the years, but I guess this one meant something to her.

It was just as special to me. This was the acknowledgement of what our life is, and how we are going to live it going forward by living each day - one at a time - to its fullest.

The cancer came and went and we dealt with it with new treatments and different doctors. It was especially difficult in 2019 after Gillian developed a tolerance for the chemotherapy that had worked so well in the past. She tried radiation, but that didn't help. She had to be admitted to the hospital a couple times and the future did not look good, so I took family leave that eventually led to my retirement at the age of 63.

Gillian began a new chemo regimen in 2020 and rebounded again like so many times over the past nine years, but we no longer make the two-hour trip to Burlington, Vermont. In January 2021, her oncologist said the results of her latest scan were "amazing" with the tumors shrinking.

Despite the pandemic, she helped with Joseph's move out of his college apartment, and into a new condominium in Texas.

We both continue to live each day to the fullest.

SCRAPBOOK PUTS US ON THE SAME PAGE

February 16, 2013

With my son giddy behind the wheel after passing his driver's test this week, I informed him he had some reading to do.

"What do you mean?" he asked.

"You have to read the scrapbook," I said. "You're not going anywhere alone in this car until you read the scrapbook."

He nodded. He knew.

My son has grown up differently from his peers, because his father works at a newspaper and was trying to make a difference in the war on underage drinking.

He was only 6 when I started the scrapbook after a series of horrific car accidents in which underage drinking was involved claimed the lives of 10 young people. That led to *The Post-Star's* series, "Cost of Fun: Stories of underage drinking." It was published in May 2004.

Before we even started the series, I had begun pasting photos of totaled automobiles; along with bold headlines of death, destruction and tragedy and an aftermath in which young people went to jail and shattered families grieved and were never the same.

I've written about the scrapbook before, often after another tragedy had claimed another life. I would review its contents, its intent for my own son and lament there was no shortage of material to fill its pages.

As he got older, my son learned about the scrapbook as I lectured about underage drinking and the terrible tragedies we were writing about in the newspaper.

He listened, but said little.

One time, I took him to Washington County Court, where I was speaking about the many tragedies my newspaper had covered and about the scrapbook I was keeping for my son. He sat in the front row, listening intently, but I never knew what he was thinking.

This past summer, I heard from a friend whose granddaughter worked with my son at the amusement park. She passed on a story she heard about my son in an email.

She said a group of teens were sitting around at work and talking about drinking and my son had exclaimed, "My dad would put me on the front page of the newspaper if I ever was caught drinking."

She said he paused, and said even more seriously, "And my dad does not kid around."

My message seemed to be getting through.

The premise for the scrapbook was simple. The day my son got his driver's license, and asked to borrow the car for the first time, I would hand him the scrapbook, tell him to make himself comfortable, and when he had finished reading he could come get the car keys.

I hoped the scrapbook, filled with victims from neighboring towns — and real people his own age — would make an impact on him. Frankly, I hoped it would scar him for life.

When we sat down for dinner the night my son got his license, he told me he had been reading the scrapbook for the past hour.

"You know what really gets me," he said. "It's not the photos of the wrecked cars. They are bad and all, but it's the photos of the kids. They are my age. Some of them were only 16, like me."

"They will always be 16," I said.

I am hopeful the scrapbook has made an impact, but I know I am not out of the woods yet. At some point, he will be tempted at a party or dance, by his own curiosity, and the memory of the scrapbook will fade. I just hope its lessons do not.

Later that evening before he went to bed, my son brought up the scrapbook again.

"The thing that really got me is that you took the time to cut out every one of those articles over the past 10 years and put them all in the scrapbook," he said.

"And why do you think I did that?" I asked.

"To save my life," he said.

P.S.

In the wake of a double fatal car accident in April 2002, I bought a scrapbook and began clipping out newspaper articles of the carnage wrought by underage drinking. The purpose was to give it to my then 6-year-old son the day he received his driver's license.

Sadly, the scrapbook filled up quickly.

Over the years, readers asked to borrow the scrapbook several times so they could copy the clips and show them to their own children. Joseph remembered me taking him to speaking engagements where I brought the scrapbook.

After he received his driver's license in February 2013, the 16-year-old asked to borrow the car that evening so he could drive himself to the rehearsal for the play he was in. I handed him the scrapbook and he began reading.

A week later, the newspaper published a guest essay by my son with a photograph of him holding the scrapbook. He was not smiling. He wrote this:

"As I continued to flip through the scrapbook, I started to understand my dad's anger over this issue, and why he takes it so seriously. I knew before, but reading the scrapbook brought me greater clarity. All I could think was: Why do we keep doing this? Can we not learn from our mistakes? Why in my five-hour pre-licensing course were we not shown these articles."

I was one proud father.

"The object of the scrapbook is not to scare, it's to educate, to remind us teenagers when we feel invincible, we're not."

My son later told me, he never drank in high school.

A YEAR OF LISTENING COMES TO AN END

September 29, 2013

Too often over the years, my mother and I had little to talk about. She asked me how my family was and I asked her how she was, and then there was silence.

So it occurred to me this week that I had spent more time with my mom in the past year than I had in the previous 30 years combined.

It wasn't intentional. I loved my mom, but that's how life works out sometimes. You go off to college, you chase a career, go where they will give you a job and live your life. With my own son about to embark on that journey, that realization is a bit unsettling.

But a year ago, we moved my mother from Connecticut to a local nursing home. She had been ill and no longer could take care of herself, although she argued she could.

It changed our lives.

Each day after work, I stopped by the nursing home and visited her while she was having dinner.

At first I carried the conversation. I would ask about her progress in rehab and if she was taking part in any activities.

At first, she didn't have a lot to say. And if she did, it wasn't very positive. Ultimately, she demanded to know when she could go home.

On Sundays, we would bring her to our house. We would watch television, have snacks and talk some before having Sunday dinner as a family.

But as she got stronger, as she settled into her new world, she started to talk.

My mom was from Belfast, proud of her Irish heritage, and so many people just liked to hear the accent she never lost.

The story of my mother and father and how they met is from another time and I still find it remarkable.

My dad joined the Navy during the Korean War because the recruiter assured him he was about to be drafted.

His ship regularly docked in Ireland, and on one of those trips my father and mother went on a blind date. My father insisted he fell instantly in love. They only saw each other two or three times before my father proposed marriage.

So at the age of 27 and in love with an American sailor, she embarked on her great adventure. She booked passage to the United States on the Queen Elizabeth, said goodbye to her mother and five siblings and sailed off to the new world. She would not see her family again for 10 years.

She stayed briefly with her new Baptist in-laws before having a falling out, then traveled to Mobile, Ala. where my father was about to be discharged. It was there that they were married in the local Catholic Church with only two witnesses present. They didn't know either of them.

Can you imagine the courage that took?

Can you imagine the conviction and how many people must have told her she was out of her mind?

It began a 45-year journey that produced two sons and a lifetime of wonderful memories. But she struggled after Dad died in 2001. After all, they had been through so much together.

So as the months passed this past year, I noticed I was doing more listening, and she more talking.

Sometimes she complained, other times she excitedly told me about how she had progressed walking. She loved to tell me the details of the conversations she had with the nurses and young aides who took care of her and the advice she often gave them about their love lives.

She was blossoming again.

One day she told me a story, and there was a reference, oh so subtle but unmistakable, and it made me laugh. She had just told a joke. But unless you were paying close attention, you would have missed it. I recognized it immediately. That was my sense of humor.

My mother called it a dry wit and I always wondered where it came from and now I knew.

One day she looked around the dining hall filled with the elderly, gray-haired men and woman — many of whom were in wheelchairs — and said, "I hope I am never old like these people."

How could I not laugh? She was 85.

She had found her voice again.

She had found joy in her new life, with new friends, reveling in each detail of her only grandson's life.

And when I showed up each evening for dinner, her eyes brightened and she showed me that smile.

And then we talked. OK, she talked and I listened.

It was a year ago this week that my mom came back into my life.

On Thursday, she passed away.

It was a great year.

P.S.

I clearly remember taking a stack of paperwork nearly a foot high to the lawyer's office.

My mother was in a nursing home and we were applying for Medicaid. What my mother probably never realized in her year in the nursing home was that our family's experience led to an award-winning newspaper project about senior living entitled, "Who will take care of us?"

When I left the nursing home that last time after my mother died, there were so many nurses and aides to thank for being so kind to my mother. They had become a surrogate family. I told them I would be back again to visit, but I never returned.

'I'LL GET THE DUCT TAPE'

January 1, 2014

As the paper towel wrapped around my index finger turned crimson, my son insisted that I immediately sit down.

"Why?" I asked.

I had just sliced my finger with the potato peeler, and my family is all too familiar with a medical history that includes instances when I've "gone dark" over what some would say are inconsequential medical procedures — like a cortisone shot or the removal of a cast.

They say I'm a "fainter" but I argue my chronic cases of light-headedness are a legitimate response to extreme medical events.

Three times I have gone lights out in a doctor's office. The good news is I was actually the patient in two of the cases. In my defense, the needle they were giving my wife in the third case was very large.

My family rarely lets me forget these episodes.

If a slasher movie is on television, they advise me to sit down and look away. If I tell them I am getting a flu shot at work, they look concerned. If someone spills the ketchup at dinner, they quickly dip a French fry in it.

I remind them that I was there for the Caesarean section that led to the birth of my child, although they did make me sit during the entire procedure, with a nurse nearby just in case.

It is not unusual for my family to apologize for me.

"He is a bit squeamish when it comes to blood," my wife will say to the doctor.

"Not true," I argue. "I'm fine with other people's blood. It's mine that worries me."

So with my third paper towel soaked with blood, I did what most men would do in the situation, I asked my wife for a Band-Aid.

I was not worried. The cut was not that deep and my wife is a registered nurse. She gives shots and stuff and looks at gross wounds all the time.

"We don't have any," I hear from the other room.

This strikes me as somewhat unusual, considering her profession, so I show her the crimson paper towel.

"You better sit down," she says.

She then announces she will get something from the car.

My wife regularly visits patients in their homes as part of her job, so she likes to have emergency medical supplies handy.

"Sorry, no Band-Aids there," she says.

The irony that a professional nurse entrusted with the well-being of so many does not have one Band-Aid in the bathroom medicine cabinet seems to be lost on her.

I show her the blood is still oozing from the cut.

She goes into the other room and reappears a minute later. She applies some disinfectant to a narrow strip of a paper towel and wraps it around the finger. She then tells me to look away from the cut. She seems to have a plan. She presses the paper towel around the finger and tells me to apply pressure on the wound. She tells me to look away again and begins wrapping the finger tightly.

My finger is starting to feel better.

I think the blood has stopped oozing.

She looks it over one last time, admires her handiwork and says, "That should do it."

I look at my finger.

It is tightly wrapped in duct tape.

P.S.

While checking out at my doctor's office about a month later, the receptionist slid a bag across the table.

"That's for you," she said with a crooked smile.

When I looked inside, I started laughing. It was filled with Band-Aids.

I turned around and caught my doctor peeking out the door with a big smile on his face.

WHERE HAS TIME GONE?

June 29, 2014

I'm pretty sure the first time was in October 1996 after my beloved Yankees won the World Series.

I was 39 and my first and only child had been in my life 8 months.

I was determined not to be that guy always writing about his kid in the newspaper, bubbling over about every milestone that makes we parents proud, but I figured this one time I might be forgiven.

Only now do I realize that first column was not so much about baseball as it was an introduction as I tried to explain who I was, and perhaps, what I hoped he would be.

Over the years, these reflections have often come bubbling up in the middle of the night when personal reflection took precedence over sleep, and getting the words right was all that mattered.

"Dear Joseph," I finally wrote on a bleak December night, and proceeded to tell my 5-year-old everything he needed to know about a grandfather he might never remember.

He wore my dad's watch Friday night at his graduation.

When I started a scrapbook filled with newspaper articles of teenagers killed in tragic accidents because of drinking and driving, I told my readers about it, I explained it was for my son and the day he earned his driver's license I would make him read about the carnage of teenagers who will never get any older. I hoped other parents would start their own scrapbooks, but honestly, it was my own selfish attempt to make a difference in his life, and keep him from making a tragic mistake.

The day he got his license, I handed him that scrapbook. He read it, and later that night told me he couldn't believe how I painstakingly saved dozens and dozens of articles over the past 10 years and pasted them carefully in that scrapbook.

"Do you know why," I asked.

"Because you love me," he said.

He got it, and I was left speechless.

The lad has shown up repeatedly in this space over the years regarding his sleep habits, voluminous consumption of anything not nailed down in the kitchen and those predictable childhood milestones we as parents find so important. He never complained or professed to be embarrassed by it.

I hope you readers forgive me for indulging myself, but more often than not I have heard my experiences mirrored your own — past and present.

It has been a rewarding, satisfying and sometimes frustrating 18 years I would never exchange.

So here in the stillness of another one of those sleepless nights with a house-full of sleeping people who have also been so important in my son's life, I find myself with the tears streaming down my face again, finding it hard to believe the years have evaporated so fast.

There is a Queensbury High diploma on the dining room table, a mortarboardnearby and time is short for late-night conversations about life, world problems and the future, just like the one we had tonight.

College awaits. He is excited. I think he is ready.

As a parent worrying about, not only the world we have today, but the one we will have tomorrow, I am surprised how many times my thoughts have returned to anecdotes about my child and how his experiences were often metaphors for the world as a whole.

I am only realizing now, how important our children are to the journey, and what we do to make the world a better place is often with them in mind.

For those of you that have followed along here, you may also find it hard to believe time has gone so quickly.

Perhaps the tears flow now because I fear I won't have anything more to write about. More likely, I wonder if these stories will lack the heart so important to our lives and how we live them.

The photo that is on Facebook today shows my boy as a graduate in the throes of appreciating a job well done, a big long arm slung over my shoulder and a smile of pure joy and satisfaction. His father, on the other hand, is shown choking back the emotion of the moment and wondering if he could possibly know the pride that I now feel.

Good luck my dear son. Thank you for it all.

P.S.

As it is with so many parents, my only son's graduation hit me hard.

Thankfully, we had plenty more time together despite his enrollment in a college that was a seven-hour drive away.

He worked on the school newspaper, swam for the varsity swim team and performed with the college orchestra. It gave us lots of excuses to come visit. It often seemed like we were at his college more weekends than we were at home.

Unlike me during my teenage years, my son was a willing participant in our family vacations to England, Ireland, Italy, Austria and Germany in the ensuing years. For a brief time his senior year in college, we were both editors of our newspaper.

MAIL BRINGS A REAL, RARE LETTER

February 10, 2015

I stared at the envelope.

I had just finished snow-blowing the driveway for what seemed like the 10th straight day, and had just freed the mailbox and the pile of bills inside.

It was the letter that got my attention.

Nobody gets letters anymore.

It was from my son in college, and although he has been away since last fall, this was the first time we had received a letter.

"Uh, oh!" I remember thinking.

I wrestled the snowblower up the hill and parked it in the garage. I dropped the mail on the table and sat down and stared at the letter again, not sure if I wanted to know what was inside.

Finally, I opened it.

"Dear Mom and Dad," it began. "First, please don't worry, everything is OK. This isn't a bad-news letter."

"Uh, oh!" I repeated.

I was sure it was a "bad news" letter.

"I just had to tell you guys something that I may have said at some point, but I think it needs to be repeated."

He told us about watching a movie in his documentary film class. It was about a Tennessee high school football team in the bad part of Memphis. He told us in detail about the kids who grew up with just a single parent, if they were lucky, and the relatives who were in prison. He told us about the broken-down homes they lived in and a future that was bleak.

"I realized it was the complete opposite of my own experience growing up."

He described how we all ate dinner together every night and how we often "bugged him" about school and what was going on in his life.

"I realize now that it was because you cared," he wrote.

The letter was handwritten in sometimes hard-to-read print and covered an entire page and a third of another.

He thanked us for his childhood.

"You guys educated me in movies, music, journalism, you name it," he wrote. "I am at a great college because of the two of you. No matter what I do in my life, I will always owe every bit of that to the two of you, and I will be forever grateful."

There was moisture welling up in the corners of my eyes. It must have been the cold.

I sat there for a long while when I was done reading, wondering how I hit the lottery with this young man.

A short time later, my wife came out and sat down.

I told her she had mail.

She was thrilled to see the letter until she was done reading the first sentence about it not being a "bad letter."

"He's not on drugs is he?" she said to me.

"Keep reading," I said.

And I went and got the tissue box.

P.S.

Because I am a cynical newspaper editor, I am always suspicious. We were in the second month of our son's second semester of his freshman year at college and we had not received one piece of correspondence until that February morning.

"I always knew I had it a lot better than many, many people," he told me in January, 2021. "But that was the first time I understood the scope of it. I'm definitely glad I wrote it."

So was I.

I saved it in the family scrapbook where I hope someday he has a son who will read it.

REUNION FLOURISHES DESPITE POLITICS

July 27, 2016

There are nine of us.

We are Joe and Ruth Tingley's grandchildren, and like the next generation of many families, we drifted apart as we went to college, started jobs and grew into adulthood. We often missed each other's weddings and the births of our children, only to be thrown together by that inevitability of life — the deaths of our parents.

In those times, we cemented the bond Joe and Ruth started, and Phyllis, Ed, Bill and Bob fine-tuned with their own broods.

When my father died — the last of Joe and Ruth's four children to pass — I remember wondering if this was it. Would we ever be together again?

But there, filling the last row of chairs at the back of the funeral home, was my family in all its unusual and diverse incarnations, laughing and story-telling and embracing each other like we never missed a beat, like we saw each other every day.

Someone suggested we should get together when there was not a funeral. It would be a great tribute to our parents.

So it was nice to be in Canada this weekend with my cousins again, carrying on the tradition we started almost 15 years ago.

We are a diverse, unusual group with unusual life experiences, and I don't pretend to know all the details of how we all got where we are today.

My cousins are regular people in so many ways, yet absolutely unique in other ways.

I'd say most of them are very religious, far more than I am. I would describe them as more conservative than liberal, but not especially political.

I don't know if they are the average American families, but I know they face many of the same challenges regarding education, health care and retirement so many of us face.

With Donald Trump's acceptance speech still fresh in our minds this weekend, it was inevitable our discussions kept returning, not only to the election, but to Trump.

It was clear they were paying attention to the presidential campaign, that they were tired of the current politics, but most of all, it was clear they were taking Donald Trump seriously.

It makes me uncomfortable to talk about politics in social situations, especially since I spend a good part of my job in that world.

At first, I changed the subject when Trump came up.

Gradually, I tipped-toed around the issue and revealed my considerable concerns about a Trump presidency.

I agreed that his acceptance speech was excellent, but I pointed out that the fact-checkers found significant problems with the accuracy of the speech.

My cousins did not seem to know that.

Most told me they did not read a newspaper daily.

Several said they watched CNN and Fox News religiously, and took seriously what they read on social media without much skepticism.

In that way, I believe they are a lot like the rest of the country.

My frustration built over the weekend.

If you are going to be a good American citizen, and an informed voter, I told one of my cousins, you have to work at it. You have to put some time into it. You have to fact-check speeches and be skeptical when you are told things that seem hard to believe.

My voice was rising and I knew I was getting preachy. Several people left the table.

Someone finally changed the subject. We talked about our grandparents and parents, and the great memories we all shared.

We laughed the night away.

When the weekend was over, we all hugged and kissed each other. It had gone by too fast.

I was most of all thankful that Trump had not torn us apart.

At least, not yet.

P.S.

In reviewing my columns for this project, I was surprised at how often my concern about Donald Trump appeared. My columns were usually about local issues and I tried to stay away from national politics.

This was one of the first about Trump, but there would be more, showing disdain and concern about his lack of morality and inability to tell the truth. Gradually, I could see his attacks on "fake news" and journalists as "enemies of the people" creeping into the dialog with our own readers. It continued for all four years.

Sadly, the cousins did not gather again after that reunion. While I don't blame Donald Trump, his election did leave some of us wondering if we knew each other at all. The contentious politics led to several cousins removing each other as friends on Facebook. I'm hoping there is another reunion in our future, especially if there is no need to talk about politics.

LETTERS FROM MY DAD

August 15, 2015

I heard from my father last week.

It was a gift from yesterday, and a reminder that my parents' generation often left a record far more profound than the "LOL" standard of today, a record that often offers a glimpse of who they were and what they truly felt.

These were love letters.

Two years ago after Mom passed, I found a vintage alligator bag in her closet. It was stamped inside "genuine alligator" and made by S&S in Cuba. I assumed it was something Dad had gotten her during his Navy travels.

It had been retired to the closet with the straps ripped at each end. Perhaps it held sentimental value, or maybe it was just the right size for its contents — 10 letters.

After two years, I decided to transcribe them for the family record.

The envelopes were familiar for anyone with family overseas. They were the old-fashioned "Air Mail" envelopes with short blue and red stripes around the border and a "Via Air Mail" label over a set of flight wings in four languages just below the postmark.

They had all been written by my father.

The script was easily legible from his time aboard the USS Corregidor.

What was especially intriguing were the four letters covering an eight-day period in June 1956, just two weeks before my parents were married.

My father met my mother on a blind date in Belfast, Northern Ireland. He said it was love at first sight. My mother said it took her a little longer. The letters showed a side of my tough-guy dad I never saw.

"My Dearest Darling" that first letter started on June 9, 1956. It spoke of longing and love, and perhaps if you read between the lines, a little bit of passion.

"Well Marie how is the one I love more than anything in the world today. I sure do miss you honey and it won't be so long now before I see you again. Boy it sure will seem good to have you with me again. You are everything I want honey and I just can't wait now."

My dad grew up on a farm and worked most of his life in a factory as a heavy machine operator. He was hard-working and didn't show his emotions very often. By the time I was 18, we had traded hugs for handshakes.

When I got mail at college, it was almost exclusively from my mother.

The letters I found in my mother's closet chronicle my father's last voyage, leaving Germany, sailing to Italy, then Gibraltar before crossing the Atlantic one final time to Mobile, Ala.

My mother had already made her way to the States and was living with her sister in Norfolk, Va. But at each port there was no word from my mother, and my father's letters alternated between profound love and profound worry that she had changed her mind.

"I sure do hope everything is all right," he wrote on June 11, 1956. "The last I heard from you was in Germany. I think it was the 21st of May. You can't imagine how it felt when I didn't get any mail. I felt empty as heck inside and I still do. ... Darling I just pray to God that you still do want me. I know I haven't wrote to you the way I should but I have tried to my best. I keep telling myself everything is all right but I have that funny feeling inside. I love you darling with every bit of love I have in my body and I wish I could talk to you now and tell you myself. ... I go on watch in the engine room and I start imagining all kinds of things. I went to bed tonight and tried to sleep but couldn't so I came down and am writing this letter. I sure hope that you love me like you always have. Because darling you are my life to me. Everything I have been planning is about you. If I should lose you I don't know what I would do."

I'm sure my dad would be mortified to see such personal words published in the newspaper. He might even feel betrayed by me sharing them, but they give me comfort now and they speak of an era when love was formally recorded for posterity.

On June 14, 1956 my father wrote he would be arriving in Mobile, Ala. in six days and he hoped my mother would meet him there. He had still not heard from her.

"Honey, I have tried hard to be good to you since you have been to this country. Ever since I met you, I haven't even looked at another girl. For me to think that you don't want me no more just about breaks my heart.

"Gosh Honey, I imagine all kind of things now. I think you might have gone back to Ireland, or you met someone new or else you are sick or a million other things that run through my mind. I just hope I am all wrong. Darling, you are my whole life to me and without you I have got nothing. So I hope you love me enough to send me a telegram and let me know what is going on. The way things are now I don't know what to do. I want to plan on getting married just as soon after I get into Mobile.

"If you will have me, we will have the rest of our lives together. I sure hope I hear from you soon darling because if I don't you will have torn my heart out. I love you Marie and want to see you so bad. I just can't wait. God bless you always my darling. Till the next time."

On June 30, 1956, Edward Arthur Tingley married Rose Marie Sally at the Cathedral of Immaculate Conception in Mobile, Ala.

Ten months later, I was born.

My dad died on Dec. 28, 2001. My mom followed on Sept. 26, 2013. My parents were married over 45 years.

Obviously, she said yes.

P.S.

After finding the letters after my mother died, I searched online and found the website for the Cathedral of Immaculate Conception - where my parents were married - in Mobile, Ala. I found that the priest who married them had spent his life there and died only a few years earlier.

The website had photos of the church and the alter and I compared them to the one wedding photo of my parents. It looked the same.

Like many people, I have a bucket list of things I would like to do before I die. On it is a certain Catholic Church in Mobile, Alabama.

SWIMMING MADE OUR RELATIONSHIP STRONGER

February 12, 2017

Over the past year, the phone calls from college have disappeared.

The once frantic emails looking for advice have ended.

And more often than not, the text messages go unanswered.

I'm not complaining, really, because my boy turns 21 next week, and for me it is a sign he is striding confidently into adulthood, and looking to stand on his own two feet.

When his mother starts weeping, I tell her it is a good thing.

I argue he is becoming his own man and we won't be around forever.

I'm pragmatic that way.

Most importantly, I believe he is happy. He has embraced his studies and taken advantage of all his school has to offer. After coming home for Christmas this year, he slipped up when he was going out the door and said he was going "home."

And the tears well up.

He decided earlier this year this would be his last season of college swimming.

He is ready for what's next.

While he is ready, I'm not so sure I am.

I remember us being in the car in the pre-dawn darkness heading to Amsterdam for that first club swim meet 10 years ago. I know it is a cliche, but it seems like yesterday.

I look back and realize those drives cemented our father-son relationship like nothing else.

As we stared through the windshield, I explained who I was, why I believed what I did and what I hoped for him in the future.

We talked about history, religion, the family, politics, journalism, relationships—we talked about life.

After the meet, we might stop at the diner in Malta to celebrate a new personal best and talk some more over a burger.

I talked, he listened.

He talked, I listened.

I've missed those talks more of late.

Since he started college, I've followed him and his teammates around western New York, Pennsylvania and Ohio. It is Division III competition and my son is not a star. He is a solid college swimmer who plugs away in distance events hoping to get a third or fourth place, so it wasn't the swimming that drove me to all those rust belt burgs. I just wanted to see my boy.

Gradually, swimming became a metaphor for our relationship. There have been ups and downs, triumphs and disappointments. More importantly, and I've told him this more than once, I've swum every stroke with him.

I think he understands that.

During his freshman year, he had a big invitational at SUNY Fredonia. It was a few weeks before Christmas and I had a lot to do. I decided to pass up the five-hour drive. The morning of the meet, I woke up and knew I had to be there.

I walked in to the arena as they were playing the National Anthem. I found a seat and saw my boy on the pool deck. He looked up and I could see him scanning the crowd.

It wasn't long before he found me. I'll never forget the surprise in his eyes.

For some time, our relationship has been morphing from father-son to something closer to best friends.

At least, that's what I think.

We just enjoy each other's company and our talks can go on for hours at the expense of others in the room.

As I write this, I am sitting in a darkened hotel room in Newark, Ohio. In a few hours my boy will be swimming his final race. Another chapter is closing.

I tried to tell him earlier this week what this all meant to me; the memories, the pride I took seeing him develop as an athlete and now a man, but the words weren't there for me.

It is fitting that this journey ends with swimming's longest race—the mile.

It is another one of those endings that seems to be coming far too often these days.

He has landed an internship that will take him away from home this summer.

Next year he will graduate college.

Then, I expect him to start living what I hope will be a wonderful, joyful life.

It's what I've wanted for him ever since that tiny little hand first grabbed my finger 21 years ago on a snowy February morning.

He is ready.

I just wish I was.

P.S.

After the final race that afternoon, I broke into tears right there in the arena.

To my delight, my son changed his mind and returned to the swim team for his senior year. He said something about finishing what he started.

Time was growing short and I was resolved that I would not miss any of the remaining time we have together. I attended every meet in three different states that senior year.

At the conference championships in one of his final races, he qualified for the evening finals with a personal best in the breast stroke. In his final race, he finished last, but with a personal best time.

This time I was smiling. He had completed the race.

UNPREPARED FOR COLLEGE GRADUATION

May 20, 2018

Four years ago, we gave our son to a college to finish the job.

That was tough.

As we drove off that August afternoon, I rolled down the window and yelled out, "Don't do drugs!"

We pulled away laughing, only to quickly dissolve into tears, stopping five minutes later at the convenient store for an emergency supply of tissues.

I'm reporting back four years later that things turned out well. There is a college diploma on the dining room table, a summer job with the National Park Service and graduate school planned in the fall at a campus too far away.

Along the way, he interned at the *Schenectady Gazette*, freelanced for *The Post-Star*, spent three weeks aboard an 1800s sailing ship on Lake Erie, teamed with two other reporters in revealing a sexual assault problem on his college's campus, swam competitively for four years, became editor of his school newspaper and interned at the Gettysburg National Military Park, where I believe he may have found his calling.

I apologize if this sounds like the random boasts of a parent, because that is not my intent. Just like four years ago when he graduated from high school, this fork in the road has left me shaken.

Last week, Wallace Paprocki of Greenwich, a letter-writer who has been kind to me over the years, reminded our readers of the column I wrote after my son's high school graduation.

He said he wrote me at the time suggesting the growth, experiences and opportunities awaiting him might compensate for the loss of his daily presence at home.

It didn't, but I understand that is part of this process.

That high school graduation column closed a chapter in my relationship with my son. I wrote of the important life lessons his mother and I tried to impart. It was an ending that left us both distraught and in tears more than once. Now it was up to him.

The experience four years later has been much different.

There were no tears on graduation day, and while I was proud, and smiled for all the photos, I felt unsettled.

In the hours after he walked across that stage, I found myself nursing a small cut of prime rib with my son, surrounded by the people who have been most important in his life, people who contributed mightily to the person he has become, people I hope will always be in his life.

I found myself staring at the 22-year-old version of my son and feeling like there was something I forgot to do.

I retreated to 39 years earlier when I walked across another stage on Mother's Day to become the first in my family to graduate from college. I don't recall thinking it was a big deal at the time, but looking back four decades later through a father's eyes, I suspect my tough-as-nails dad felt differently.

What perplexes me now is what's next.

Not for him.

He has a plan, a direction and a passion for history that he wants to follow. When he visited graduate schools this past year, mom and dad were waved off.

He had this one. No need for us to make the trips.

So I wonder where it all goes from here. Where do we fit into the equation?

I suppose there is no way of knowing.

The time spent together the past few weeks has been wonderful as he closed out his college career and we all said goodbye to a time that was very special.

But he will be leaving again soon, building the beginnings of a career and a life as he charges bright-eyed into the future.

Over the past four years, the three of us have adopted this "group hug" tradition before we say goodbye. We wrap our arms around each other — the three of us — bounce up and down and begin making an odd whooping, guttural chant until we have drawn just enough attention to cause a public scene.

From swimming arenas to dorm rooms to restaurant parking lots, we have repeated this embarrassing tradition over and over again. My son never backed away.

I can't bear the thought of that ending as we turn the page on another chapter.

The one thing that has not changed four years later — my boy is ready for what is next, but once again, I am not.

P.S.

My son enrolled in West Virginia University's public history program the next fall and graduated with a master's in 2020 in the midst of a pandemic. There would not be another graduation to attend.

He worked that summer for the National Park Service at Gettysburg National Historic Park as a seasonal park ranger and returned home afterward to look for a job. That fall he was hired to work at the San Antonio Missions National Historic Park and moved to Texas.

I joined him on the cross country journey as we visited historic sites along the way. We stopped at the Flight 93 Memorial in Pennsylvania, Andrew Jackson's house in Nashville, the National Civil Rights Museum and Lorraine Motel in Memphis and Dealey Plaza in Dallas.

But what I will always remember is the selfie we took outside Palmer Hall at Eastern Kentucky University. Forty-one years earlier, I had my photo taken with my dad at the exact same spot on my graduation day.

KNOCK ON THE DOOR

December 24, 2019

The Sorrenti family moved into the raised ranch across the street from us when I was 11 years old.

We had only been in our new house a year or so.

Our new neighbors had a boy my age and a girl about my brother's age. We all quickly became friends.

It turned out that Mrs. Sorrenti worked in the office of the factory where my dad worked, and they also attended our church.

We were neighbors, but I don't recall it being anything more than an occasional wave from across the street.

Until Christmas Eve.

I'm going to guess it was 1969, and the record shows a mild recession started that December.

There was little understanding of economic ups and down in those days. The men just whispered about "only getting 40 hours" and "work being slow."

That's how things were in small factory towns dependent on manufacturing.

Many of the details of how we ended up on Rosalind and Tony's front porch that Christmas Eve have been lost to time.

But I remember it being unusual.

My mother and father didn't drop in on people, especially neighbors they didn't know that well. They were homebodies.

But there we were on the porch, ringing the doorbell, and I didn't know what to expect.

I think the discussion started because Rosalind and Tony didn't have any Christmas lights up. There was quiet as father talked about how Tony had been "furloughed" because "things were slow."

I think that is the word they used in those days to tell you there would not be a paycheck this Christmas season. That meant the presents would be in short supply.

For Rosalind and Tony, there was also the burden of a brand new mortgage.

Standing on that porch, I sensed our visit was not one of celebration. I wondered if we were intruding.

But Rosalind and Tony opened the door and greeted us with smiles and a warm embrace.

They were warm, gregarious Italians at a time and place where everyone had to be labeled by their ethnic origins.

I think it was the first time I ever saw my immigrant Irish mother eat Italian food.

She was shocked to hear my brother and I rave about this new exotic dish we had discovered at Rosalind's house — lasagna.

It was an evening of revelry and great cheer.

At the time, we had no idea what it meant to our neighbors.

Years later, visiting the Sorrenti family became a regular part of our Christmas Eve where the wine and the Italian delicacies flowed.

Inevitably, over some Christmas cheer, Tony would talk about that Christmas Eve when he had just lost his job.

He would explain how there were few presents under the tree and he was moping around the house.

And then the doorbell rang.

And for a few hours, we all laughed, ate and celebrated the holiday.

Tony said he would never forget my father for that visit. I don't think he ever did.

I had not thought about it for some time either, until this past week, and I wondered about Rosalind and Tony. I knew they had moved away after the kids were gone.

A few searches online found that Tony died in 2018.

Rosalind left us last January after battling Alzheimer's for a number of years.

They were both 89 and I had not seen either of them since my dad passed away in 2001.

But that memory persists of one neighbor reaching out to another.

Every year after that first Christmas Eve, the raised ranch across the street glowed with Christmas lights. Inside, there was food, laughter and great cheer.

It still makes me smile.

P.S.

After writing this I searched social media trying to find Rosalind and Tony's two children in Connecticut. I finally found Randy and sent him a message with a link to the column, but I never heard back.

EPILOGUE

EDITOR FINDS A FUTURE LOOKING TO THE PAST

July 19, 2020

This final chapter starts with me in front of an elevator one Sunday morning 19 years ago at Glens Falls Hospital.

I didn't want to be there. I was only there out of a sense of obligation. One of our editors had been very sick and it didn't look good. But I didn't know what room she was in and there was no one at the information desk. I had my excuse. "I'llcome back another time," I thought to myself, and I turned to leave.

I stopped.

To this day, I don't know why.

I found Mary in her room with her mother. She was struggling to breathe. Her mother said they were about to move her to intensive care. Nurses hurried in and out of the room.

I told Mary we missed her.

I told Mary we needed her back soon, and I started to leave because I was just in the way.

Mary stopped me with her eyes and choked out a reply:

"I really ... miss ... working ... at ... the paper," she said.

Her gaze stayed on me.

At the time, the words seemed unremarkable, but over the years they stuck like none other. Perhaps, it was the context as she struggled to get out each word between breaths.

Perhaps it was something in the way she said it, in the intensity of her gaze, as if she needed me to understand what I had, and she soon would not.

That was Nov. 18, 2001. Mary Joseph died a few hours later at the obscenely young age of 39.

So now, 21 years later, I hesitate as I walk away from a job that I adored much like Mary.

I wonder now if Mary would ask, "Are you crazy?"

Oh, the people I have met.

And the arguments I have had.

And the love I have been shown, especially over the past two weeks from so many readers who took the time to say simply they would miss reading my words.

You can't ask for anything more.

I'd like to think some of Mary's spirit stayed, not only with me, but was transported ethereally to every editor and reporter who walked through those doors at Lawrence and Cooper Streets over the past two decades.

I'd like to think her untimely passing pushed me to get the most out of myself, and in turn our staff to appreciate the opportunity to make a difference every day.

Leaving the newspaper, like any significant decision, was made incrementally, in dribs and drabs over the past three months as I wondered how much I would miss the paper. In order to go forward, I had to look backward.

What started as a pandemic cleaning project in my basement became an exploration of the work we have done over the past 21 years as I unpacked boxes, read through old files and marveled at the scope and quality of the work done — some of which I had entirely forgotten about — by dedicated reporters and editors.

Time had fogged so many of the details, so I picked up the phone.

I wanted the retired Maury Thompson to tell me how this fry cook on the way to nowhere 30 years ago ended up poignantly portraying the final days of his wife's life in a series of heartbreaking columns.

I wanted Matt Sturdevant, now a public relations executive for an insurance company, to tell me how a 25-year-old kid with just a couple of years of experience, managed to be a decade ahead of his time in reporting about "Growing up Gay" in the North Country nine years before same-sex marriage became state law.

Konrad Marshall, now an elite journalist in Australia, took me back with him alone to *The Post-Star* newsroom as he delicately interviewed 23 victims of domestic violence, telling me he could still see their faces and hear the anguish in their voices even today.

T.J. Hooker, just a 24-year-old photographer at the time, spoke in slow, halting tones as he described the 14 bodies lined up along the shore of Lake George after the Ethan Allen sank, and I knew he was reliving it all over again.

And there is my friend and former colleague, Mark Mahoney, taking me back to the murder he and his daughter witnessed at the Cumberland Farms parking lot, and my surprise that I had forgotten the most important part of the story. How this father pledged to his frightened 9-year-old daughter that he would go to the convicted murderer's sentencing personally so he could assure her that the man who stared her down after murdering his wife was never going to be able to harm her.

A few years later, Mark Mahoney won the Pulitzer Prize.

What a charmed life I have led. How lucky I have been to have the privilege of walking in the shadows of such men and women on a daily basis, to cheer them on, to challenge them, to pick them up when they stumbled, defend them when they were attacked, but more often than not, watching them succeed beyond their wildest dreams.

They turned over rocks to expose community problems with drug abuse, underage drinking and the stigma of suicide. We all wanted to make a difference. We would be a far poorer community without their efforts.

So here's a little confession. I'm not the best journalist at *The Post-Star*. I never have been. There have been dozens of others who were far better. Will Doolittle, Bob Condon and my partner in sports in those early years, Greg Brownell, have been with me on this ride from the beginning. They could have gone anywhere and done anything, but lucky for me — and you too — they stayed in Glens Falls.

It allowed me to pursue my dream of being a columnist and telling people's stories.

To do that, you need to be trusted.

So when the Rev. Paul Mead called years ago, we were making a pact to trust each other about a checkered past and a hopeful future.

Others followed.

All I had to do was answer the phone. I like to think they were all characters in a long-running drama that is our community story.

I have been humbled over the past two weeks that so many of you have reached out to me to tell me you will miss reading my words. I can't think of a greater compliment, but there is also a gnawing feeling I have let you down.

I've tried to be authentic and honest as I addressed community and personal issues alike. Along the way, I opened my heart to you about my own trials and tribulations in being a son, a husband and a father. And while it was cathartic for me at times, I believed many of you related to these stories about life, death and heartbreak because we all have them.

That is life.

Three months ago, my wife's nine-year tug-of-war with ovarian cancer was getting the better of her and I stepped away from the newspaper completely.

My son was forced to come home from graduate school because of the pandemic, and the three of us were together again.

Some nights we set the Scrabble board up in my wife's bed so she could be more comfortable. It was in those quiet moments when we tried to form a new word that we were closest, where the word we all are looking for was so obvious — family.

Early in the morning as they slept, I would bury myself in my files in my office to sort through the past and, I guess, look for a future.

I think I found that. It was the work I had been doing for the past 21 years. It was those people I had worked shoulder to shoulder with, so many of them, who told the stories of this community so well and made it better. There is a bigger story here and it should keep me busy for some time.

So each morning I would write alone in my basement without interruption, and then meet my wife upstairs on the porch for lunch.

She has started a new regimen of chemotherapy and the results have been encouraging as she plays ball with the dog, putters with her flowers and attacks the evil vine at the edge of the yard.

We continue to do what has become our routine all these years, living each day to the fullest.

Only now, I will be there to share it. That is the best thing of all.

Ken Tingley was the editor of The Post-Star from 1999 to 2020.

P.S.

After I announced my retirement, I received more than 100 emails and letters from readers, many saying they would miss my column. Several sent books for me to read. Only one said "good riddance".

At the Glens Falls Common Council meeting at the beginning of my last week, Mayor Dan Hall and the Common Council declared Friday, July 17 to be "Ken Tingley Day" in the city of Glens Falls.

Over the next five months I buried myself in a book project called *The Last American Newspaper* that celebrated the work of the reporters and editors at my newspaper and the importance it had in the community. By the end of the year, the newsroom's staff had dwindled to just eight.

I was not replaced as editor.

My wife continued to respond well to her new cancer treatment, my son started a career with the National Park Service and I plan to keep on writing.

ACKNOWLEDGEMENTS

The best part about my newspaper job was writing my column.

By 2008, I had been editor at The Post-Star in Glens Falls, N.Y. for nine years and was feeling restless. I believed I needed to do a better job of telling the stories of the people in my community.

Within a week, I got a call from a young pastor named Paul Mead – the subject of the first column in this collection - who wanted to talk about his past, and his future. Although we had never met, he put his trust in me and opened his heart. He told his hard-to-believe evolution from crack addict to minister at the Gospel Lighthouse Church in Kingsbury, N.Y. It was a story of redemption.

The work reflected here could not have been done without the scores of individuals who put their trust in me to tell their stories. I am in debt to all of them.

I hope this collection of columns gives you a small sampling of the people I have met on my own 30-year journey.

Along the way, Will Doolittle became my own personal editor and writing coach and I benefited from it daily. That relationship continues to this day.

Over the years, this column became my own personal scrapbook for my family and the life we lived. My wife and son shared their lives - often with some trepidation – without objection or complaint. I sensed over the years "my family" became part of my readers' family as well. What I hope it showed is the common journey we all have in this life.

Being a newspaper spouse is challenging even in the best of times. Too many times after a long day at work, my conversation with my wife Gillian started with the promise that as soon as I was done with the latest project at work, there would be time for her and my son. Far too often, that did not come to pass.

Gillian was there at the beginning keeping sports statistics on frozen football fields, taking photographs at basketball games and being an unwavering anchor at home. Most importantly, she made her own later struggles with illness routine.

Recently, after my son finished college and started a job in Texas, I asked him about the difficulty of growing up as the occasional subject – sometimes embarrassingly so - of his father's newspaper column. He shared with me a conversation he had with a teacher in high school who once asked him about being the subject of so many of his father's columns. He told the teacher it didn't bother him, but then added, "I'm probably the only kid in school who has to say to his dad, 'Hey, this is off the record.'"

ABOUT THE AUTHOR

Ken Tingley was the editor of The Post-Star in Glens Falls, N.Y. from 1999 to 2020. During his tenure, the newspaper won a Pulitzer Prize in editorial writing in 2009, was recognized by the New York State Associated Press Association with its "Newspaper of Distinction" award nine times while winning more than a dozen national awards for its journalism.

During his tenure, Tingley also wrote an award-winning local news and sports column that was regularly honored by the New York State News Publishers Association and the New York State Associated Press Association. When Tingley retired in July 2020, his column had been named a finalist by the National Society of Newspaper Columnists in 8 of the past 10 years. It was honored with a first-place award in 2016.

Tingley has also been active in state and national journalism organizations. He was president of the New York State Associated Press Association in 2010 when it merged with the state broadcasters association. He also served twice on the board of directors of the American Society of Newspaper Editors and was a Pulitzer Prize judge from 2008-09.

Before becoming editor in Glens Falls in 1999, Tingley was sports editor of The Post-Star from 1988 to 1999 and the sports section was annually honored as one of the best small-newspaper sports sections in the country by the Associated Press Sports Editors. Tingley was honored nationally for his sports writing 11 times - including five times for columns – by APSE. Tingley served as third Vice President for APSE from 1995-97.

Tingley started his newspaper career as a sports writer at the Ashland (Ky.) Daily Independent in 1979 before moving on to the Press-Republican in Plattsburgh, N.Y. (1980-82), The Daily Star in Oneonta, N.Y. (1982-87) and the Kingsport (Tenn.) Times-News (1987-1988).

Tingley grew up in Seymour, Conn. and graduated from Seymour High School in 1975. He attended college at the University of Connecticut's Waterbury branch for two years, before transferring to Eastern Kentucky University where he became sports editor of The Eastern Progress his senior year and graduated with a degree in journalism in 1979.

He married his wife, Gillian, in 1982 and they had a son, Joseph, in 1996. This is Ken's first book.

CPSIA information can be obtained
at www.ICGtesting.com
Printed in the USA
LVHW010417230821
695784LV00005B/8